PROJECT MANAGEMENT

A Deep Guide to Help You Master and Innovate Projects with Lean Thinking, Including How to Dominate Agile, Scrum, Kanban, And Six Sigma.

PETER BROWN

No part of this book may be reproduced or transmitted in any form or by any means, electronic or mechanical, including photocopying, recording or by any information storage and retrieval system, without written permission from the author, except for the inclusion of brief quotations in a review.

Limit of Liability and Disclaimer of Warranty: The publisher has used its best efforts in preparing this book, and the information provided herein is provided "as is." This book is designed to provide information and motivation to our readers. It is sold with the understanding that the publisher is not engaged to render any type of psychological, legal, or any other kind of professional advice. The content of each article is the sole expression and opinion of its author, and not necessarily that of the publisher. No warranties or guarantees are expressed or implied by the publisher's choice to include any of the content in this volume. Neither the publisher nor the individual author(s) shall be liable for any physical, psychological, emotional, financial, or commercial damages, including, but not limited to, special, incidental, consequential or other damages. Our views and rights are the same: You are responsible for your own choices, actions, and results.

Copyright © 2021 by Peter Brown. All rights reserved.

Table of Contents

WHAT IS THE LEAN THINKING? 7

THE TOYOTA PRODUCTION SYSTEM 14

TOTAL QUALITY MANAGEMENT 19

ADVANTAGES AND BENEFITS 26

TOOLS AND METHODOLOGIES..............................33

UNDERSTAND THE PRINCIPLES OF LEAN 39

PROCESS...45

KAIZEN 51

SIX SIGMA 58

KANBAN 65

ANALYTICS 73

TIPS FOR SUCCESS 79

LEAN ANALYTICS CYCLES 84

TYPES OF KANBAN SYSTEMS 93

RUNNING A PROJECT WITH KANBAN.................102

BUILDING A LEAN TEAM 111

KAIZEN EVENTS **120**

SIX SIGMA SCALE **133**

TIPS TO MAKE SIX SIGMA WORK FOR YOU **137**

KANBAN COMBINED WITH LEAN MANUFACTURING **144**

KAIZEN AND THE CAPABILITIES OF THE ORGANIZATION **153**

BUSINESS ANALYSIS TECHNIQUES **163**

THE METRICS THAT MATTER FOR YOUR BUSINESS **171**

CONCLUSIONS ABOUT LEAN **177**

WHAT IS AGILE PROJECT MANAGEMENT **181**

ADVANTAGES AND BENEFITS **186**

UNDERSTAND THE PRINCIPLES OF AGILE **199**

TOOLS AND METHODOLOGIES **215**

SKILLS AND SOFTWARE DEVELOPMENT **230**

MONITORING AND TIPS FOR SUCCESS **245**

THE AGILE PROCESS **255**

WHAT ARE THE REASONS WHY AGILE PROJECT MANAGEMENT COULD FAIL? 263

TOOLS FOR GREATER TEAM EFFECTIVENESS IN AGILE PROJECT MANAGEMENT 271

THE AGILE DEVELOPMENT PROCESS 277

BENEFITS OF AGILE METHODOLOGY 292

DISADVANTAGES OF AGILE METHODOLOGY 300

HOW TO AGILE: THE WORK ETHIC AND VALUES 309

THE AUTHENTICITY OF AGILE MANAGEMENT .. 317

CONCLUSIONS ABOUT AGILE 321

WHAT IS SCRUM? 324

ADVANTAGE AND BENEFITS 329

UNDERSTAND SCRUM 334

SPRINTING CYCLE 340

TOOLS AND METHODOLOGIES 351

MONITORING 366

SYSTEMS OF CONTROL IN SCRUM 380

APPLICATIONS OF SCRUM 387

METRICS IN SCRUM 403

HOW TO BUILD A SCRUM TEAM 416

NON-CORE ROLES IN SCRUM 430

SCRUM MANAGEMENT ERRORS TO AVOID 433

USEFUL RESOURCES 437

CONCLUSIONS ABOUT SCRUM 444

What is The Lean Thinking?

Lean thinking is a practice that promotes the idea that we should always on the lookout for things that can provide more benefit and value to society and individuals while reducing if not outright removing wastes.

Kanban is a fundamental practice in Lean thinking because it allows you to identify where waste occurs in the workflow to prevent further unnecessary costs and use of resources. It enables employees to be aware of which projects need to be done right away while avoiding overproduction. Implementing Kanban is a great way to practice Lean thinking, empowering employees to meet changes in market behavior.

The term was coined by Daniel T. Jones and James P. Womack as a representation of the insights they gained after an in-depth analysis of the Toyota Production System.

Toyota's way of training their managers throughout the years focused on developing its employees' abilities of reasoning instead of pushing them to follow systems developed by specialists. The company also has a group of elders and coordinators who are dedicated to aiding and teaching their managers on how to think differently and how to do better at their job by focusing on core aspects.

History of Lean

The Lean Methodology originated from the Toyota Production System in the 1950s. After World War II, Kiichiro Toyoda and Taiichi Ohno from Toyota revisited the manufacturing techniques of Henry Ford and the statistical quality control processes of Edwards Deming to set the foundation for the Toyota Production System (TPS).

The Toyota Production System shifted the focus from improving individual products or machines to optimizing across the entire value stream. This system was established based on two major concepts – Jidoka and Just-in-Time. The term 'Jidoka' means 'automation with human intelligence' or 'autonomation'. With Jidoka, the equipment stops when a problem arises which forces workers to solve the problem in order to start the production line. The 'Just-in-Time' concept is to produce only what is needed, when it is needed, and in quantities needed.

Basics of Lean

The Workplace

Focusing on the workplace entails making regular visits to the place where specific tasks take place. Being in the place and experiencing firsthand what happens there gives the managers and other employees the idea of what happens there. This also enables management to get a bird's eye view of the project. As a result, they acquire the capability to assess the works in progress and determine if there is room for improvement.

Additionally, being present also gives the employees an avenue to express their concerns regarding the work in progress and other things to the management. These concerns being addressed gives the impression to the employees that they have support and respect from the management.

Visiting the workplace and engaging your people leaves them the impression that you genuinely care, value and trust them. This also boosts morale, as it gives employees more confidence. Having confident and dedicated employees is good for your business.

Value

Value refers to what a customer is willing to pay to acquire certain products or services. For a business to be profitable, it must create something of value at the least amount of cost. This requires a two-pronged approach.

First, you must get an understanding of your customers. That way, you can create something that they would deem useful. You need to implement a system that would help prevent the production and delivery of defective work. This is a way to prevent the likelihood of customers spending money on your products and being dissatisfied with them. Lean management practitioners refer to this practice as building value through built-in quality is tied to this.

You should remove as much waste as possible. Make sure that you are conserving the company's effort, time, energy, and resources. This means putting a stop to something in the process once you see there is something wrong or doubtful in the process of the item being produced.

Value streams

A value stream refers to the entirety of the product's life cycle, which spans the collection of raw materials, the period in which the finished product is in use, and ultimately, the disposal of the product. This means that you'll need a good understanding of your "takt" time. Note that in management systems such as Lean, Takt time refers to the rate at which a production team should complete a product in order to meet demand. The takt time rhythm results in the creation of stable value streams in which the stable teams are tasked to work on stable sets of products with given stable equipment instead of optimizing the usage of specified machines or processes.

Lean thinking must be practiced studying this stream in detail. All processes must be examined to verify if it adds value to the product. Note that any part of the value stream can be either of this three:

1. *Will clearly create value*
2. *Will not create value but the waste is unavoidable due to the current technology*
3. *Will not create value and is easily and immediately avoidable*

Flow

Another aspect essential to the elimination of waste in the process is the complete understanding of the flow of processes. If the stream seems to have stalled at a certain point, that means waste will be or has been produced. Sometimes, that is unavoidable.

Unfortunately, almost all traditional businesses are addicted to batch processes, wherein processes are aimed to produce as many items are possible with the goal of reducing the unit costs to a minimum value. Lean thinking approaches the matter in another way, wherein the focus is on the optimization of the workflow that the general cost of the business is reduced at a dramatic rate through the elimination of the need for transportation, subcontractor usage, systems, and warehouses.

Pull

Lean thinking has the goal of ensuring that every step in the process is executed because it is needed at a precise point in time. No step will be performed well ahead of time, preventing the buildup of Work-In-Progress inventory and bottlenecks. The synchronized flow will be maintained as a result.

This means that decision-makers need to envision the differences between ideal and actual scenarios at any time in the workplace. This is where the use of visualization tools such as Kanban card boards will be handy. With such a board, you can pull work from upstream depending on what you takt time dictates.

The suppliers of Six Sigma propose a venture rendition of its items, which might be instilled into the whole association structure. You shouldn't be befuddled by the cost of a big business framework, in light of the fact that a volume of total compensation it brings is extremely worth it. Additionally, you shouldn't stress, since Lean Six Sigma preparing will give all of your important data you need so as to advance another framework and how to stay in contact with the most recent data about Lean Six Sigma.

Additionally, it also requires efficient ways of voicing what is required in each step in the value chain. Sure, there is tension created because having a pull system requires flexibility and short design-to-delivery cycle periods.

Nonetheless, pulling will enable the team to edge closer to a single piecework. The team can identify issues as they show up, which can lead to the prevention of bigger problems. This can also contribute to complex situations being solved over time.

Excellence

Lastly, Lean thinking is about instilling the kaizen spirit in every employee in your company. Kaizen refers to the notion of changing for the better albeit in small and sustainable ways. The kaizen spirit means looking for the 1% change for a hundred times from every team member instead of an instantaneous 100% change. Through the practice of kaizen, self and the collective confidence to face larger challenges are developed.

The ultimate goal of Lean Thinking is not to the application of the tools to all processes, but by seeking perfection by changing for the better. Smart systems or go-it-alone people are not the main contributors to perfection and are not sought after. It is the dedication from everyone in the company to improve things hand-with-hand little by little that matters. By applying Lean thinking in the overall workflow, the monitoring and reduction of wastes will be ensured.

The Toyota Production System

The Toyota Production System (TPS) is Lean Thinking 1.0 because in 1988 a graduate student, John Krafcik at MIT, said it was by naming TPS "Lean Thinking." The 1990 publication of The Machine That Changed the World by James Womack and Daniel Jones tossed the term into the mainstream of American manufacturing.

Manufacturers have sought efficiencies for five hundred years, if not longer. But our brief Lean history begins in 1913 with Henry Ford and his plant in Highland Park, Michigan, where his moving assembly line and standard parts, machines, and work created flow production. Although this method limited alterations in the production process and thus the variety of products—you could have any car in any color as long as it was a Model T, and it was black—it was a jumpstart to increase efficiency in production processes. This approach worked best when large volumes of the same product were in demand. Ford controlled and minimized variation to the smallest detail. But when product options became important, Ford shrugged his shoulders. Until then, however, his genius and obsession with efficiency was king.

Another oversized element in the development of Lean Thinking 1.0 was the automatic weaving loom invented by Sakichi Toyoda, the first machine that reacted like a human (autonomation) by stopping automatically if a thread broke.

Thus, minimizing defective cloth and reducing the number of workers needed to monitor machine functioning. The income from licensing the loom's patent enabled the company to enter the world of automotive manufacturing in 1935. About fifteen years well along, Eiji Toyoda studied American manufacturing and with Taiichi Ohno, who had joined the company during WWII, began the many steps to create the Toyota Production System. In the mid-1950s, consulting engineer Shigeo Shingo joined the effort to reduce waste and became a significant contributor to Lean processes and Lean management.

Womack and Jones identified five principles of the Lean Thinking process:
1. *Value is defined by the customer*
2. *Identify the value stream needed to create the product and eliminate the waste it contains*
3. *Enable the product production process to flow smoothly*
4. *Create a pull flow rather than push*
5. *Goal, never reached, is perfection*

Early in its development, the TPS had two basic pillars: just in time and autonomation. Today, the two pillars are continuous improvement and respect for people. Respect for people means to listen to the suggestions of the people who do the work and to make sure they are well trained and confident—with the intent to improve production processes, not people interactions.

Through the years and up to the present day, the Toyota Production System (Lean Thinking 1.0) has created or emphasized many now-standard tools and concepts. They include a single-minute exchange of dies, value streams, Five S, poka-yoke (mistake-proofing), total productive maintenance, Kanban (signaling information), level loading, visual control, and the relentless elimination of waste (nonvalue-added work, overburden, and unevenness). Tools and concepts are only workarounds until the ideal flow is achieved.

Taiichi Ohno, the often-described "Father of Lean," listed seven wastes to be eliminated in all production processes:

- **Transportation**
- **Inventory**
- **Movement**
- **Waiting**
- **Over-production**
- **Over-processing**
- **Defects**

Managers and employees identified and did whatever was necessary to reduce or eliminate each waste. There was some overlap in defining wastes, but naming wasn't important; uncovering the waste and getting rid of it was. The worst waste is over-production because it includes all the other wastes.

In "Decoding the DNA of the Toyota Production System" (Harvard Business Appraisal, September 1999), Spear and Bowen listed four rules of the TPS, which are paraphrased below:

- *All work is specified to content, sequence, timing, and outcome*
- *The customer-supplier connection must be clear and direct*
- *The pathway for products must be simple and direct*
- *The scientific method will be applied to potential improvements*

These four rules mask the real genius of the approach. Toyota focused on finding the most effective response to real problems—unbound by a philosophical or standardized approach, using only what worked best—and would adjust anything as needed to reach pre-defined outcomes.

The TPS shifted the focus from large stationary machines to the flow of products through assembly. Toyota right-sized machines for demand, moved them for correct sequencing and optimally located operators, and externalized set-up to lower cost, improve quality and respond to changing customer interests.

Below is a graphic of what Lean Thinking does.

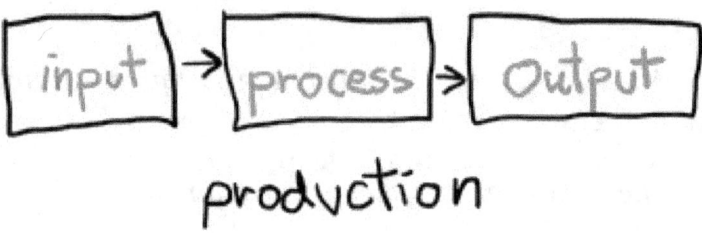

production

It ensures input is what is needed when it is needed. The process adds value to the material without waste, and the product is what the customer wants.

Toyota continues to improve and expand Lean Thinking 1.0 and has become the most successful automobile manufacturer in the world.

Total Quality Management

Lean management is one of the ways that you can approach your startup or organization. This is going to take all of the principles that we have been looking at and applying them at a management level to allow yourself to better achieve the small, incremental changes that would be needed to improve the quality and the efficiency of your startup.

If you want to run a lean business, this is one of the most important starting points for you—you must be able to ensure that your system is going to work properly, and to do so, you will need to implement lean principles from top to bottom. While you could begin working hard on using lean analytics to improve the data and profits that you have, you can also further optimize with the use of lean management. Remember, lean systems care about more than their bottom line—they seek to create a culture of efficiency which can really only be attained by providing everything that everyone needs. This means that you are going to want to have management also aiding in this process as well.

Within this part, we are going to address lean management and how they can be a major value for your company and setup. By applying lean management, you will be taking the time and effort to allow your startup to thrive.

What Is Lean Management?

Lean management is sort of the other side of lean analytics when considering a startup company. When you are working with lean management, you are working with the personal side. Rather than focusing on the numbers, you are focusing on the people as well. You are looking for better leadership, facilitating it to enable the entire process to work in the first place.

It is following to impossible to have your lean startup if you do not also employ lean management. You are going to want to ensure that your lean management will allow for the sharing and disbursement of responsibility while also putting a major emphasis on being able to do so while moving toward continuous improvement.

Many of the principles of lean management are the same as the ones that you have seen thus far. The managers within the organization will be applying those same five principles yet again in ways that will allow for the facilitation of efficiency.

These principles in lean management appear as the following:

Identify the value: This step is once again about finding the problem that needs to be solved. The lean manager is going to be looking for the problem that the customer needs to solve and then figuring out a product to market as the solution.

The product must be something that is a part of the solution, and it must be something that adds value.

Value stream mapping: This is once again the process of cleaning up the system to find any waste. Managers make great use of this—it allows them to see which teams are doing what and how they can optimize the processes and the team, allowing them to facilitate the build that they are going to need. It will help them see where they need to focus on getting people up to speed, or how they could possibly allow their processes to flow smoother than ever.

Creating continuous workflow: The manager's job is to facilitate this workflow. If they see any sort of bottlenecking—an area within the production line that gets backed up or narrowed, causing a buildup of work—they must figure out how to solve it. This is often done with Kanban—the use of visual cues to trigger actions when problems arise. The manager is going to be the one that is responsible for breaking down the work and visualizing the proper flow to allow for the removal of any interruptions that would otherwise arise.

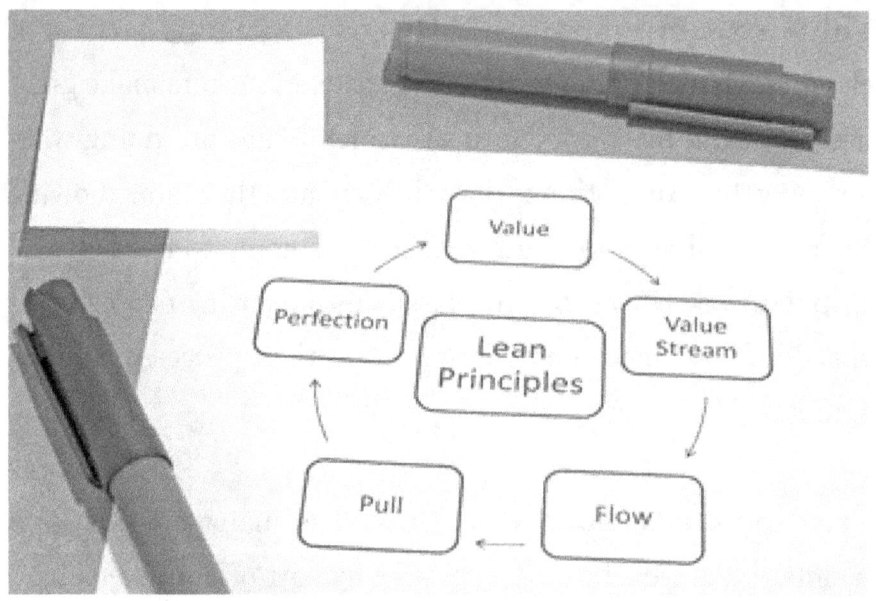

Using a pull system: This is ensuring that the workflow is consistently stable. This is going to be done by precisely determining just how much work needs to get done and then figuring out how they can facilitate it to work better. When you see this, you are going to be decreasing the waste of any processes that arise. It ensures that the work that you are doing is going to be narrowed down and processed accordingly to minimize overhead.

Facilitating continuous improvement: Because the manager is going to be the one responsible for everything, they are naturally responsible for ensuring that continuous improvement is always happening.

They do this by putting together techniques and work that will help the system run effectively.

You are going to be looking at how people are able to be organized. It is taking a look at areas that could be improved and applying the gains from optimizing some areas and applying them to others as well. These are very important aspects that the manager must apply. They must be able to ensure that all employees are actively contributing to that constant improvement that is within the workflow. With this attitude, the organization is then able to be agile enough to deal with any roadblocks that may arise at varying points.

Applying Lean Management

Ultimately, lean management will advocate for three fundamental business issues. In focusing on all three of these, you are able to ensure that the entire organization is transformed at the same time into something that is going to be more efficient in general. These three focuses are purpose, process, and people.

When you focus on purpose, you are considering what it is that you are doing. What will solve this problem that you see do? Will you be able to up supply to meet demand? Upping supply does not matter if there is no demand in the first place, so that is not always the best place to look. You will be considering whether or not you are solving customer problems or internal problems here. When you are able to alleviate the problems at hand, you can then make sure that your process is more efficient in general.

Process refers to being able to organize everything that needs to be done. You are looking at the major value that you are serving by ensuring that all flow is valuable, capable, and available. Is everything there? Is the work flowing properly?

Finally, people focus on everyone that is involved in the process. How can your current organization allow for every process that must occur, there is also someone that is able to manage it? It is putting people in charge of certain areas to ensure that they can keep everything flowing regularly. It is aiming to have everyone that is involved be able to state, with truth to it, that they are able to engage in operating the system correctly while also continuing to improve it, while not stepping on anyone else's toes.

There are many different ways that you can really facilitate these points as well, and we will be considering all of them here. Some of the easiest implementations of being able to facilitate lean management in a meaningful manner include all sorts of strategies for ensuring that your business continues to run well. We are going to go over these strategies and tactics now.

Advantages and Benefits

Becoming lean as an individual can make a big difference in your tasks as an employee. When you apply its concepts consistently enough, they're bound to affect your life's other aspects positively. Over time, you'll find that you're able to process decisions in a more systematic way. If lean concepts can have such a profound effect on a personal level, you can just imagine the possibilities if you scale the leanness all the way to an enterprise.

Shifting to Lean: What's in It for You?

Lean thinking encourages people to apply doable changes in small increments. The ultimate goal is to speed up all the workflows within a system without compromising product or service quality. Lean is certainly not a quick fix for eliminating company wastes. It involves being in a long-term commitment with continuous growth and improvement.

Even if a particular lean technique has been proven effective by many companies, changes certainly didn't happen within a few months of applying the methods. It usually takes far longer than that for anything significant to be noticeable. Of course, it's also understandable how people may feel discouraged to stick with the new methods if the benefits aren't that obvious. To help you stay lean when you're tempted to think that it doesn't work, here's a list of its short-term to long-term benefits:

Short-term Benefits

Improved Management: Even though problems will still come up every now and then, lean makes the work environment more convenient to deal with if you're a manager. With better task standards in place, it will be easier for you to pinpoint anything that's disrupting the flow of the value stream. Most of the time, you will be able to figure out that something isn't quite right just by looking at an area's set-up or layout.

Improved Efficiency and Productivity: As a result of standardizing every piece of the workflow, it becomes automatic for employees to know what exactly they need to do — and when they need to do it. It reduces a lot of redundancy and overlaps that stem from task confusion. It also ensures that they are doing their work correctly every single time. They no longer have to constantly ask whether a particular task is under their responsibility. They can just focus on their own task list without worrying about anything else.

Safer and More Convenient Layouts: Since literal wastes will be decluttered, turning lean gives your company more space to move around. This will instantly make task movements a lot more convenient. Additionally, it will provide your staff with a safer space for working when the layout is reorganized to eliminate hazards.

Involvement from the Whole Company: Lean is something that isn't applied only to one team or department. When a company decides to go lean, every level of the hierarchy is involved — from those on the top all the way to the ones on the bottom. After all, lean systems depend on the cooperation of everyone involved.

Medium and Long-term Benefits

Improved Cash Flow: Once you get rid of DOWNTIME, you can now focus your energy on ensuring that the value-adding steps of your value stream flow as smoothly as possible. In the absence of roadblocks, workflow bottlenecks, and delays, not only will you be able to deliver products in a just-in-time manner, but you'll also improve the cash flow within your company.

Customer Satisfaction and Loyalty: Customer satisfaction is one of the most immediate results of applying lean, so they become more likely to trust your brand again in the future. If you keep on doing what works, you're bound to gain their loyalty in the long run.

Employee Satisfaction and Loyalty: While lean systems are mainly focused on the desires of the customer, it also promotes better mood and morale among employees. The changes may be met with resistance at first, but once they see that it takes them far less time to complete tasks compared to before, they'll become more open to the overall idea of lean. Additionally, since lean is all about constant improvement and collaborations, they tend to feel better about themselves because they're part of a team that actually cares about others. Lean systems give them a safe space to voice out their concerns and provide suggestions for further improvement.

Marketability for Collaboration: What makes something marketable? In terms of companies, marketable companies are usually unproblematic ones. You need to be that company if you wish to be a part of a lean enterprise. After all, lean is all about efficiency, and you need to be an efficient team player to ensure that you don't disrupt the flow of the entire system.

Lean is not merely an exercise in cost-cutting. It is more of a long-term opportunity for consistent growth. Once you have smoothed out your lean processes within the company, you will eventually become the preferred suppliers of particular products and services.

That's because your consistency and standards translate well to your products — something that lets both customers and collaborators know that you're a company that they can trust.

Main Principle

While the Lean process was originally developed to help with the industry of manufacturing and production, Lean has been so effective that many other businesses and industries have found ways to adapt it to their own needs. Every business wants to increase profits, reduce waste, enhance the customer experience, and just become overall more efficient. The Lean Process can work to make this happen.

Before you adopt any of the Lean processes, you must understand the two primary tenants. The first one is to focus on the importance of incremental improvement. The second is that the company needs to have a high level of respect for people, both those who purchase the product, and for their own employees.

With regard to the businesses' focus on its incremental improvements, the improvements do not have to be done overnight. However, the business needs to strive in order to steadily and effectively improve their processes so that there is less waste present. You must take a good look at the processes that you currently use and see where things can be improved. Is there to much waiting time in one area? Are the suppliers not getting things in on time? Is there a lot of movement for one part, such as a paper needing approval from three different areas before starting? Are some of the departments that should be working together on different sides of the business?

All of these can lead to more waste in your business, and it is important to avoid them as much as possible. When you take a step back and look objectively at the system you have in place, you are likely to see several spots where you are able to make improvements. Even if these are small, or incremental changes, you will be amazed at what they can do to eliminate waste, speed up your process, and even help customers enjoy a better experience.

But when working on the Lean methodology, we can't forget that there needs to be a high level of respect for people. This tenant is meant to be applied not only to your customers but also to your own people, the employees. When we show respect to the customers, it means that we go the extra mile any time there is a problem. We listen to them and then work to make the experience better. We help to fix the problem, and maybe even throw in something extra to help it get solved.

This same idea needs to be applied to your employees when you are working in the Lean process. When a company wants to respect their team, they will work on creating a strong internal culture that is dedicated to teamwork and treating the employees fairly.

Employees will learn that they are valued, and that their opinion means something and that they aren't just another number that brings in the money.

Any business that wants to implement the Lean process will need to improve employee morale, teamwork and more because they realize that by improving the team, they are able to effectively improve the company as well.

Tools and Methodologies

Many techniques and simple creative thinking are done to develop tools that help make the process and business lean. Lean tools, basically, are just a practical application of common sense in business management to make it more impactful, efficient and profitable.

Some tools of lean are enlisted below:

- The 5S
- Mistake-proofing
- Kanban
- SMED
- Andon
- Bottleneck analysis
- Continuous flow
- Muda (waste)
- Root cause analysis
- SMART goals
- Jidoka
- KPI
- Production leveling

- Gamba
- Hoshin Kanri
- Value Stream Mapping

Detailed description and analysis of the tools used in the lean methodology might require a separate volume of its own, however, a brief discussion on some of the most important and extensively used tools of lean is done in the proceeding paragraphs.

In order to further comprehend Lean thinking, we must look into the tools and terms used in the Japanese Toyota Production System. The TPS methodology is essentially geared toward understanding how processes work, identifying ways of improving them, and making the processes smoother and faster. If any activities in the process are unnecessary, then they have to be eliminated.

On the other hand, every business that adopts the TPS approach must realize that it is not a panacea for all the problems within the organization. It is not about the elements on their own, but how they are all brought together to create a system that is consistently put into practice daily. The principles must be embedded in the thinking of everyone within the organization. There must be action and implementation.

Utilizing the Human Potential

People form the core of the TPS approach. In order to achieve excellent organizational results, the employees must be trained on how to adopt values and beliefs that will bring about a strong and stable organizational culture. The company has to make an effort to constantly reinforce this new culture so that it becomes a permanent feature of its business landscape.

Every organization must always remember that it is the people who create value. It is people who implement processes and use equipment and technology. To root out waste from within requires establishing the right culture and setting, where employees are innovative, engaged, and perform work that is meaningful.

The Lean philosophy is often mistaken as a set of tools and techniques. However, Lean is first and foremost about people. There are companies that have failed to grasp this simple idea and have suffered the consequences. Lean requires everyone in the organization to change their mindset and then use the tools to eliminate waste and improve customer value. The organization must respect its people, continually educating, training, challenging, and empowering them. Any organization that thinks itself Lean has to see its people as its most prized asset, and this asset must be stimulated, celebrated, and compensated properly.

Let's introduce now some terms you need to know.

Heijunka

Heijunka means "leveling" in Japanese and is the foundation of the TPS model. It is designed to help organizations meet customer demand with minimal waste in the production process. Most experts agree that heijunka should be considered during the latter stages of implementing a Lean strategy. It works best after the organization has identified, solidified, and refined their value streams, and the Lean philosophy is already entrenched into the organizational culture. It involves three ideas:

- **Leveling** – This refers to minimizing variations in the volume of production so as to make planning easier. It is aimed at ensuring that production is a predictable process throughout the month rather than a "peak" and "trough" affair. In other words, a company should produce the same average number of a product every day rather than vary its production numbers.

- **Sequencing** – This refers to combining the type of work done. The aim is to create a process where production matches consumer demand. Every product is produced according to a particular sequence, and this sequence is a by-product of customer demand. Tasks are processed according to date so that customer demand is met.

- **Standardization and Stability** – This refers to ensuring that work standards are maintained at a constant level. It involves reducing variation in the standards of processes and continuously employing best practices. Once standardization has been accomplished within an organization, the business processes can then be stabilized, and finally improved.

Jidoka

Jidoka means humanized automation and involves preventing defects in products and stopping work if any are detected. By stopping the work process the moment a problem occurs, the cause of the problem can be identified immediately. The root causes can then be eliminated, and the process improved. Jidoka is one of the two pillars of the TPS system and has two major elements:

- **Automation** – This means automation with human intelligence. The equipment being used in the production process is designed to automatically differentiate between good and defective products. There is no need for a human operator to stand and watch over the machine, thus allowing one person to supervise several machines at once. This form of innovation can be seen with printing machines that automatically stop printing when the ink runs out.

- **Stop at every abnormality** – If a defect is spotted, an employee can stop the entire production line so that the problem can be resolved immediately. This may seem like an extreme measure, but if the company is batch-processing a product, the potential for massive defects is averted by fixing the root cause as early as possible.

Lean thinking provides an organization with effective ways to enhance value for customers by eliminating waste and smoothening out the process flow.

Understand the Principles of Lean

The Lean philosophy is a group of business methods, strategies, and practices that are primarily focused on continuous improvement and eliminating waste within a company. Despite popular belief that the Lean model is the preserve of the manufacturing and production industry, it is a concept that can be adapted to suit any type of business. Lean encompasses the various aspects of operations, such as internal functions, supply networks, and consumer value chains.

Due to its origins, the Lean philosophy tends to make a lot of references to manufacturing situations. In reality, however, the Lean approach is one that every type of business organization can find useful due to its vigilant and rigorous methods of reducing waste and improving efficiency. Lean is now used in almost every industry, including construction, healthcare, aerospace, retail, banking, and government.

In order to appreciate the Lean philosophy fully, it is important to look back at its origins. This management philosophy came out from the Toyota Production System (TPS), which had a very successful automobile manufacturing and operations system. The core aspect of the Lean philosophy was to try to reduce three types of variation in manufacturing: *muda, mura, and muri.*

Muda is a Japanese word that means uselessness or futility. In business, this would represent waste. In order to reduce and eliminate waste, it is necessary to first clearly separate activities that are considered value-adding from those that have been identified as being wasteful.

Mura refers to unevenness in business workflow processes. This form of waste can cause needless downtimes or phases of unnecessary strain on employees, processes, and equipment. From a managerial perspective, unevenness leads to one of the biggest challenges for businesses – uncertainty. It is difficult to plan ahead and run a successful business if the levels of uncertainty are too high. Any kind of interruption in the workflow process can easily lead to a reduction in the ability of an organization to respond to customer needs. If a customer orders a product and the expectation is that delivery will be made by a set date, throwing uncertainty into the mix suddenly causes chaos and delays. For a manufacturing organization to overcome mura, it must seriously consider the layout of its facilities and assembly protocol. For any other kind of business, there has to be a methodology for understanding processes better and improving the ability to foresee potential problems.

Muri refers to waste resulting from overburdening a system or through a lack of understanding of its capabilities.

If a production system or business process becomes overworked, it is inevitable that wear and tear will occur, both on the machines as well as personnel.

An extremely high workload can result in system failure and the production of a high number of defective products. When mura and muri combine, bottlenecks crop up all over the organization. The best way to avoid straining the machines or employees is to make sure that the focus remains on only those activities that add value. The organization must also minimize waste in other relevant areas.

Another Lean concept that goes hand-in-hand with waste identification and reduction is Kaizen. Kaizen refers to continuous improvement. It involves creating a culture where an individual or organization chooses to improve themselves on a consistent basis. This is a concept that has been adopted by almost every industry, from global multinational businesses to personal trainers.

The Lean philosophy incorporates numerous tools, but the major factor affecting its impact on an organization is an attentive mindset. Everyone in the organization, from CEO to shop steward, must be vigilant when it comes to eliminating waste, continuously improving, and effecting positive change.

Implementing Lean

Here's what you need to clarify with them:
- What are the changes that you'll be implementing?
- Why are you implementing them?
- How are they going to benefit from these changes?

- How will it benefit the whole company?

Lean thinking all sounds good in theory, and it can be exciting to continue applying it once you've seen how great it can be in practice. However, the tasks between teams or entities cannot always be as conveniently executed as getting from Point A to Point B in a clean, straight line. Their involvement with each other goes back and forth, which emphasizes how every component must be free of wastes to ensure a smooth flow.

Of course, shifting to lean has its own set of issues and challenges. Like any other form of change, you should resist hoping that it would do its "magic" in just a few weeks or months.

Technically speaking, when every factor is ironed out right from the beginning, it can be possible to have everything sorted out in just a short time. But that only applies when the scenario is ideal. Experience will tell you that situations are rarely ever ideal, especially when transitions are concerned.

Here are some issues that you might have to deal with on your way to implementing lean:

Cultural Resistance

This may be the biggest hurdle that you have to get through when transitioning from wasteful to lean. When a status quo has already been set, most people are resistant to any change in the company culture.

That's usually a result of staying in their comfort zones for long enough. They feel that change is unnecessary since they already like the current workflow.

To gradually ease the workforce into the lean system, training (or retraining) people must be prioritized.

Although all four of these are important considerations, they're likely going to be most concerned about the third point, as this involves their role in the company. However, if you can clearly explain the good things about these changes, then people will be more inclined to accept it.

Costs and Upkeep

On a personal level, there are cases in which you'll need to spend money today to be able to profit or save more money in the future.

Going lean requires the same thing. Eliminating wastes will need money because going for the long-term fix requires money. Eventually, however, the money you spent will eventually go back to you in the form of increased profits from minimized defects.

And, just like your home needs yearly maintenance, lean also requires upkeep. Proper planning and execution will ensure that you won't have to worry about running out of certain parts or having outdated systems.

Talent Gaps

Since lean processes may now require updated technologies, companies that are going lean must bridge the talent gap. This means that they may have to let go of general-labor employees in favor of those who have licenses and certifications to operate lean system equipment. These employees are adept not only at handling these systems, but they are also capable of performing maintenance, inspections, repairs, and designs.

Process

This is another fun part of the process that we can spend a bit of our time on. You will find that there are a lot of tools and options that we can use when we bring out Lean and try to utilize it for some of our own needs. This is a simple process that can work along with a lot of the other parts that we need to improve our business and cut down waste.

When it is time for us to determine what is considered a wasteful process in our business, we want to make sure that we are going with some of the right stuff and that we aren't throwing away processes that are good for us, or keeping ones that we need to get rid of in the process. While we work on all of this, it is so important that we double-check and look to see whether the work environment that we use is in the optimum shape that it can be.

5S is regarded as a foundational component of the Toyota Production System because it helped keep the workplace neat and highly organized. This methodology was put in place because they knew how difficult it was to produce consistent results when a place is utterly messy.

The 5S cycle for systematic neatness in the workplace.

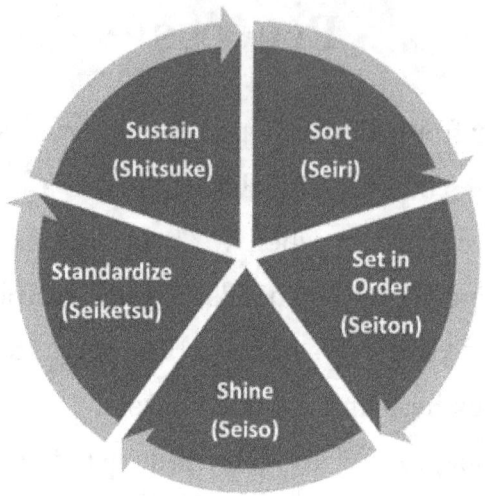

This is exactly what the 5S process is for. Each S in the cycle aims to organize workspaces such that all tasks can be performed safely and efficiently. It operates on the idea that if the workplace is kept clean and things are where they should be, it will be easier for employees to accomplish their tasks without wasting their time on non-value adding steps or exposing themselves to safety hazards.

Like Kanban, just-in-time, and jidoka, 5S is a concept that started out as a tool at the Toyota production floor.

Mistakes, delays, and accidents are probably not immediately blamed on all the clutter in the workplace. However, if you really think about it, all the mess usually prevents people from focusing on their jobs. Consequently, this only impedes the flow and it's only a matter of time before everyone gets stuck on the same spot.

Hence, to ensure the functionality of a workspace, the 5S can be used as a standard for maintaining order and structure. The terms were originally in Japanese, but close equivalents are used for the English translation. Here's what they stand for:

Sort (Seiri / Tidiness)

The first stage involves the examination of all the tools and equipment that are currently present in the area. The goal is to determine which of them should stay and which of them should be removed to free up some space. At the end of this process, only the necessary tools should be left behind.

Thus, it's worth asking:
- *What's the purpose of this particular item?*
- *Who's using it?*
- *When was the last time it was used?*
- *How often do people use it?*
- *Is it really a necessity in this workspace?*

The best people to ask regarding the items' value would be the people who are actually working in that area. For items that have been tagged as "unnecessary", these may be given away to another department, recycled, sold, thrown away, or put into the storage.

Set in Order (Seiton / Orderliness)

Now that you've set which tools or equipment will remain, you can now proceed to organizing items based on what reduces motion wastes the most. The key is to remember the statement, "A place for everything; everything in its place."

This means that things shouldn't just be grouped together in a logical manner, but they should also be placed in a logical location. For instance, if an item is used frequently, it should be located in a place where it's easy to pull out.

Shine (Seiso / Cleanliness)

Of course, keeping an area clean and organized requires work. Although it sounds very trivial, general cleaning is important enough to actually be involved as a crucial step in this process. This stage emphasizes the regular cleaning of work areas, which includes putting items in their storage, sweeping, mopping, wiping, etc. This also includes regular equipment maintenance. Cleanliness ensures that problems don't go hidden by clutter, while maintenance prolongs the lifespan of your tools and equipment.

Standardize (Seiketsu / Standardization)

In order to know which strategies are really working for you, detailed documentation must be conducted. This helps you establish standards that serve as an instant reference for how 5S can be maintained in your company.

Oftentimes the workplace instantly transforms when you've completed the first three stages of 5S. Making the changes permanent is usually the following challenge. To turn the new habits into a lifestyle, standards must be put in place. These can be in the form of setting schedules or assigning routines. Standards ensure that all your efforts towards order will not go to waste.

Sustain (Shitsuke / Discipline)

When the cleanup process has finally been standardized, you must then do the necessary work to maintain your new routines and update them as the situation deems fit. This final stage is all about keeping 5S going with the help of the entire workforce — from the managers to the employees.

The goal is to make 5S a long-term commitment, and not just a short-term solution for workflow efficiency. When people are disciplined enough to stick with 5S, it usually yields remarkable improvements.

Although 5S is relatively budget-friendly, its full effectivity still relies on your available resources. At the very least, it will involve expenses during the cleaning process. Additionally, you will need to train your employees regularly and acquire supplies such as labeling, shelving, floor markings, etc. to sustain the new practice.

In theory, the 5S methodology is very similar to a general house cleaning. In the workplace, however, there is this added consideration of whether item placements help in any way with movement and employee convenience. The general consensus is, the more convenient it is for everyone to get what they really need, the better.

Of course, starting the whole process can be daunting at first, especially if your workspaces haven't been neat for quite some time. Fortunately, implementing 5S can start small, and you only need to assign a few individuals — or one team at a time — to begin the process. A training module is highly recommended to show the full benefits of 5S over the long term.

Ultimately, the 5S methodology believes that a clean workspace is a productive workspace. If people never have to waste time looking for things ever again, then a general cleanup is indeed a great investment.

Kaizen

There are a lot of great options that we are able to work with when it is time to handle our businesses and even our own ways of life. And many of them are going to be able to help us to see some amazing results as well. But one of the best options that we are able to take a look at here is going to be known as Kaizen. This Kaizen is a Japanese word that means "continuous improvement" or "Change for the better." This is a philosophy that is found in Japan and talks about all of the processes that we are able to work with to help us improve operations. And when they are done well, they are going to also involve all employees in the process as well. Kaizen is going to work well and provide a huge improvement in productivity by going in a methodical and gradual kind of process.

The concepts that come with Kaizen are going to include a lot of different ideas along the way as well. It is going to involve us making the work environment that we have more efficient and can help improve some benefits with the help of creating a good atmosphere for a team to work with, by improving some of the procedures that happen in your company all day long. It can also include ensuring the satisfaction of the employees, rather than ignoring them, which can help to make the job that they are doing more fulfilling, safer, and less tiring.

Understanding Kaizen

While the options and discussion that we had above are going to provide us with a lot of information on Kaizen and what we are able to do with them, it is time to dive more into some of what this is all about. Some of the key parts that we need to remember with this kind of philosophy includes quality control, standardized ways of doing work, delivery that is just in time, the use of equipment that is efficient and safe, and the elimination of waste in the workplace as much as possible.

There are a lot of parts that are going to show up with this, but the overall goal that we see is that kaizen is supposed to help us to make some small changes, ones that are going to happen over time in order to help improve the company and the way that they do things. Keep in mind with this one that the alterations are going to happen. The idea here is that it is going to recognize that some small changes that we make right here and now are going to not just impact us now but will also help to make some big impacts on the future of the company as well.

There are actually a lot of companies that have adopted the kaizen concept. One notable option of this is Toyota.

The Requirements for Kaizen

Another thing that we need to take a look at here is the requirements that are meant to come with kaizen. There are a few things that companies who would like to work with Kaizen will need to consider. Some of the traditional ideas that come from Japan concerning Kaizen are going to come with five basic parts that we need to focus on along the way. These are going to include:

1. **Teamwork**
2. **Personal discipline among all the members**
3. **Improved morale of employees at all levels**
4. **Quality**
5. **Suggestions for improvement from anyone**

All of these are going to be important to what we can do with the kaizen process. First, we need to have some teamwork in place. When we have everyone on our team on the same page, and they are all able to work with one another, some beautiful things will happen. If they work separate from one another and do not value the ideas that each one brings to the table, then this will spell disaster for your business Kaizen encourages lots of teamwork.

From there, we have to make sure that the employees are able to handle their own personal discipline. You do not need to hire someone who will micromanage the employees in this kind of process, because you will have enough trust in your employees to know that they can step up to the plate and handle themselves. This kind of freedom can increase morale and helps the employees feel like you value them as an important part of the team, rather than seeing them just like another number, which is easy to get rid of.

As we mentioned, this is a system that will require us to have our employees as part of a team, and that we have to allow the employees' room to make decisions, bring up suggestions, and do their work without being constantly supervised. When we are able to create this kind of environment in our business, it ensures that we see higher morale for these employees. Higher morale is something that a lot of companies would like to have because it is so beneficial, but since they are not following the rules of Kaizen, it is something they have to go without.

Then we need to focus on quality. Yes, we want to increase profits and make a good product while reducing waste. But if we are not able to do this while also making a quality product to offer the customer, then you may as well give up on working with Kaizen because you are not using it well

And finally, when it comes to suggestions and ideas on how to improve the business and the processes, you need to take them from anyone. Don't have meetings on this that are closed door and don't kick anyone out of it. Each person is valuable in all of this, and you need to recognize that, or you are missing out on some of the best parts of the Kaizen process.

These five tenants are going to lead us to see three outcomes that can be so important to your company. They can help us to create some standardization, good housekeeping within the business, and the elimination of waste. Ideally, Kaizen is going to be so ingrained in what the company is doing that it becomes a part of the culture of the company, and it is going to become natural to the employees as well. This will ensure that it is going to work well in no time.

The concept of Kaizen is that it says there is not a perfect end and that there is room for improvement for everyone to enjoy all along. People need to strive in order to evolve and make innovations at all times.

The basic principles that come with this are that most people who perform certain tasks and activities are the ones who are going to have the most intimate knowledge about that activity and task, including them to effect change is going to make sense.

So, if there is someone out there who has spent a lot of time working on one part of the whole process, then these are the individuals you should go through and ask for suggestions and help with making changes. They are likely to have a lot of really good suggestions that we are able to utilize along with this and will ensure that we are going to make changes that work, rather than ones that make sense on paper but won't help us along the way in real life.

You will find that the different improvements that are going to happen with this will follow the format of PDCA. This is going to stand for the plan do check act. This plan portion of the whole thing is going to work on including us mapping out some of the changes that we have so that anyone who is working on that plan, no matter where they are in the whole process, know what they should expect when teams try to solve a problem.

They do part of this is going to mean that we want to work on implementing some of the best solutions to our own problems. And then we get to work on the check step in this. This step is important when we want to evaluate a solution to our problem and then see whether or not it is working how we want.

This is going to be so important because we do not want to go through and work on the whole process without being sure that it will work the way that we want.

Six Sigma

Six Sigma is the name that is given to a system we can use to measure the quality of a goal of getting as close to perfection in our processes as possible. A company that operates in perfect synchronicity would be able to generate as few as 3.4 defects per millions in the hopes of having very few unsatisfied customers in the process.

There are different levels of this based on where your business is and where they would like to go. The ultimate goal is to reach that perfection level that we talked about above, but for some companies, any kind of improvement will be a good thing and being able to move up in this, and come with fewer defects on your projects, will be a good goal to work on as well.

The Certification

The first thing that we will take a look at when working with this Six Sigma process is the certification levels that you and members of your team can get. This will have a few options depending on how much knowledge the person has about the process and even how long they have been able to work with it. You would have the executive level, for example, including your managed team members who would then be responsible for setting up Six Sigma and all of its parts within your company.

Then we can move to the Champion in this, which will be the person who has the knowledge and the ability to lead projects and even be the voice for the project if it is needed.

White belts would be following, and they will basically be the rank and file workers. They understand what Six Sigma is about, but they are just getting into this process and may not be as well-versed as some others who work with this. They are still important because they will often be the ones implementing some of the plans that come up through this process.

Then we move on to the yellow belts, which will be the active members of the team who works on Six Sigma. They can also spend some time to determine, in a few areas, where some improvements are necessary. Then we can move on to some of the green belts, who will work along with the following level, the black belts, in order to get things done and decide which projects to work with.

The black belts are following, and they will be able to lead some of the projects that are considered really important or higher up in your business while supporting and mentoring some of the other belts as they do more and more of their own work. Then we can end up with the master's black belts. These will be the individuals who are usually brought onto a project or business specifically to help implement it along the way. they will be there to guide and to mentor everyone else on the team so they can handle this project.

All of the belt levels are important, and they will be able to take on the necessary work to learn about Six Sigma, implement and use the project, and do all of the other steps that are necessary to make this as successful as possible. No one is really more important than the others, and everyone has a voice and something important to add to the conversation as we go through this process.

Implementing Six Sigma

When we are done setting everyone up to have the right belts and to know how to handle all of this process, it is time for us to jump on board and start implementing Six Sigma and all of the steps that you need for it. Giving your team a really good and compelling reason to go with Six Sigma and showing them how much it can benefit them will be so important to how much success you are able to get with this. If you don't have everyone on board with this, then you will not see a good amount of implementation when it comes to making things one work. It is important through all of this to motivate and help your team see why this is such a good thing for all of them.

A burning platform is a motivational tactic where you are able to explain the situation that the company is in right now and why that situation is so dire in the first place. Then you can show how Six Sigma is the only method that can help get the company out of that predicament and them the company to see some better results in no time.

Sometimes you may have to go through and do the process on a trial basis. Your management may be the ones who struggle with seeing why this is a good idea in the first place, and they may not want to jump on board and give it a try. You could get them to agree to do a small part of this, seeing how it works in one department, and then implementing it. This helps to save money and can make it easier for you to really show how great Six Sigma will be for everyone.

While we are going through all of this, you also have to make sure that all of the tools that your employees need for self-improvement are readily available to them. Once you are done with that initial round of training for Six Sigma, then it is important to have other tools that can help your employees keep up to date and can also be there to support them and help them move up the ranks. Reward this, offer some good mentorship to help others obtain this, and just make sure that your employees are not being stuck because of the processes or rules that you make.

Without this, you risk having your employees walking into this confused. And if you want to make this work out well, then the resources, the self-help, the mentorship, and anything else that your employees need have to be present the whole time to them without issues. There will be some questions that come up and your employees may get confused by some of the parts. If you offer the right resources from the beginning, you can avoid some of these issues while ensuring that your employees see the great benefits that come with Six Sigma.

The Key Principles

Now that we have a basic understanding of how this process works, it is time for us to move on and look at a few of the key principles that will show up with Six Sigma so we can better understand how this will fit into some of the work that we are trying to do. Lean Six Sigma will work based on the common acceptance of five important laws. We need to talk about all of these here.

That first law will be known as the law of the market. This means that the customer needs to be the one considered before you make any decision. If you try to make some decisions without first considering the customer, then you will end up in some trouble as we go through this.

Then we are able to move on to the second law. This will be the law of flexibility, wherein the best processes will be the ones that you can use for the greatest number of disparate functions. You need to be flexible in any business. This allows you to adapt and make some of the changes you need along the way and can be a fantastic way to not get stuck in the old.

Then we see the third law here. This is the law about focus, which will help make sure that we don't try to take on too much all at once. This one will state that a business should only focus on one problem for the business, even if there are a lot of potential problems that you can fix. You want to also focus on just the problem and not the whole business. This helps you to maintain your focus and not get taken in by too much at once.

We can then move on to our fourth law here. This is the law of velocity. This one will tell you that the greater number of steps that you add into the process, the less efficient it is. There are times when the process does need more steps than others, but if you just add in steps to make it look good, then you create a lot of waste, and that is a problem. This one will have us take a closer look at the process and then determine whether we can make some changes to it or not to eliminate the steps that cause the waste.

And then we will end this with the final step, the law of complexity. This one is a lot of fun, and it is potentially the place where you will find a lot of waste.

This one states that the simpler or the easier a process is, the better. We do not want a lot of complications in our system because this leads to more mistakes and a lot of waste in the process.

We then need to make sure that we choose the right processes. Just like with the Lean method that we have talked about through this guide, Six Sigma wants to be able to get rid of the waste as much as possible. And choosing the process that is right for our needs will make sure that this can actually happen. When it is time to decide which process you should apply to the method of Six Sigma, the best place that you can start is with any of the processes that you already know ahead of time are defective, and the ones that you would really like to reduce how many times the defect occurs in the first place. These must be obvious issues that you need to work on if you already know that they are a problem, so that can be some good news.

From this point, it is then just a matter of looking for instances where your takt time is not working all that well. When you find these places, you can then look into the steps where the number of available resources can be reduced and see whether you can make this a bit more effective in the process.

Kanban

Kanban refers to a software that is not just used on a whiteboard for listing out tasks using differently colored cards. It can do much more than that and help an organization in different ways, but it is important to stick with the principles laid down by the system.

As you know, Kanban is used in a plethora of industries, and its popularity is steadily on the rise. Right from established firms to start-ups, everybody is using Kanban to their advantage.

Kanban System

Now, you may wonder as to how Kanban can be implemented in software firms as it has its roots in the manufacturing industry. For this, we have to examine the differences between Kanban and other agile methods.

To start, the main difference between Kanban systems and SCRUM is that there are no time boxes in Kanban for tasks. The tasks that are a part of the Kanban system are larger and can be fewer in number. The time period assessment in Kanban systems is usually optional, or there will be none at all. There is no speed of team in Kanban systems, and only the average time is assessed for implementation.

These specifications make us think about what will remain of agile methods if all the main elements are removed. Increasing dimensions and reducing counting speed of a team will leave us with nothing. One will wonder as to how it is possible to consider supervision if the majority of tools have been taken out.

Most project managers tend to think about control and try to maintain it even when they do not have it. It is just a myth that a manager's supervision over development is mere fiction. If his team is not interested in working, the project is bound to fail even if he has full control over the team.

If the team is having fun when working on a project with proper efficiency, then there will be no need for control, as it will only increase costs.

Say, for example, one problem that is associated with SCRUM is the higher costs resulting from discussions and meetings and can end up leading to loss of time and at least one entire day being wasted to finish the sprint and another day to start the following one.

Kanban systems are different from SCRUM as they focus more on tasks. The main aim of Kanban systems is successfully completing a sprint. Tasks are the main focus. There is usually no sprint. The deployment is usually made when the completed work is ready for presentation. The team working on the tasks should avoid engaging in estimating the time taken to fulfill a task, as it can be incorrect and result in time wastage.

A manager should not worry about time estimates if he has faith in his team. The main objective of the manager is to prioritize tasks and fulfill objectives. That is his main job. There is no need for him to control anything else. The manager has to add items to the board based on their priority. This is the responsibility of a manager who adopts the Kanban system.

The team board of a Kanban system can look as follows. The following are placed from left to right.

Goals

This is an optional column but will be quite useful on a Kanban board. Goals that are high level will be placed here so that everybody on the team will know what they are going after and have a constant visual reminder. Some examples include increasing work speed by 15% or the name of the task.

Task Queue

Task queue refers to tasks that are ready to be started. The highest card that is placed in the queue is given top priority and is then moved to the following column.

Acceptance

This acceptance column and the columns before the 'Done' column might vary based on how the work is flowing for the team. Tasks that are currently being carried out need to be finalized in this column. Once the discussion about the same is done, it will be moved to the following column.

Development

The task is maintained here until it is completed. Once done, it will be moved to the following column. If the structure of the task is not correct or it is somewhat uncertain, then it can be moved back to this column.

Test

The test column in a Kanban system is one where those projects are being mentioned that are being tested. If there are any issues in this column, the tasks are moved to the development column. If there are none, then they will be moved to the following column.

Done

This has cards of tasks that are completely finished. People do not have to worry about these tasks anymore. Priority tasks might also appear in this column. They are those that need to be performed on a priority basis. If the task needs immediate attention, it should be mentioned under "expedite" tasks. These must be completed as soon as possible.

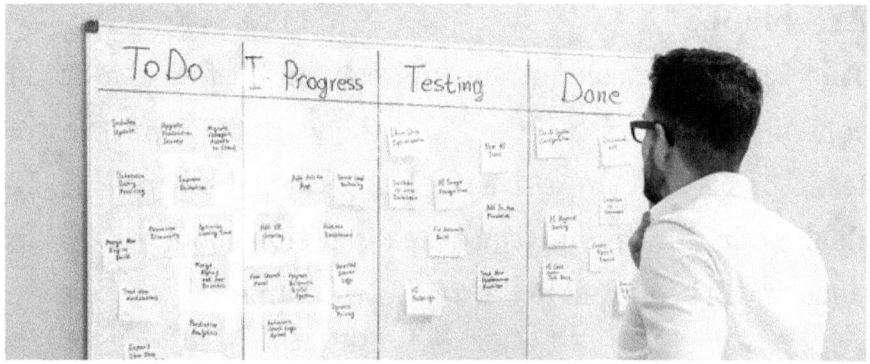

We have deliberated WIP limits throughout this manuscript and why it is important for all managers to set WIP limits. Under each task that is pinned on the board, it is important to place a number, which will stand for the number of WIP tasks that can be assigned at any given point in time. These figures are usually chosen based on a team's capacity. A project manager will be aware of the numbers to be placed based on trial and error.

Say there are ten programmers who are a part of a project, the tasks under Development will carry a number between 4 and 5, depending on the team's capacity. This number has to be ideal, that is, not too small or too big. If it is too small, the team can get bored, and if it is too big then they might not be able to finish the tasks.

A good way of coming up with the right number is dividing the number of developers into a team of two and then coming up with a figure based on past project experiences.

Similarly, tasks have to be assigned for personnel belonging to other departments such as sales and marketing, amongst others.

How Teams Benefit from Kanban

Here are some of the benefits that a team can derive by adopting the Kanban method.

To start with, it is important to reduce the number of tasks that are being performed at once in order to focus on finishing a majority. There will be no need to go into details of two or more tasks as it can lead to confusion. The manager will have planned the story queue, and all it takes for the team members is going through it to ensure that tasks are carried out on time. As you know, not everything in the test column will end up being a success. Some of it can throw up problems. In such cases, you must work as a team to solve the problem. Once that is done, you can move the items to the following column.

The time that is taken to finish a task has to be calculated. For this, the dates must be logged based on when a card was added to the task queue and when it was completed. The average waiting time will be calculated based on the time that was taken to finish a task. The manager or product owner will calculate this based on the figures at his or her disposal.

As we know, Kanban systems require a manager to adhere to a few basic principles, such as visualizing the product to divide the work into different tasks by placing colored cards on the board, limiting the WIP limit on each task at every subsequent stage of production, and measuring the cycle time to improve the processes involved, and to reduce the overall time. These are the basic terms of using Kanban, whereas when it comes to SCRUM, there can be nine terms, 13 terms in XP method, and 120 in RUP methods.

Kanban is not a project management or software development tool and does not tell people how projects should be carried out. It does not tell people how different processes should be planned and executed. It only provides a visual representation of the work and measures the progress of each team.

As opposed to SCRUM, Kanban can help to organize teams and improve their overall work. Microsoft has used Kanban since 2004 and has employed it in developing operations across the organization.

The best part of this system is that it can be applied to different departments and processes. If an organization is used to make use of agile techniques such as SCRUM and XP, or traditional ones such as waterfall, then Kanban can be extended to these methods to improve their overall functioning viz. quality of work, time taken to finish tasks, cycle times, etc. It can help the organization produce quality work in shorter periods of time.

Kanban in Software or Product Development

Applications software development teams use Kanban to implement Agile and Lean principles. Kanban systems give teams certain principles and practices that can help them visualize their work and deliver quality results within short times.

Teams who use these systems will have access to constant feedback that can help them improve their working standards.

They will also have access to market research and customer likes, therefore further speeding up delivery times.

Kanban systems have evolved over the years and have become more adaptable to different industries. The IT industry has greatly benefited from it and continues to invite takers. It might take some time for a company to adopt the different aspects that are a part of the system, but once done, it will prove a good fit.

Kanban systems also provide teams with the necessary tools and techniques to improve their service level agreements and reduce the risk involved in processing and the cost of delay of delivering end products to customers within the right times. Kanban systems help delivery teams to match customer expectations.

Many businesses have now started to use Kanban for portfolio management. It can provide them with agility and allows teams to perform tasks much faster.

Analytics

Lean Analytics is an approach to improve your business. It relies on you focusing on one single metric to measure your progress toward your goals. The manuscript refers to that metric as the One Metric That Matters. It's pretty straightforward, don't you think?

To start with Lean analytics, you should have great knowledge of the industry you're in. You should also know the current state of your business. Is it on its way to success? Is it failing? Or everything is doing fine with no signs of sudden success or failure?

The following step is to set a goal. It can be better sales, or it can be company expansion. Once the goal is set, you will need to determine your One Metric That Matters. If your goal is better sales, your One Metric That Matters is the number of sales your company will make.

Lean analytics isn't a static approach—it was before. Every business has its own unique needs and it changes, depending on the state it is in. This means that you need to change your One Metric That Matters from time to time. You need to reevaluate your company's performance and goal to know the proper metric to use following time.

Startups and Lean analytics

Lean analytics restrains a business from losing its focus on its goal. Startups benefit from it. It helps them overcome the initial pitfalls of starting a business. That pitfall is the fervor to do all things at once and recover investments made.

Lean analytics pushes startups away from going through premature scaling or growth. Instead of expanding, it pushes a business to establish a solid foundation. Businesses using lean analytics become solutions specialists.

It gives the company a direction, and a very narrow one at that. As mentioned before, lean analytics uses a single metric to measure progress. This approach has been developed from a business methodology called Lean Startup.

Lean Startup

Lean startup is a business methodology that promotes running a business as lean as it can. Steve Blank and Eric Reis helped popularize it.

The methodology encourages an entrepreneur to start a business with minimal resources. This includes minimizing employees, products, and services.

Regular and large-scale businesses use a Swiss knife to operate. A lean startup only uses a sharp and flexible single knife.

As the business operates, it improves and adds elements to the business when needed. Progression means the business obtains essential tools to help the single knife.

Build, Measure, and Learn

When it comes to product and service development, a Lean Startup uses lean analytics. Lean analytics follows a simple build, measure, and learn development cycle.

For example, if the entrepreneur has an idea for a product, he'll start to build. He'll then measure and test the product. He'll then gather data from the measurements. And then he'll learn how he can improve the product based on data and lean analysis.

The improvements learned are ideas that he'll use to build again. The cycle repeats until he creates the perfect product.

During the measurement and learn cycles, companies undergo five stages:

Empathy: Connecting to customers and knowing what they want.

Familiarity: Making your brand, products, and services stick to customers' minds.

Virality: Making non-customers discover your brand, product, or service.

Revenue: Developing methods to further improve revenue from your products and services.

Scale: Enlarging your reach and customer base.

For example, you have built a new car model. You will first deal with the customers and test the product. Once they finish testing the car, you will gather data from them by asking for feedback. You then enter the learn and build phase again.

In the following measurement phase, you will then make your way to introduce the car to more people. You'll do that by making the car more appealing. Then another cycle goes by.

After that, you will focus on the revenue aspect of the new car. If you learn that the model is viable for your business, then you can start scaling your production.

To move through the stages, you need to follow the hook model. The hook model has four phases.

They are:

Trigger: Event that needs to be done to start the lean analytical stage.

Action: Action that needs to be done to act upon the trigger.

Variable Reward: Motivator to make the action continue.

Investment: Motivator to make the stakeholders proceed to the following stage.

The Pitfall

Amateurs, like me before, always tend to get trapped in the wrong mindset. When they start a business, they tend to think that it's as simple as:

- Think of a product
- Develop the product
- Sell the product
- Profit!

Mind you, that's not a bad mindset to have. After all, you can simplify a business like that. The only problem is that they get stuck with that simplification. They fail to see or discover the intricacies behind every process.

For example, an entrepreneur wants to start a coffee shop. He finds a location for it. Build the shop. List the menu he wants to be present in the shop. And opens it. And like before, his business fails. Why did that happen?

The problem is that the coffee shop owner thought that he's done after the initial stage. He thought that the business will grow by itself.

Unfortunately, you can't plant a seed, water it for a few days, let it grow by itself, and harvest the fruit after. You can't treat a business that way. You don't stop and wait.

For one, you should never end the connection between you and the customer after he buys your product. Your job isn't done yet if someone gets your service and product. You should get feedback.

Customer feedback is the most important element in a successful business. The wants of the customer are your ticket to success.

For example, do you still remember Twilight? Do you remember the time when it was the most popular romance manuscript title on the market? Because of its immense popularity, many amateur and veteran authors had an idea. They took it to themselves to write manuscripts about vampires. What happened? Did another vampire story become popular? No. What happened was that Fifty Shades of Gray took the throne. Was that a vampire story? No. So why did it become popular?

The author of that manuscript is a fan of Twilight's author. And she knows well what made Twilight good. She was a customer. It wasn't about the vampires. It was about the kind of romance that made the manuscript sell well.

It's the same for other products. Just because bubble tea is popular doesn't mean that people will buy bubble tea from you. Customers have individual needs. And if you want your product to sell, your product must meet those needs. If a certain bubble tea is popular, get one and analyze it. Talk to the people who drink that product and ask what they like.

Use the feedback and imitate the tea. Sell it. And you now have a higher chance of having a successful business.

Tips for Success

Why aren't more big companies adopting this lean Start-up approach when it comes to the development of new products or services? For many big companies, process and culture vary in significant ways. A Start-up typically has smaller groups working on a project. These smaller groups can more quickly make decisions, obtain funds, and work more efficiently because they are just a small group of individuals. Many large companies are either unable or unwilling to work with a small group mentality.

In large companies, it takes a great deal of time for decisions to be made because the groups are large, so communication is slowed down and more challenging. Keeping everyone on the same page is nearly impossible because the number of people that need to be aligned is so great. The most common setbacks many large companies encounter, according to a study published in The Harvard Business View website, when trying to adopt a leaner approach include:

1. **Showing customers, investors, or stakeholders a product too early.**
2. **Being unable to create viable products.**
3. **Lacking necessary resources.**
4. **Having a business model that is not flexible.**

Customer relationship shifts. Additionally, another major concern for larger companies comes from the top executive who feels this approach to product creation takes away some of their authority both among the employees but also through the eyes of the customers. They fear that when showing products too soon to customers, their credibility is at stake. Relying on data and analysis makes them feel as though they do not have the knowledge to make the soundest decisions when bringing a product to life.

Large companies also lack innovators in the company. While many of the individuals are skilled in the operations aspects, not many have the talent to create unique products, services, or systems to keep up with the changing market. There is a wedge that divides the concept of a Start-up business and incorporating these concepts into a big business that has more structure, policies, executives, and standards.

With the many challenges, it is obvious why many large companies or established companies fail to implement or properly implement the concept of a lean model. More often than not, there is a greater misunderstanding of what actually needs to be measured and what should be learned through product development. Companies may fail to understand the lean analytics or the measure and learn aspects of the lean cycle. This focuses on what you should measure and why and how to properly track what is important.

It doesn't matter if you are just starting out or have been in business for years because, although the lean Start-up idea is the best way for many businesses to grow faster, it can also be the solution for an established business to come up with more innovative products in a less amount of time. Here are three simple steps you can take to incorporate the lean Start-up method into your small business.

1. Identify the customer problem and create a solution.
Every business is constantly trying to come up with new ideas, products, services, and marketing strategies. This is done by talking to your customers. You can't understand what they need if you don't talk to them first. As with the case of the Swiffer creation, this doesn't always have to mean conducting interviews; it can just simply be watching what your customers do and how they do it, then paying attention to a way it could be made easier for them.

Once you have identified the potential problem your customers face, you need to see if it is a valid problem. For this, you simply need to ask random people if they think it is a good idea or if they would use it. If you find that more people would be interested in this idea, then you move forward to testing it.

2. Develop your MVP

The MVP is where many companies have an issue with applying the Lean Start-up Method. How can you put a product out on the market before it is 100% completed? This is the number one concern of most businesses that hesitate to adopt a lean approach. Many established businesses believe that putting out an MVP will discredit their accomplishments since the MVP is often the bare minimum demo of a product. The value of testing out an MVP is also not understood by older generation entrepreneurs. This is because they are set on the way business has always operated and just accept that some ideas succeed, and some fail. An MVP forces them to change this way of thinking. This is often due to a misunderstanding of what the MVP actually is or can be. Your MVP gives a select group of your target audience a sneak peek of the most important features. This can be done through a video introduction, small scale model, or preorder sign-ups. The idea is to get the product out to a small portion of the public to determine if it will be successful or not and what you can change or adjust to make it more successful.

This MVP will help eliminate wasted time developing a full product that ends up being useless to your customers. The MVP shouldn't take long to develop, and it doesn't have to have all the bells and whistles; it just needs to do what it is intended to do. Get it seen and gain feedback to determine whether it is worth pursuing.

3. Experiment and measure results

Experiment, measure, repeat. This is the core of the Lean Startup method. By conducting experiments, you take the major risks out of the equation. You determine what issues you may run into, come up with a solution, and then test out the solution to see how valid it is. This is where you can begin to develop your ideas and concepts on a particular product fully and how things will run when in full production. These are low-cost experiments that should take a short amount of time to get started. The more experiments you can run in a shorter time frame, the more information you can gain and the more confident you can be before moving forward.

Lean Analytics Cycles

The Lean analytic cycle is similar to that of the scientific method. Through the cycle, you begin to piece together all the data, concepts, and information you have thus far and begin to execute the best way to approach each business problem. For each stage, you will begin a new cycle where you will identify the main problem, choose the one metric, and get to work.

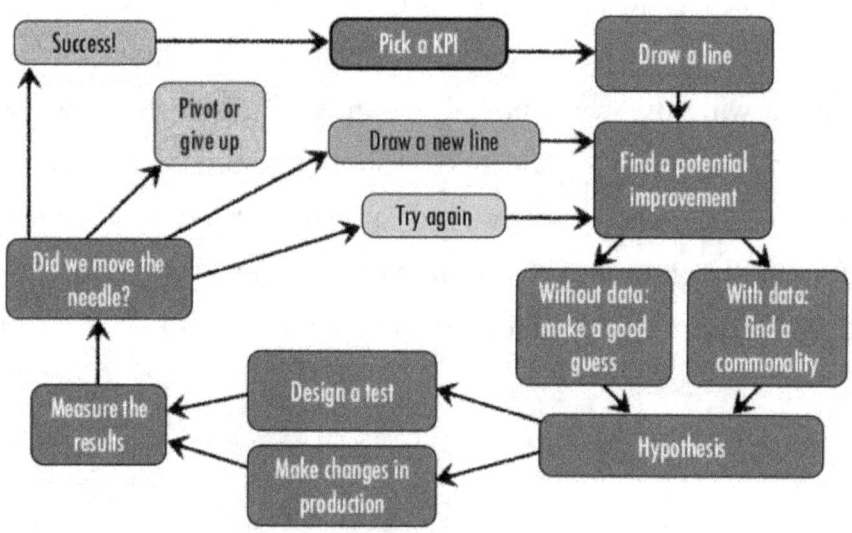

The Lean Analytics Cycle is vital in helping you get started on this part of the Lean support methodology with your business. Four steps will come with this process and following each one can be crucial in ensuring that this works for you.

The Lean Analytics Cycle will be incredibly helpful when you begin going through the entire process. Let's take a look at the steps that you need to fulfill to use the Lean Analytics Cycle.

Form a Hypothesis

The hypothesis is when you create different ways to test out your KPIs. This can be by developing a marketing campaign to test features on a product or changing your pricing, just to name a few examples.

This is a stage where a level of creativity needs to come into play. The hypothesis gives you the answers that you need to move forward. You will need to look for inspiration, and you can find it in one of two ways. You can look for an answer for something like "If I perform ____, I believe ____ will happen, and ____ will be the outcome."

The first place you can look into is any data that you have available. Often, this data will provide you with the answer that you need. If you do not have data at all, you may need to do some studying to come up with an answer. You could use some of the strategies from your competitors, follow the practices that have worked well for others, do a survey, or study the market to see what the best option will be.

What you need to keep in mind here is that the hypothesis is there to help you to think like your audience. You want to keep asking questions until you understand what they are thinking or learn to understand the behavior of your audience or customer.

You can often turn toward data collected to come up with the best way to improve your KPI. Look at what your customers have in common. Focus on the customers that are doing what you want. For example, if you are focusing on lowering your churn rate, or the yearly rate of how frequently customers stop subscribing to your services, then you want to understand why the customers that stay is staying. Where do they come from; what is their buying process? Get inside the head of your customers to form your hypothesis.

If you do not have data collected, then you can turn to several other sources to make the best-educated guess. Do this by:

- **Understanding your market.** Surveys, feedback, or just getting out there and talking to your audience can give you enough information to create your hypothesis.

- **Look at what your competitors are doing.** While you have your unique idea in mind, it doesn't hurt to rely on what is already being done to understand how it can be improved. Your competitors may be doing something well that you can implement but also improve upon; you won't know how to improve it if you don't test it out yourself first.

- **Get up to date on what the best practices are.** You can gain inspiration from reading up on the ways different companies are doing business. How are they using content marketing? How have they been able to grow quickly? Understanding the best practices in your industry and the business world can lead to a hypothesis that truly accelerates your growth.

- **You create your hypothesis by considering the action you will take and what the result of the action will be.** The result should lead you to the desired outcome. It should be written out in this way:

- **If I do (insert action), I believe (insert result) will happen, which will get me (desired outcome).**

- **This hypothesis should be placed in a location where you and your team can view it daily.** Having it visually present will remind you what you are working towards.

Experiment

Once you have your hypothesis set, you will begin to come up with a way to put it into action. This may require making changes to the production process to test the product out with half of your customers.

When choosing an experimental path, you need to be able to answer the who, what, and why about your target audience.

- **Who will your experiment be for?** You need to know what target audience you want to test your experiment out on or which target audience you are expecting to act in a certain way. You need to know if the audience you are trying to reach is the right one if you appeal to them and if their behavior can be changed.

- **What do you want this target audience to do?** You need to be clear about what you will ask this audience to do. You will want to determine if there is something that might get in the way of them completing what you expect them to and how many of them will do what you want them to.

- **Is what you are asking worthwhile to them?** You need to be sure your targets understand why they would want to do what you are asking them. What is their motivation for doing it, or what makes them do the same thing for a competitor but not you? Your target audience wants to know what is in it for them, and if what you offer is more appealing or convenient than what your competitor already offers.

The answers to these questions are derived from your customer development, which is how you can fully understand your customers.

After answering these questions, you should have a statement that looks like: WHO will do WHAT because WHY.

The who, what, and why should result in improving your KPI. If you have a solid hypothesis, then you will come up with a solid experiment to test this hypothesis. Once you have decided on the experiment, you move on to determining how you will measure the outcome. Before you can begin to measure, you need to have a starting baseline to compare to.

Types of experiments can include:

- *Marketing campaigns*
- *Application redesign*
- *Change in pricing*
- *Location of shipping costs*
- *Testing out different platforms*
- *Wording or word usage*
- *Rest new features*
- *How your business appeals to customers.*

Measure your Outcomes and Decide

Was your experiment a success, or did you learn what did not work? If you had success with your experiment, then you can simply move on to determine the following metric to test and start experimenting again.

You can't just get started with an experiment and then walk away from it. You need to measure how well it goes to determine if it is truly working; if some changes are needed; or if you need to work from scratch. You can then decide on the following steps you need to take. Some of the things to look for when measuring the outcomes during this stage include:

- **Was the experiment a success?** If it is, then the metric is done. You can move on to finding the following metric to help your business.

- **Did the experiment fail?** Then it is time to revise the hypothesis. You should stop and take some time to figure out why the experiment failed so that you have a better chance at a good hypothesis the following time.

- **The experiment moved but was not close to the defined goal.** In this scenario, you will still need to define a brand-new experiment. You can stay with the hypothesis if it still seems viable, but you would need to change up the experiment.

If you did have much success, it doesn't mean you just give up. You now have several options as to how to move forward:

- If the experiment was of no success whatsoever, then consider first what you learned, then revisit your hypothesis. You may need to come up with a new target audience, a new action taken by the target audience, or a new motivating factor.

- If you had slight success with your experiment, again first look at what you learned, then make minor adjustments to your experiment and try it again. If you saw some success with your experiment, it might not be that your hypothesis is completely wrong; it might just mean you need to tweak a few things.

Through the experiment, you will be able to determine if the result moves you closer to your end target. If you are moved closer to the end target, then you can move forward to the following metric that matters. If, however, you notice you are moving farther away from the target, you need to evaluate your data and make a shift in your business, your model, or your market.

Decide

After studying all the data and determining whether your experiment was a success or not, you now need to decide: *Do you pivot or persevere?*

Sometimes, you need to change your strategy to meet the overall vision you have for that product. This may require simply adjusting a part of your experiment and repeating the process. You may need to pivot in a new direction in one or more areas.

Pivot does not mean failure; it is a way of bringing to focus on what is working or is not working in the process. When you can catch what isn't working, you can make adjustments to experiment in a new direction.

You can also persevere. In this case, you don't need to pivot but move forward. When your experiment is a success, you can feel confident that you are on the right path to developing the right product.

Types of Kanban Systems

Many organizations have started to use Kanban systems to improve their productivity. There are different types of cards that can be used in a Kanban system since Kanban, unlike 6-Sigma, is not a fixed methodology. It is for this reason that it can be used for different purposes. The different types of Kanban systems are listed out in the part. This is not an exhaustive list of the Kanban system can mean different things to various organizations.

Supplier Kanban

A supplier is an organization or individual from whom another organization sources material to make its products. This system moves directly towards the supplier and is often entered as a representation of the manufacturer.

Regardless of the type of Kanban system used, it is important to note that a Kanban system is a way to increase the productivity and quality of the products and services provided by an organization.

Through Kanban

Kanban systems comprise of both production and withdrawal Kanban systems.

These systems are used in situations where both the workstations associated with the two Kanban systems are adjacent to each other.

This system speeds the process of production. For example, if an organization has the area of production and area of storage subsequent to each other, the system will pull parts from the two systems and operate on those parts across the production queue.

Withdrawal Kanban

This system is also known as a conveyance or move cards Kanban. If any component needs to be transferred from the production Kanban to another type, this system is used for signaling. The cards are connected to different tasks that must be taken to a workplace when they should be completed. Once the tasks are complete, the cards are returned.

Emergency Kanban

This type of system is used to replace any defective parts or to signal to the entire team that the quantity of a product or service required to be manufactured has either increased or decreased in number. Organizations often use emergency Kanban systems when a particular part of a system has stopped functioning the way it is supposed to or when there are any changes made to the process.

Production Kanban

This system is made of an exhaustive list of tasks that must be completed to ensure that a product is delivered on time. This system brings in information on different materials and parts that are required along with the information from Withdrawal systems. This system allows the team to start with the production of the product and also explain the services or products that must be produced.

Express Kanban

This system is one that comes into the picture when there is a shortage of parts within the system. These systems send signals to the teams to increase the number of parts that are required to complete the process in hand. This system aims to ensure that the manufacturing process or production process is not slowed down. These systems are often called signal Kanban systems since they are used to trigger any shortage or purchase.

Kanban Board

The Kanban board allows teams to visualize the work and the workflow. Teams can use this board to optimize the workflow. If you want to use a physical Kanban board, you can use a whiteboard and sticky notes.

These notes will communicate the progress, issues, and status of every task. You can also use online Kanban boards, but these are only a refinement of the physical Kanban board.

The Kanban technique only emerged in the 1940s when Toyota re-imagined its approach towards engineering and manufacturing. The line-workers used actual Kanban cards to let their suppliers know there was a demand for some parts in the assembly line. This made it easier for teams to communicate with each other about what work needed to be completed and by when. This process also helped with maximizing value and reducing waste.

As mentioned earlier, the application of Kanban was not only influenced by the Toyota Production System, but also by Lean thinking. This new version of Kanban came into existence in 2005. The core principles of Kanban, covered in the first volume, are the same in most industries, including human resource management and software development. The following are the principles of Kanban:

- **Visualize your work**
- **Limit the work in the process**
- **Focus on the workflow**
- **Practice continuous improvement**

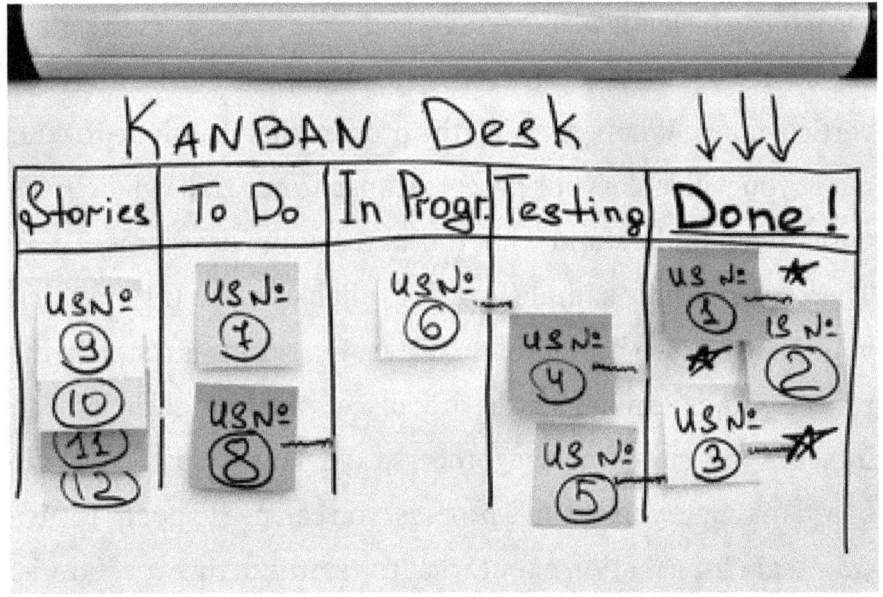

Visualize the Work and Workflow

When it comes to manufacturing, the complete workflow is always visible. One can view the workflow through the production line. In work that requires some knowledge, the process is opaque. This means that you will need to map the process on the Kanban board, and use cards to represent the work. This provides visibility into the workflow and also gives people a chance to look at the different aspects of work.

Since most teams have their own process to complete their tasks, Kanban boards will give teams the freedom to map their workflow.

You will need to lay the simple processes out on the board in the form of vertical lanes.

If you have complex processes, you can use horizontal and vertical lanes. When you map the process that is unique to your team, you will make your process transparent. This will help the entire team understand what the status of the process is.

There are multiple sample boards available on the Internet that you can use to see how Kanban works. Every lane is a step in the process, and Kanban cards are placed against each lane to indicate the status of the process. When you customize the board to reflect your team's process, you can use to board to give your team information about what the status of the workflow is.

You should know that the card color can determine the type of work or its priority. Any visual indicators, like avatars or user icons, can be placed on the card to indicate who the work is assigned to. You can also use these icons to indicate the class of service, source of demand, and any other detail that is relevant to the work your team is doing. You can always decide what your board should look like and how each card should represent the work you are doing.

There are many benefits to visualizing your workflow and your work. You can start with understanding how your brain processes information. The human brain can understand any visual information 60,000 times faster than it can understand the text. Since you can create a picture of your work using a Kanban board, the visual display makes it easier and faster for team members to understand the progress and status.

You can display these visual details in one place, which minimizes the time the team takes to track the progress. This will also reduce the number of status meetings that you will need to have. The stakeholders and team members can use the Kanban board and cards to communicate high-value information in a simple and transparent way.

Optimize the Flow of your Work

The above benefit is only one of the many benefits of using the Kanban system and Kanban board. Through Kanban, teams can get rid of visual to-do lists. They can effectively optimize their workflow and tools, which will improve collaboration. This is because teams can limit the work in progress, be transparent about their work, and gather the necessary metrics to improve and measure productivity and efficiency.

The objective of the Kanban system is to limit the quantity of work that is under process so that the work that flows into the system can be managed easily. In simple words, systems can handle only some amount of traffic, so it is important to ensure that the traffic moves smoothly through the various steps of the process.

When the system is overloaded with work, things will certainly slow down, and the flow will turn into a jam. It is easy to spot the work that is stuck on a Kanban board since any backlog will affect the work that is in the lanes. This will give the team clarity about what work needs to be completed immediately to remove any backlog.

You can use more than one work in progress limit on a Kanban board. This limit is more of a constraint that is applied to some parts of the workflow or to the whole process. When you use these limits, you can improve how the workflows through the steps that you have defined on the board. This will help to improve the efficiency of your team.

When your Kanban system is correctly implemented, it will become the center for continuous improvement. A team can always measure its effectiveness by tracking its lead times throughout, quality, and more. Analysis and experiments can help the team, and the organization changes the system. This will help the team improve its efficiency and effectiveness.

Running a Project with Kanban

When setting out to incorporate Kanban into a project, it's important to note that the project itself does not have an iterative nature under the Kanban methodology. Rather, Kanban is a type of workflow management system that enables you to carry out tasks in a sequential and linear manner. As a result, your task flow management becomes much more efficient, thereby enabling you to reduce time and waste.

How so?

The reason for this is that Kanban isn't an iterative methodology in the way that Scrum is. As such, the way a project is run under the Kanban principle is meant to be incremental. So, one task gives way to another, and so on. As we have stated earlier, there is a clear need for one task to be cleared off the Board before another can begin. If there are too many tasks on the Board at the same time, then the project may end up falling behind schedule.

It's important to note that a Kanban has one beginning and one end. Unlike Scrum, there are no sprints. There are, however, cycles. Each cycle is completed every time a User story is done. When a User Story is completed, the customer can be summoned to get an update on the process of the project. Thus, the beginning of the project is marked by the official kickoff while the end of the project is marked when the customer gives the final "okay."

Getting Started with a Kanban Project

Kanban-based projects start out pretty much like any other project. There is a customer that want something done and a project team that can do it. Just like Scrum, the customer can be external or internal, depending on the dynamic of the project.

Here is where things diverge somewhat from Scrum. In a Kanban project, there is the leader of a "project manager" who is the owner of the project, so to speak. The project manager is tasked with being the person who coordinates the administrative side of the project. Unlike the Product Owner, the project manager may be an internal stakeholder who is responsible for ensuring the project gets done.

The project manager is responsible for producing the project charter and any other relevant documentation that may be needed as part of the project's governance. Please bear in mind that documentation ought to be kept to a minimum. So, only the required paperwork should be put together in order to make sure the rules of the game are clear.

Then, the project manager can go about searching for a Service Request Manager. The SRM can be an additional person that is dedicated solely to the project itself, or the project manager can double up in this role.

In fact, it makes a lot more sense for the project manager to double up in this role as it means that there is one less line of reporting.

This reduces the time wasted among the various interlocutors communicating. As such, this concept diverges from Scrum as the stakeholders, and Product Owners are different individuals. In Kanban, it doesn't really matter, especially when stakeholders are keen on ensuring the project gets done.

The project manager, or SRM, is then in charge of defining the project's scope and deliverables. By sitting down with the customer, the project manager can determine what needs to be done. This workflow management leads to the creation of User Stories. The User Stories, just like Scrum, are the description of the end users who will interact with the final outputs delivered by the project. In the end, the User Stories create the project Backlog. The Backlog is comprised solely of User Stories as tasks are determined far along on by the project team.

Once the scope of the project and User Stories have been defined, the project manager can go about assembling the project team. It should be noted that there is no prescribed number of team members, as is the case in Scrum. The number of team members can be as high as it needs to be. In fact, large projects work well under Kanban as there is no restrictions in the dynamic of the workflow. Since Kanban is sequential in nature, the project manager can simply go about determining what needs to be done and how many people need to do it.

As such, the project manager needs to be an experienced individual in the project's field. The project manager needs to understand the needs of the tasks that will be completed in order to determine how long tasks will take and how they should be completed. While the project team has the freedom to determine their workflow, the project manager needs to be the guide for the overall tempo of the project.

Assembling the Team

As mentioned earlier, the project manager is tasked with bringing the team together. Since the project manager is the main interlocutor with the customer, they cannot be fully immersed in the project. This means that they cannot have a functional role within the project team through the project manager may be able to contribute any way they can.

The profile of each team member needs to fit the needs of the project. So, if the team is building a house, there is a need for plumbers, masons, electricians, carpenters, and so on.

The actual number of each type of member is determined by the overall scope of the project. As such, a small project would require a smaller number of members, while a large project would require a larger team.

On the whole, the project team is self-regulating. This means that they are able to distribute the workflow as they see fit. This means that team members are encouraged to rotate from task to task so long as they are able to complete them in a timely manner. The last thing that you want to have is a rigid structure in which everyone is typecast into a role they cannot get out of. By fostering collaborative communication, the team can determine who does what and when.

Although, it should be noted that the project manager has the official ruling in which User Stories are prioritized. The prioritization of the tasks related to that User Story depends on the project team. The thing that matters is that each individual task is completed within the allotted time (time boxing) and that the User Story is completed within the timeframe established at the outset of the project.

As for the Service Delivery Manager role, the SDM ought to be a project team member that is doubling up on this role. Since the main purpose of this role is to ensure quality and continuous improvement, it makes sense to have a team member perform this role.

Of course, this role has no authority, so it's not meant to be a "boss" that supervises everyone else. If you wanted to go about this role democratically, you could rotate the position among members who are qualified and willing to do it. This divides up the responsibility and does not place the burden solely on one person.

Divvying Up Time

Since Kanban is sequential, time is managed by determining how long individual tasks ought to take. So rather than fitting X number of tasks in X amount of time, X amount of time is assigned to X number of tasks. This means that the time needs to be cognizant of how much time they really need to get things done. That's why it's a good rule of thumb to overestimate task time by around 20%. If there is ever any time leftover, this time ought to be allocated to testing. Please keep in mind that testing is of the utmost importance under the scope of an Agile-based project.

As for the number of days and hours that a project team plans to work, this is determined by the team itself. This means that the team needs to figure out how much time they are going to devote to individual tasks. Once a task is completed, they can move on to the following. Doubling up on tasks, or multitasking is discouraged as this can lead to the "In Progress" column getting jammed.

Lastly, it's worth noting that since Kanban focuses on incremental progress, cycles will never be distributed evenly. As such, some cycles may take longer than others. This is something that the customer needs to be aware of.

Project Cycles

In short, a project cycle refers to the transition of a User Story from Backlog all the way to the "Completed" column. The overall cycle is determined by the User Story going from a sketch to a working piece of kit. This is when the customer can see what the team has produced at every stage of the process.

Here are the main stages of the cycle:
Backlog. The User Stories are created by the project manager and assigned to the Backlog. Depending on the nature of the User Stories, the project manager may decide to prioritize one story at a time, or perhaps tackle multiple stories simultaneously so long as the project team is able to handle it.
Planned. At this point, the project team comes together to plan how the User Story will be completed in terms of the tasks that need to be done. Work is divided up and assigned to individual team members. The SDM can be named at this point and tasked with keeping track of time.

In progress. The User Story is moved to this column along with all the cards that correspond to the tasks in progress. The SDM needs to ensure that the Board is updated constantly as tasks are completed and moved on to the following column. It should be noted that anything that is still being worked on is in progress.

Developed. The finished task is considered to be developed when there is no additional work needed on it. Then, the card is moved to this column while the task waits for it to be tested.

Tested. Generally, there is a testing team that is assigned to this task. The testing team should only test as many tasks as they have the capacity for. Often, they cannot test multiple tasks a time; this means that they might need to test one task at a time. Once the tasks have been tested and pass criteria, the card can then be moved to this column. When all tasks have been tested, and the complete User Story has been tested out, the User Story card can be moved to the "Tested" column.

Completed. Lastly, once all the testing has been completed and the customer gives the green light, the User Story can be moved to the "completed" column. Individual tasks that have been developed, tested, and approved also go to this column.

Building a Lean Team

Regardless of whether you are working in a startup or working on building an internal project in an established organization, the lean team approach will maximize the efficiency and the results in uncertain times. That said, it is hard to assemble a group that can execute this vision. This process also comes with the routine challenges and questions that are unique to the methodology. Now, look at seven steps you can use to build a Lean team.

Start Small

Amazon follows the "two-pizza team" approach. In this approach, you must always start with a small team if you want to work on developing new methods. You should aim to develop a team that you can feed easily with just two pizzas. When you have a smaller team, you will see that the members bond faster, which will improve the communication within the team. A small team also ensures that a decision is made quickly, and new methods can be tested faster. There is also better accountability since every member of the team is aware of what they need to do.

Make the Team Cross-Functional

Yes, there are very few people on the team. This does not mean that you do not capitalize on their abilities. Every lean team should be cross-functional, which means that different members of the team should bring out a different ability or skill that will represent the different departments in the company. In enterprise organizations, the teams have employees from the same departments, and once they complete their work, the results or the output will be shared with the following department. This is an inefficient approach since ideas are not shared between departments, which will lead to subpar solutions.

If you want to build a cross-functional team, you should first sit down and understand the needs of the project. You must understand the project and identify the different departments that must be involved to make some progress. You should also identify potential roadblocks and see how they can be avoided. Eric Rise, in his above manuscript, talks about an industrial project. For this project, the team should include a product designer, a member with manufacturing expertise, and marketing or a salesperson who understands the needs of the customers. A project in a different industry will require a different set of people. There are numerous combinations that you can look at, depending on what needs to be achieved at the end of the project.

Every project manager or team leader must be aware of what the project is and also see if they need to obtain some permissions from the legal department. Make sure that you identify the different departments that need to be involved in the project at the start so you can avoid any delays. You can always ask for volunteers if you have issues with finding a person from a specific department to join your team.

Never Over-Rely on Team Players

Most project managers make the mistake of depending on the same employees to ensure that the team works together. This will impact the productivity and satisfaction of those employees since they will be overloaded.

A study was conducted by the Harvard Business Evaluation to understand employee satisfaction.

The study concluded that employees who are always in high demand because they are seen as collaborators in their company have the lowest career and engagement satisfaction scores. Some experts say that it is easy to prevent overload by reducing some unnecessary meetings, and let individuals know that it is okay for them to say no and let someone else take their place.

Train People to Be Team Smart

It is important to ensure that every employee in a team excels in that team. To do this, you must invest in training. Companies make the mistake of focusing on helping a team member develop professionally at an individual level. They develop training programs that do not focus on teams, but only on people. Managers and employees are never educated on how they can contribute effectively to the team or how to build a better team. Many companies are team dumb since the collective intelligence of the team is independent of the intelligence of the members of the team.

A company with the smartest employees can still have terrible teams. A paper published in 2010 in the Science journal showed that the collective intelligence or "c-factor" is correlated with the communication and environment within the team.

This factor is dependent on how the conversations take place in the team, the social sensitivity of the group, and the number of women in the group. This research also suggested that teams that fail at completing one task are likely to fail all other tasks as well. You, as the project manager, can increase the c-factor in the team by guiding the different members of the team about how to work together.

Creating a Pro-Risk Environment

If you want to create breakthroughs or find some innovative solutions, you need bold ideas and the willingness to make mistakes. Individuals in lean teams should learn to welcome both failure and risk. It is difficult to create this mindset in teams since most organizations still follow the principle of "failure is not an option". The dynamics of the team will make it hard to change this mindset since every member of the team will want to play it safe. Nobody will ever want to look like a fool in front of their colleagues. That being said, you could use some pragmatic tools and psychological insights to coach your team into feeling brave about failing and taking risks.

Each member of the team has a different trait, but since everyone is a human being, most of their behavioral and psychological patterns are the same.

This may seem obvious to you now, but the truth is that people often overlook this insight. Companies only focus on the personalities, capabilities, and expertise of the individuals they hire, but research states that people with different capabilities can work together and deliver projects on time if the right environment is created for them.

It is important to let your teams know that their decisions will not result in litigation or a loss of millions of dollars. You must help your teams understand what can be undone and what cannot. A team should have a reverse button at some point where they can step back, accept that it is not going to work, and try a different approach. They should, however, make those decisions quickly. If the team works on identifying the reversible risks, people will not be bogged down because this will reduce the chance of a blame game.

Understanding the Needs of the Team

Every member of a team will join that team with specific assumptions in mind, and they work on trying to understand how to get their work done. They also have some assumptions about how the communication in the team should work.

If you want to ensure that your team works as a cohesive unit, you must understand the different assumptions that each individual is working with.

Every team member walks around the team with an assumption about how each member of the team should behave. If there is an individual who constantly interrupts people, the other members of the team may believe that he or she is a jerk.

It is for this reason that experts recommend that every team should develop a charter of norms. These norms will answer simple questions like:

- How do we want to work together?
- How do we react to a situation where we disagree with each other?
- Are we going to make some proposals?
- Are there going to be arguments about tasks?
- How do we come to a decision?

When you develop the charter, identify the different scales that you want to cover. Ensure that you cover the scales surrounding evaluating, scheduling, communicating, disagreeing, trusting, persuading, deciding, and leading.

Measure to Learn and Improve the Team

Regardless of whether you want to build a new team or improve an existing team, you cannot simply start without considering the team and measuring the team.

Your measurements do not have to be elaborate, and they can be as simple as assessing the current sentiment in the team. By this, you should try to understand how people feel about the team spirit.

You can assess this during every team meeting. Ask your team members to give the team a rating between one and five. If they are not comfortable about sharing the rating in front of the entire team, you can ask them to rate the team on a piece of paper. When you receive the information, you must act on that information. For instance, if most members of the team have rated the spirit as one, you should spend some time to understand why they feel this way and work towards developing a solution to cater to the problem. When you do this, you apply the build-measure-learn lean startup methodology to your team.

Teams do vary across a company, but a lean team will only be effective if it is small, and the members have diverse capabilities. It is important for you, as the project manager, to create ground rules, ensure that every member contributes, and check in with the team to assess how individuals feel about the team and the environment. From here, you can work on the feedback you receive and improve the processes. You must remember that you and your team should work towards continuous improvement, and this means that you can never accept that your team is perfect.

Kaizen Events

Standard 5 Day Kaizen Event

Standard 5 Day Kaizen Events, also referred to as Kaizen Blitzes or Rapid Improvement Events (RIEs), are targeted improvement activities (PDCAs) used by teams to implement improvements quickly in a specific area. Teams use the Standard 5 Day Kaizen Event to implement significant improvements in a relatively short timeframe.

The following is the Standard 5 Day Kaizen Event Quick Determination Checklist to ensure this is the type of Kaizen Event required given your specific situation. Ensure the majority of Characteristics are checked as Yes or Likely in the Your Situation column.

Standard 5 Day Kaizen Event Quick Determination Checklist

Characteristic	YES or LIKELY	Your Situation	Characteristic	YES or LIKELY	Your Situation
Large Scope (crosses departments)	✔		Management Involvement	✔	
			5S Applied	✔	
Small Scope (within the department)	✔		Training Costs a Factor	✔	
			Requires Detailed Planning Meetings	✔	
Immediate Attention Required	✔				
Process Immediately Accessible	✔		May Require Statistical Methods to Determine Root Cause	✔	
Root Cause Known					
Specific Training Required	✔		Web-based Collaboration Application Main Form of Communication		
Broad Training Required	✔		Team Required	✔	
Team Members Physically (Locally) Available	✔		Value Stream or Process Map Required	✔	
Meeting Times < 4 Hours			Likely Will Impact Balanced Scorecard or Performance Dashboard Metric	✔	
Process Change (PDCAs) Continuously Applied Over a Few Days	✔		Team Charter Required	✔	

A successful Standard 5 Day Kaizen Event must have the following conditions present:

- Process or area available during the time period.
- Good communication with everyone involved.
- Nearly all team members are local and available.
- Resources such as time, training, other departments for support, etc. will be available.
- Management committed and engaged in the project.
- Process area employees' ideas are considered (as only a few will be on the team).
- All employees are treated with dignity and respect.

The Standard 5 Day Kaizen Event was very popular in the 1990s when Lean (i.e., The Toyota Production System) became a widespread improvement platform (outside of Japan). Manufacturing was implementing significant change in their production facilities by reducing inventories and consolidating floor space through the implementation of the Lean tools of cell layout, continuous flow and Kanban's, visual controls, etc. This required a major physical change requiring a tightly controlled and focused effort in a relatively short time period. Also, management wanted to demonstrate a commitment to continuous improvement by dedicating resources and people. The Standard 5 Day Kaizen Event was a perfect platform to do this. However, this is not the case so much today; therefore, the "standard" Kaizen Event has evolved into these other types of Kaizen Events to meet today's demand for continuous improvement. The Standard 5 Day Kaizen Event is still considered a valuable tool for those organizations that require a significant change in a short period of time.

Steps and Forms
The following steps and forms should be used as a guide to customizing a Standard 5 Day Kaizen Event to fit your organization requirements. There are many variables to consider, some of which are:
- Number employees that are part of the project team as well as the process area employees that require training

in Lean and/or Six Sigma (which may require two levels of training)
- Number of Continuous Improvement Specialists, Black Belts, or Lean Sensei's available for support in training and/or facilitating improvement projects
- Managers or supervisor's ability to lead continuous improvement projects – they may be great as a departmental leader, but lack the facilitation skills to get employees effectively engaged
- Availability of time to be dedicated to a Kaizen Event
- How management will stay involved in the project, especially during the Standard 5 Day Kaizen Event of the event
- Team members' availability
- Complexity of the project
- How to address preceding negative experiences with team projects
- How to effectively manage change
- Other departmental needs

Rolling Kaizen Event

Rolling Kaizen Events are targeted improvement activities (PDCAs) used by teams to implement improvements or solve a problem in a specific area that can only be accessed infrequently and/or the resources are not available for immediate use; therefore, resources and improvements must be allocated over time. The Rolling Kaizen Event may start off with a 2 - 4-hour meeting, and then meet weekly for 1 - 2 hours throughout the course of the Kaizen Event (typically three months).

The following is the Rolling Kaizen Event Quick Determination Checklist to ensure this is the type of Kaizen Event required, given your specific situation. Ensure the majority of Characteristics are checked as Yes or Likely in the Your Situation column.

Rolling Kaizen Event Quick Determination Checklist

Characteristic	YES or LIKELY	Your Situation	Characteristic	YES or LIKELY	Your Situation
Large Scope (crosses departments)	✔		Management Involvement	✔	
			5S Applied	✔	
Small Scope (within the department)	✔		Training Costs a Factor	✔	
			Requires Detailed Planning Meetings	✔	
Immediate Attention Required					
Process Immediately Accessible			May Require Statistical Methods to Determine Root Cause	✔	
Root Cause May Be Known					
Specific Training Required	✔		Web-based Collaboration Application Main Form of Communication		
Broad Training Required	✔				
			Team Required	✔	
Team Members Physically (Locally) Available	✔		Value Stream or Process Map Required	✔	
Meeting Times < 4 Hours	✔		Will Impact Balanced Scorecard or Performance Dashboard Metric	✔	
Process Change (PDCAs) Continuously Applied Over a Few Days			Team Charter Required	✔	

A successful Rolling Kaizen Event must have the following conditions present:

- Process or area available for only short periods of time.
- Good communication with everyone involved.
- Team members available for limited lengths of time (typically 1 - 2 hours a week).
- The Just-In-Time concept utilized for all activities.
- Management committed and engaged in the project.
- Process area employees' ideas are considered (as only a few will be on the team).
- All employees are treated with dignity and respect.

The Rolling Kaizen Event can be thought of as the One-Minute Manager for meetings on steroids. In that regard, the team must look at everything (i.e., meetings, improvements activities, gathering data, creating reports, etc.) in time "buckets." These time "buckets" or "meeting and activity standards" will be determined by the team or by the team leader, process owner, facilitator and/or Black Belt, Lean Sensei, or Continuous Improvement Specialist at the beginning of the Event. Typically, these buckets will be 1, 2, or 4 hours. (Or, if team members are experienced in Lean Sigma concepts, and this is not their first improvement project using these tools, then time buckets can be in 15- or 30-minute increments.) Regardless of the type or amount of time buckets used, the key point is to think of all activities in slices of time. In so doing, it will create a good foundation for the subsequent meetings. For this type of Kaizen Event, all activities for each of the Phases should have very definitive time buckets.

All types of Kaizen Events require creating a schedule (time buckets) to train, brainstorm, pilot improvements, etc. However, for the Rolling Kaizen Event there is a renewed focus to succinctly use the Just-In-Time concept for all activities. For example, many times during a Standard 5 Day Kaizen Event, all the Lean (and Six Sigma) tools may be briefly evaluation as well as additional activities such as simulations, daily report outs, teaming exercises, etc. will be conducted.

Activities such as this likely will not be part of the Rolling Kaizen Event, or if they are, they will exist in a condensed version. Therefore, categorizing as many activities as possible in these time buckets will make for a successful Rolling Kaizen Event.

If the team decided to use 1-hour buckets and an improvement activity requires 4 hours, then that would entail 4 buckets. Organizing and conducting a Kaizen Event in this manner allows the team to start thinking in "standard" times to maximize all resources. Each phase of this Kaizen Event will provide suggested times for the various activities required. However, the more experience the process owner, team leader, Lean Sensei, Black Belt, etc. has with these activities, and the easier it will be to "right-size" your time buckets.

As with any Kaizen Event staying on schedule is crucial, but even more so for the Rolling Kaizen because of the shorter time bucket "windows" that the team has to conduct its work as well as the frequency of the team meetings.

Timelines should be drawn up for meeting activities and adhered to by the team. Buckets of time should be specifically scheduled for each activity, and the sequence of meeting events should be planned prior to the meeting and put into the meeting agenda to keep the team accountable for maintaining the timeline.

No meeting should be conducted without a written agenda. Ultimately, it is the team leader's responsibility to ensure that all the activities that need to get done are completed in a timely fashion, but the team leader should also elicit the help of the team in this regard. Assigning roles such as timekeeper and scribe to team members will help to keep the meetings flowing. As with any meeting, some flexibility needs to be built into the schedule. The less experienced the team, particularly the team leader and/or facilitator, the greater the amount of flexibility that should be factored into how long it will take the team to accomplish its necessary tasks. Initially, the team leader should try to determine how much time each activity will take and prepare the schedule for about half to three-quarters of the allotted meeting time, which will allow some "slack" to make up for unexpected events and activities taking longer than expected. As the team grows in its knowledge and experience, the team leader will gradually be able to accurately schedule about ninety percent of the team's time (always leaving some flexibility for unforeseen events and needed discussions). At the end of each meeting, the leader should evaluate progress with the team and assign the specific Action Items to team members or small subgroups of the team (referred to as sub-teams). The Action Items should be completed prior to the following scheduled Kaizen Event meeting.

One of the key differences in the Rolling Kaizen Event over the Standard 5 Day Kaizen Event is that the process changes (PDCAs) happen over a longer period of time (for the Rolling Kaizen Event), not 80% of the process change (or pilot) occurring within a 3-to-5 day time period as in the Standard 5 Day Kaizen Event. The Rolling Kaizen Event is becoming the more common type of Kaizen Event for organizations today because of the time constraints for most employees. Many of the activities comprised in this type of Event will be allocated to groups of 1 – 2 team members (sub-teams) to be completed between meetings. This type of Kaizen Event goes beyond just using a detailed project management program due to the following:

- Lean and/or Six Sigma tools are understood and used as needed
- Training is conducted as needed
- Team members and process area employee's ideas are part of the Lean approach to continuous improvement and engaged as necessary
- Management is involved
- Project duration limited to approximately three months
- Steps and Forms
- The following steps and forms should be used as a guide to customizing a Rolling Kaizen Event to fit your organization's requirements. There are many variables to consider, some of which are:

- Number of employees with Lean and Six Sigma or problem-solving experience
- Unknown root cause
- Change management principles applied
- Process availability (The process is not immediately available for process change)
- Team members' availability
- Complexity of the project
- How to address past negative experiences with team projects
- How to effectively manage change
- Other departmental needs

Web-Based Kaizen Event

Overview

Web-Based Kaizen Events are targeted improvement initiatives with team members using emerging technologies to plan, implement, and sustain improvements or solve a problem over time. The Web-Based Kaizen Event may start off with a 2 - 4-hour meeting via a Web conferencing and/or emerging technology platform, then continue to meet weekly online for 1 - 2 hours throughout the course of the Kaizen Event (typically three months).

The following is the Web-Based Event Quick Determination Checklist to ensure this is the type of Kaizen Event required given your specific situation. Ensure the majority of Characteristics are checked as Yes or Likely in the Your Situation column.

Web Based Kaizen Event Quick Determination Checklist					
Characteristic	YES or LIKELY	Your Situation	Characteristic	YES or LIKELY	Your Situation
Large Scope (crosses departments)	✓		Management Involvement	✓	
			5S Applied	✓	
Small Scope (within the department)	✓		Training Costs a Factor	✓	
			Requires Detailed Planning Meetings	✓	
Immediate Attention Required	✓				
Process Immediately Accessible	✓		May Require Statistical Methods to Determine Root Cause	✓	
Root Cause May Be Known					
Specific Training Required	✓		Web-based Collaboration Application Main Form of Communication	✓	
Broad Training Required					
			Team Required	✓	
Team Members Physically (Locally) Available			Value Stream or Process Map Required	✓	
Meeting Times < 4 Hours	✓		Will Impact Balanced Scorecard or Performance Dashboard Metric	✓	
Process Change (PDCAs) Continuously Applied Over a Few Days			Team Charter Required	✓	

A successful Web-Based Kaizen Event must have the following conditions present:
- Team members have access to Web conferencing tools
- Team leader or facilitator proficient in Web conferencing tools and/or other emerging technologies
- Good communication standards for everyone involved
- Team members available for limited lengths of time (typically 1 - 2 hours weekly)
- The Just-In-Time concept for training, meetings, etc.

- Management committed and engaged in the project
- Process area employees' ideas are considered (as only a few will be on the team)
- All employees are treated with dignity and respect

Six Sigma Scale

What is the Sigma Scale?

As you saw in the former manuscript, the Sigma scale is an invaluable tool by which you can see and evaluate the progress of your business and the defects that your business is creating. This scale allows you to actually quantify the performance of your team so you can make the vital necessary changes to your business that will allow you to surpass all your former numbers and quality.

Now, as formerly states Sigma is known as a statistical term which is used to represent a standard deviation or the measure of a variation in a dataset. When your business and team can rate higher on this scale, you will find that it means you're producing a higher quality product.

Obviously, no business wants to be known for producing things that are only effective 60% of the time, but it's better than half and it's a place to start! This scale will help you to modify that number.

It should be noted that if a business can reliably produce only 31% defects, then that business rates at Two Sigma for defects. The Sigma Scale measures the overall number of opportunities on a scale of millions, then analyzes the defects at a rate of one per million.

This means that if you were to produce one million of something, or if you were to go through one specific process within your business one million times, you could expect a specific number of defects to be yielded from that. The table below illustrates the scale with the percentage of defects, the defects per million, and the Sigma scale:

The Sigma Scale

Sigma Level	Defects per Million Opportunities	Percent Defects
1	691,462	69%
2	308,538	31%
3	66,807	6.7%
4	6,210	0.62%
5	233	0.023%
6	3.4	0.00034%

As you can see, Six Sigma is the best rating on this scale. 3.4 Defects per Million Opportunities means that your business is producing a staggeringly low 0.00034% waste!

Defects per Million Opportunities (DPMO)

The term "defect" is not necessarily strict in definition.

You can break it down to mean any deviation from the ideal and it doesn't only apply to production on a manufacturing line, for instance. It can mean anything from filing to cars washed, if that's something you want to track.

A defect in filing could mean that it was filed late, that the item was placed incorrectly, or that the item couldn't be located when it was needed. It could mean that someone scratched a car, someone forgot to vacuum the back-passenger's side floor mat. As you can tell, it's a fairly loose definition. It does, however, indicate any type of variance that your customers could and should take issue with.

Now, why would that be helpful? If you're able to track the areas from which you're getting the most defects, you can devise ways to keep those defects from popping up in front of your most important or sensitive clients. Any variance, any defect can cause a customer to ask for some form of concession from you or your business as repayment for subpar service. This translates to a loss for the business.

When a company first evaluates their loss, they are looking for things they have to give their customers a "freebies," and they look for things that they have to do over again in order to make things right after failing to yield an ideal, satisfactory result in the first place.

If your business finds, upon your first evaluation, that it is somewhere between three and four Sigma (which is about average), that your business I am absorbing 67,000 units of loss in each million that is done. That is 67,000 units your business now has to pay for.

Think about whether or not your business can pay for 67,000 units right now in one lump sum. If that thought makes you uncomfortable, then you should realize that you're going to be paying that amount anyway, over time. That is the kind of loss that stacks up over time and that is the kind of loss that can sneak up on your business and keep it from growing, or worse.

Tips to Make Six Sigma Work for You

Six Sigma, especially when we combine it together with Lean, is something that can do a lot for our business. It is a method that is there to reduce most, if not all, of the wastes that or business may produce. When that happens, we can really provide some better products and services to our customers, while increasing the amount of money that we bring in each month. However, there are sometimes when you hear about this option, but you are still a little confused by the steps and what it all entails.

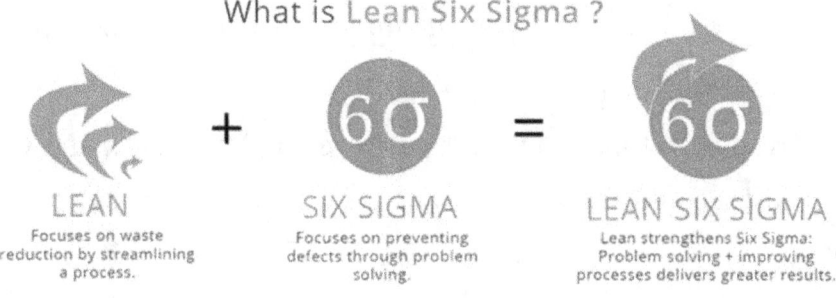

The good news is that there are a lot of tips and tricks that you can follow to make sure that you get the most out of Lean Six Sigma. This is a process that takes some time and resources, and you don't want to waste those hoping that you get it right and finding out in the end that you did something wrong. That is why we will take some time in this part to look at the best tips and tricks that you can use to make Lean Six Sigma as safe and effective as possible.

The first step is something that we have talked about a bit before, but we still need to bring it up a bit more to make sure we understand what is going on with this. We must make sure that we have the right amount of commitment from the leadership there to see results. Make sure that everyone at the top of the company is committed to working through all of this. These same people also need to be convinced about all of the benefits of Six Sigma and why they would want to go with this method over some of the other options in the first place.

Along with some of the options that we just talked about; your steering committee needs to be formed right from the start. This is done to ensure that:

The goals of the company will still align well with some of the projects that you can do with Six Sigma.

The resources that you need to use are all planned out and you already account for the roadblocks and move them out of the way.

The one person needs to be there to help lead them all, though they are not allowed to sit there, and bark orders out while not helping others during this. You need to pick out a black belt to do this and you should pick out someone who is going to do the best job with all of this.

Along the same lines here, we need to make sure that any of the leaders of our projects are trained well. they need to be the Six Sigma Champions at the minimum, which will be another level above the master black belts and is reserved for the managers who work with this process as well. This is a training session that will take two days and can help the management of your team learn how to lead and run some of their groups in Lean Six Sigma.

There also has to be someone there who will be able to train all of the other belts who will run around your company. And you have to pick the right person who will be able to handle this and do it well. There are a lot of programs out there who will promise that they can do the best job ad will provide you with some good options. But most of them are not that important and not that good, but you can still find some good ones if you do some research. You need to pick out the right person, or the right options, that will make it easier for you to go through and really train all of your employees on how to work with Six Sigma.

While we are going through and picking out the program that we want or employees to work with, we need to check what the return on the training investment should be. If you see a program and it is less than 20 times the training investment for your return, then this is just a waste of your money. Or it is a sign that you are picking the wrong project to spend your time on.

A good way to make sure that you get this new Six Sigma movement going and to ensure that it is successful is to start it down on the shop level, and not just with the management. There are too many times when the management is the one who get to decide everything. And often this is done without the discussion or input of those who work in the shop. This is really hard and can make people feel like they are not that valuable. *How good would you feel if you were just told what to do without any help along the way and without anyone asking your opinion at all?*

This is why it is a good idea to get this started right from the shop level. You do not just want to have a few green belts or a few black belts who are doing all of the work during this either. You need to take some time to train the necessary supervisors or operators on the shop floor so that they are able to work with all the techniques that come with Six Sigma. You can use the white belt program to help them get it done without them having to waste a lot of time learning the parts that don't pertain to their jobs.

Doing this is great for your company though because it will help them to feel like they own a bit of the process and like they are able to make some of the improvements as well. you can also reward some of the team members and the leaders who decide to get this certification to help encourage them to see what this is all about and why it is such a good thing to work on.

Along the way, we need to consider a new mentoring process that we are able to work with. This is going to help make sure that anyone who is working on this process, and wants to learn more about it, will have the right guidance to make it all happen. In addition, make sure that there are some options for course corrections on a regular basis and that all of the projects that are decided on and set up will get done on time as we go.

Some companies have found that when they implement the Six Sigma process that having some financial validation to this project will help to increase their chances of success as they go along. There has to be some kind of financial leader in place, someone who is able to sign off on how much the project will cost and how it will come in and save the company some more money. This is something that needs to be implemented during the control phase to make sure that the spending on any project doesn't get out of hand.

A big mistake that some companies are going to make here is that they will use Six Sigma, but they will classify it in the wrong manner. For example, they may decide to make it the job of the quality manager. The quality manager does come in with a distinct role to get things done, and they are not really there to help manage all of the processes that come with Six Sigma, at least not all on their own. The projects will work so much better when you make sure that you have the right team, and then they have the right training, so that they can handle the project and make it work well.

Create a goal that you share in common with everyone on the team. Once you have decided that it is time to implement the process of Six Sigma, the following thing that you should do is make sure that anyone else who is qualified on your team is aware of the goal and that everyone is on the same page. This common goal is not something that has to be that complicated, but you must show it through an executive directive, and you need to make sure that it is a goal that all employees, no matter their levels, have to follow. The pint of this is to reduce some of the variability so that you can reduce your waste.

Part of working with Six Sigma and Lean is that you need to take some time to add standardization into all of this. Any methodology that you implement during this has to include some standardization in order to work. To make sure that you are successful from the start, you must have an approach that is defined and standard as much as possible. If you forget this part, then there are a lot of people who may be on the same team, but they will spend a lot of time redefining it and trying to make some changes.

Standardization is something that seems like it takes out the creativity and some of the fun that can come with a process.

That doesn't have to be the truth though. This just sets up some clearly defined labels and ideas of how to get the work done that everyone on the team has to follow to make sure they get some good results in the process.

As long as the team stays within those standardizations, you will still be able to encourage you to try something new and be creative.

Remember here that standardization is the process that we need to use in order to allow the people who are on the same team to focus on reducing the standard deviation in the projects that they work with, rather than having to think about how to do the method and pick which one they would like to use to be as efficient as possible. This standardization may take more time in the beginning as everyone is going to learn how to make this work. But as time goes on here, it will make sure that all employees and managers have an approach that is common. And as we learn how to work with this and the steps that we need to take, it can help to reduce the execution time in no time. Then it is time to map out the plan that you want to work with for Six Sigma. Any plan that you do is focused the whole time and will keep things running on time. To do this, you need to make sure that the plan is mapped out well. you can also make sure that all of the different teams you would like for all of the projects are sorted out and they know what they need to do for each part of the process. And then you can schedule out all of the steps of the process.

Kanban Combined with Lean Manufacturing

Within the world of Agile, Lean Manufacturing is one of the most relevant approaches put into place by companies. Understanding Lean Manufacturing is about understanding how an organization can essentially keep on what it's been doing but doing so with less waste and more efficiency. The underlying issue here is time. Ideally, organizations would be looking to improve their overall efficiency in terms of resources used up. But the truth is that the most valuable resource any organization can boast is time. Saving time not only saves money, but it also enables the company to continue expanding its production.

As such, Lean Manufacturing is all about seeing where the organization can be more efficient. It should be noted that efficiency under this concept is more about working smarter and not necessarily harder. Let's exemplify this concept in the following manner:

A company is looking to expand its operations. It has determined that they want to improve their volume of production.

Currently, the company is working two full-time shifts. So, there are two options on the table. The first one is to add a third shift and all the associated costs that come with it, mainly the depreciation of machinery and increased labor costs.

The second option is to improve the efficiency of both current shifts by reducing the overall time it takes to produce the same amount.

This is where the company has decided to embrace Lean Manufacturing. In short, the company has decided that they will improve the efficiency of both current shifts by redesigning processes, making updates to machinery and software, while allowing workers to determine what areas of improvement could be made.

All told, the company was able to cut down the time it needed to produce the same amount by one hour. This meant that the company now had one extra productive hour, so to speak. All of it lay in the fundamentals of Lean Manufacturing and Kanban. The company moved from a centralized organizational structure to one in which individual squads could work collaboratively. Also, they improved communication by allowing real-time assessment of workflow. For instance, if one part of the process becomes backed up due to an unforeseen issue, members of other processes could go over and support them until the issue had been resolved. Then, everyone could return to their original post.

The underlying principle in this approach is to allocate resources in the areas that are needed when they are needed. Consequently, individual teams are able to self-regulate and support one another when there is a need for it.

The Five Core Principles of Lean Manufacturing

Lean Manufacturing is supported by the concept of "kaizen." Kaizen is another Japanese term that means "constant improvement." When organizations operate under the Kaizen banner, they are never content with the way things are done. This means that there is always a better and more efficient way of doing things. So, no matter how good something is, it can always be better.

That's why Lean Manufacturing is predicated under the assumption that process can always go through some type of transformation which can enable the organization to reduce waste and improve its overall production levels without having to sacrifice quality. The overall impact that this has on the bottom line means that organizations can not only produce at a lower cost but also boost profitability.

So, let's take a look at the five core principles of Lean Manufacturing.

Value as seen by the customer

All too often, companies get caught up in personal hubris. This means that companies think they know what their customers want. Truth be told, fact, some companies boast about knowing their customers so well that they don't even need to ask them what they want.

Needless to say, this is a huge mistake.

When an organization takes the time to understand what value represents to their customers, they strive to produce the value that customers are looking to derive from the products and services they produce.

For instance, a company that produces beverages ought to be inclined to consider what customers want in terms of flavor and nutritional characteristics as opposed to assuming what their customers are looking for. In the end, when a company looks at its products from the perspective of what the customer wants, it will be able to stop producing unnecessary features and items while focusing on what actually sells.

Mapping out the value stream

Generally speaking, production processes set out with a seed, that is, the raw materials that must be transformed into the finished product that is delivered to customers. Consequently, companies need to figure out where value is added throughout the entire production process. If a company fails to identify this clearly, then there is a greater risk for waste throughout the product's lifecycle.

And while most organizations do have this process properly mapped out, it's important to update it as much as possible and with as much detail as possible. This not only ensures that consistent metrics are supporting the information contained within the process itself, but also decisions are made on objective criteria rather than assumptions.

In addition, a clearly mapped out value stream can help an organization determine where the most critical portions of the process lie. This will enable the organization to figure out where bottlenecks may lie and address them accordingly.

Workflow management

This aspect of Lean Manufacturing is all about reducing the potential interruption of the production process. This implies that everything must be done to ensure that all barriers are stripped throughout the process. While this isn't about exploiting workers, it's about eliminating barriers that could potentially hinder the free flow of production. For instance, automation of manual tasks is one of the most common ways in which lead times can be improved. In addition, artificial intelligence (AI) has become more and more prevalent throughout repetitive tasks thereby allowing human labor to take care of more complex tasks that AI is still unable to support.

Think about it this way: if you had the option between using a typewriter or a computer, would it make any sense to use a typewriter? By using an automated tool such as computers, there would be no reason to insist on using a computer, that is, unless you didn't know how to use it.

Nevertheless, the main point of workflow management is not to automate for the sake of reducing workforce; it's all about finding any, and all, means available which can facilitate process thus allowing human labor to handle truly complex tasks in which robots and AI are not able to perform adequately.

Pull rather than push

Traditional production planning systems are based on a "push" system. By "push" we mean that production is forecast based on assumptions, modeling and other types of statistical tools. The issue with this type of system is that there is no guarantee that estimations will be accurate given the fact that there is any number of variables that may come into play.

That is why a pull system is more effective as it means producing based on actual requirements. Of course, this means that production needs to be able to address customer needs as efficiently as possible. This is why Kanban is utilized in manufacturing in which suppliers follow a "just in time" approach.

The biggest advantage of utilizing a pull system is that there is no residual inventory. So, what is needed is ultimately produced. At the end of the day, the organization does not have any inventory piled up as what is needed is produced. This is one of the best ways in which organizations can avoid having unsold inventory gather dust in storage.

Continuous pursuit of perfection

This refers to Kaizen. Of course, absolute perfection is unattainable. But that doesn't mean that it can't be pursued on a consistent basis.

We highlighted how Kaizen is the underlying principle of Lean Manufacturing. As such, it's important to support Kaizen by implementing the right set of metrics that can help the organization determine the right degree of perfection. For instance, the lead time is a perfectly good metric that can be utilized to determine the effectiveness of efficiency.

Ultimately, it's up to the organization to determine which metrics it can use to accurately assess the overall effectiveness of the processes put into place. This can provide objective feedback into the pursuit of perfection.

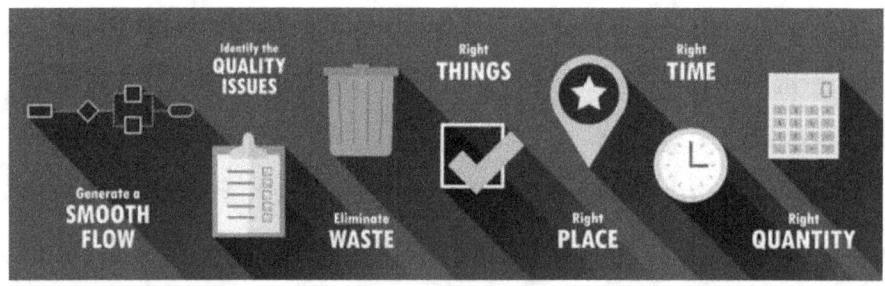

The Wastes of Lean Manufacturing

Lean Manufacturing considers a total of eight "wastes" that are the result of the production process. As such, Lean Manufacturing practitioners ought to strive to reduce them as much as possible. So, let's discuss them one by one.

Needless transport. This not only implies the transport of finished goods from one place to another but also materials within the same production cycle. The main goal to keep in mind here is eliminating as many potential barriers as possible.

Overstocking. This implies keeping inventories to the absolute, bare-bones minimum. That way, waste can be significantly reduced.

Needless steps in the process. This is a rather straightforward idea. If there is a step that can be cut out without sacrificing quality, then it must be done. By the same token, any people or equipment that is not needed can be better allocated elsewhere.

Idle time. There is nothing worse in Lean Manufacturing than having idle people or equipment. Everything must in motion to reduce lead time.

Overproduction. This harkens back to overstocking, but it also implies adding features and components that are not needed or worse yet, the customer hasn't requested.

Over-processing. Much like overproducing an item, this is about using overly complex processes or technologies that can increase lead time especially when looking to add components that customers don't want or don't need. The rule here is to keep things as simple as possible.

Defects. Any defects are considered a waste of resources.

Underutilized talent. Yes, this refers to having workers not living up to their full potential.

The Link Between Kanban and Lean Manufacturing

When Kanban and Lean Manufacturing are combined, you get a methodology in which communication is the core means by which efficiency is achieved. As a result, the organization is able to optimize its processes by being able to streamline the entire process. As each step communicates, the entire process flows a lot more freely.

As Kanban and Lean Manufacturing mesh together, "just in time" production becomes a reality. This enables every step of the process being ready just when it happens to be; no sooner, no earlier. Just the right type of production as conditions dictate. The ultimate output is the most efficient route possible from raw materials to the end-user.

Kaizen and the Capabilities of the Organization

Is innovation less likely to occur in most developing countries compared to more advanced economies? One particular theory is that when firms lack capabilities, innovation is less likely to occur. The level of firms' capabilities, which are organizational and managerial practices make innovation work while the level of government capabilities is related to the formulation of policies that are effective and can support the firm's level of innovation.

The capabilities of an organization are defined as the working practices and the knowledge which are used by firms in production and the development of new products. The capabilities of any organization manifest in productivity and quality.

In organizations that lack capabilities, if an entrepreneur comes up with a brilliant innovative idea, it is not entirely possible for the idea to be transformed into a product.

For this particular product to be installed in the market, the continuous effort of the Plan-Do-Check-Act (PDCA) cycle is needed for the trying out of the different prototypes and then modifying them to satisfy the needs of the market.

Every step, every process, every activity is known as the Kaizen activity and it enhances the capability of the organization. In summary, kaizen is an approach for the enhancement of the capabilities of organizations.

Fundamentals of Policy and System Development for the dissemination of Kaizen

In a lot of countries around the world, Kaizen has been disseminated under the leadership of the government, though private organizations took the initiatives of the quality and productivity movement and the Total Quality Control (TQC). Kaizen was implemented by Japanese companies without help and also the expansion of their businesses overseas. They also hired foreign consultants when the need arose. Considering Africa's current industrial level, which is increasing by the day, not many companies and organizations can undertake these measures. Also, low management capabilities with little or no recognition of the importance of improvement prevent the private sector from taking the Kaizen dissemination initiative. In many countries in the world, kaizen activities are carried out under the assistance of kaizen promotion firms that are within the framework of the public support system.

The government works on the improvement of quality and productivity while adding support measures that target different countries and their organizations as part of their industrial policy. According to research, the manufacturing companies are not actually the ones that need productivity and quality improvement. It is also required in the service industry as well as in the public sector. Do you know that the need for productivity and quality improvement is also needed in the lives of the general public? This gives reason to why it is important for the spread of kaizen thereby promoting the changes in the attitude of people towards productivity and quality as a movement worldwide. An example is the government-led dissemination and promotion of kaizen in Ethiopia and Singapore which resulted in highly successful results.

Activities Necessary for the Promotion of Kaizen
Policy and Finance Support by Relevant Government Agencies

For nationwide dissemination of kaizen, the first step is to involve the selection of some organizations that are responsible for the development of mechanisms and systems that support the activities of kaizen, secure and train the human resources, otherwise referred to as kaizen trainers.

To begin these steps, the government is expected to implement policies to support the promotion of kaizen and also to support operations and activities of the promotion organizations of kaizen financially. Through understanding, cooperation, and the demonstration of strong leadership of government officials towards the dissemination of kaizen, it can be realized. With the support of the government, the promotion organizations of kaizen can help develop plans and strategies for the dissemination of kaizen in order to secure the government's approval. The plans and strategies must be in line with the framework of the national development plan of the country. With this, the kaizen can effectively spread throughout the country. During the development of the framework of the dissemination system of kaizen, the promotion organization of kaizen is expected to establish effective yet detailed action plans with the national development plan of the country and its industrial policies.

Kaizen Promotion Organizations' Dissemination Activities

The activities of dissemination are to be carried out by every individual in the company for the improvement of productivity and quality and also to enhance the organizations' capabilities and its industrial competitiveness.

The effectiveness of the activities of kaizen is to be recognized and implemented continuously in order to establish the culture of Kaizen.

The creation of the kaizen culture through the dissemination and increase of awareness is important for the kaizen dissemination as a national movement in the country. It is expected for the promotion organizations of kaizen to start with the communication of information and the increase of awareness on its concept and significance to the world through the use of equipment such as radio, bulletins, television, government-organized events, the Internet and also Social Networking Service (SNS).

These promotion organizations should be able to organize conferences and seminars for other organizations and companies so as to offer training and consulting services when it is needed. In the introductory phase, it is important to raise awareness by increasing opportunities for companies and people in order to acquire more knowledge of kaizen. For future marketing purposes, it is necessary to try to offer services at a low cost or free of charge. It is an effective way of spreading the word and getting people to listen. Another way of spreading the news and increasing awareness is to organize kaizen conferences to commend Kaizen trainers and companies that have been performing excellently.

Training Kaizen Trainers

While trying to disseminate kaizen through the use of publicity tools and seminars in order to stimulate demand for kaizen, it is important to train Kaizen trainers who are to provide services that are kaizen-related to meet the created demands of the company. The kaizen trainers can be employees of the promotion organizations or even private consultants who have already completed their training which was conducted by kaizen promotion organizations. It is important and expected of them to acquire theoretical knowledge through Classroom Training and also obtain practical skills through In-Company Training. Such knowledge can be acquired in vocational schools, higher education institutions and other institutions of learning. Some practical methods of kaizen and techniques can be acquired by practically applying them through In-Company Training; so, prospective trainers must gain as much practical experience as possible to gain practical skills that would allow them to deal with issues related to kaizen. The level of kaizen techniques that are required in business areas in a country differs depending on the level of industrial development of the country. For this particular reason, it is advised that they must determine the scope of training to develop and enhance the contents which come in the form of manuals, primers, curriculums, guidelines, etc., based on the needs of the enterprises. Kaizen trainers are divided into two; those who belong to the private sector and those who belong to public agencies. As they are of different types, it is necessary that kaizen promoting countries provide strategic training for them and also to document the roles in which they are expected to play when providing individuals in companies their consulting services.

Consulting Services to Support Businesses

Once the creation of a level of kaizen demands through activities created for awareness and dissemination, the trainers are to provide consulting services for companies and other organizations in the selected countries. The activities are to be conducted through concerted team efforts among every individual in the company and the kaizen trainers and not via the efforts of the trainers alone. For these activities to be implemented effectively and to bury its roots in the organization, the trainers should be able to conduct training on the various levels of management. While the training is in progress, it is vital to allow employees to develop mindsets to think and also conduct activities of their own and also make the management support the activities.

The promotion organizations of kaizen are to be able to organize a series of events in order to share the outcome of kaizen to the public. For the support of businesses, it is important to make use of some mechanisms so as to encourage voluntary promotion activities.

Collection, Analysis, Evaluation, And Release of Data

Once kaizen activities have been implemented in various organizations, the outcome is to be collected, analyzed, evaluationed thoroughly in order to see and understand the impact of the activities on businesses in each company kaizen was implemented before releasing the data. Sorting through the kaizen data by business size and the industry provides the private sector, the general public and the government with useful information on the contribution the dissemination has on national welfare and the economic growth of the country. The data generated can help encourage the companies to sustain and maintain continuous kaizen activities and top use that opportunity to motivate companies that are striving to meet them.

It is expected that the data generated from the kaizen activities should be quantitative for an easier understanding of the degree of impacts. This can also be achieved if the promotional organizations of kaizen have a mechanism and the capability to collect and accumulate the right yet reliable data.

In addition to this, it is important to study and compile qualitative outcomes too. Some of these qualitative outcomes are the employee's attitude, mindset and mentality with the customer satisfaction levels as a bonus.

Every kaizen activity is expected to increase the dissemination of kaizen and also improve the productivity and quality of industries and organizations, thereby enhancing the industry in the country and also their competitiveness. It is somewhat difficult to measure the impact the activities of kaizen have made directly for the growth and enhancement of the competitiveness of industries and the reduction in the unemployment rate and the Gross Domestic Product (GDP) growth. The promotion organizations of kaizen should aid in the implementation of kaizen and its accumulated data in other companies in order to present visible results. Kaizen activities allow for the enhancement of the capacity of industries, help build credibility and achieve social recognition. Such activities can be conducted intensively and more extensively in every society when it is done with the help of a wide range of stakeholders which includes trade associations, government-affiliated organizations, financial institutions, educational institutions and private instructions also. With this, it is advisable to build strategic partnerships with stakeholders.

I believe that with the understanding of how kaizen can be disseminated, we would see its importance and use it wisely. Before the government can be allowed to put in their efforts continuously, it is very important for them to be ready to support kaizen activities and to show how committed they are. There are things that are to be considered in order for the government to assist the promotion organizations. They are;

- *How can kaizen promotion organizations be selected?*
- *Budgetary measures*
- *Strong leadership of high-ranking government officials*

Business Analysis Techniques

Since every new product or project is created in response to a business need, correctly understanding those business needs is just as critical in a Lean and Agile environment as it is in traditional software development. Unfortunately, the English language is full of ambiguity and misunderstandings.

It is the responsibility of the Product Owner, the Business Analyst, or whoever is defining the business needs to make them as clear as possible to the developer community and the Stakeholders.

Developers need to understand them to correctly code the solution

Stakeholders need to understand them to evaluate whether the solution fits their needs

Unfortunately, you can rarely just look up business needs. You cannot apply the same methods as you would for authoring a research report. Most business or technical requirements are not documented anywhere. They exist in the minds of Stakeholders and in feedback that has yet to be obtained from end users.

This was a challenge in a traditional development environment. In today's Lean and Agile environment, we face a paradigm shift in business analysis that makes some major inroads into that.

In this part, we will show you a few of the most important LEAN business analysis techniques. However, there are many more available online as well as taught in classroom courses.

You can never know too much. Even after doing business analysis for the past 30 years, we (the authors) still add new tools and techniques to our BABOT3 (Business Analysis Bag of Tips, Tricks, and Techniques) on a regular basis.

The Product Vision Statement

Before any technical product development can start, the Agile team needs to understand where they are going and why.

A widely used tool to share a product's goals and purpose is the Product Vision Statement (sometimes called "the following Big Thing"). It shows the future of the new product (or new features), what problems it will resolve, and what needs it will fulfill. It answers the WHAT, WHY, WHO, WHERE, and HOW of the product.

- **WHAT** is the business need that this product is going to fill?
- **WHAT** is the key benefit?
- **WHY** would it add value to the customer?
- **WHO** is the target customer?

- **WHO** are the competitors?
- **WHERE** does this product fit in the organizational strategy?
- **HOW** is it different than competitor products?
- **HOW** will it be a competitive advantage?

These are the fundamental questions that the Product Vision or "the following Big Thing" must answer.

One of the quotes that we love from the late, great Steve Jobs is:

> **Steve Jobs**
>
> "If you are working on something exciting that you really care about, you don't have to be pushed. The vision pulls you."

In our opinion, this is an extremely powerful statement. A great vision will ignite that human creativity inside of us. Keep that in mind when you write you're following Product Vision.

However, if you are the Business Analyst, it is important to realize, that creating the Product Vision is not usually the job of the Business Analyst. It is the responsibility of the Product Owner, Product Manager, or Product Leader.

Several Lean business analysis techniques exist to use the Vision Statement as a basis in creating the Product Roadmap and getting the Product Backlog started (seeding the Backlog).

And don't forget:
Keep it Lean!
A Product Vision is not static. It gets rewritten and adjusted as the team gets customer and stakeholder feedback. A Product Vision is the steppingstone to a Product Roadmap.

The Product Roadmap

The Product Roadmap is not a Lean or Agile invention. It existed long before the Lean movement. In traditional software development approaches (i.e. Waterfall), it detailed what to build for months or even years in advance of the launch.

However, like everything else, Product Roadmaps changed with the Lean movement. Many companies discovered a lot of waste in their Roadmap methods especially in the modern software development environments. Most Product Managers moved to a Lean/Agile approach for building their Roadmaps.

LEAN Product Roadmaps

Developing Lean Roadmaps means constantly considering product and Feature iterations based on customer feedback. In a Lean / Agile environment, a Product Roadmap is a living document that is updated when needed.

An effective Product Roadmap solves an important customer problem or offers new opportunities to customers. It does not focus on detailed Features that depict how to solve the problem or provide a new opportunity. Rather, it gives guidance on the product strategies and priorities.

Detailed Product Features belong in your Product Backlog. It is the responsibility of the Product Owner, together with a Business Analyst and/or business side teams, to define detailed Features and User Stories that will enable the technical team to build the product.

A typical Lean Product Roadmap includes:
- Product strategy and goals
- High-level product features
- Product feature timelines
- Feature responsibilities
- High-level priorities

A Product Roadmap should be simple and easy to understand. It should tell a coherent story about the envisioned growth of the product. It serves as the basis for another important concept in Lean and Agile software development - the Minimum Viable Product.

The idea behind Lean and Agile development is not to plan everything out to the nth degree but to go with the flow. As you get feedback you improve the product.

Once you have a product that people are using, you can think about adding new Minimum Viable Features (a.k.a. Minimum Buyable Features). The whole idea is to grow the product quickly and delight your customers with new Features on a regular basis.

When defining a Minimum Viable Product, a good place to start is by focusing on solving a problem for one persona. Make sure that the persona you pick is representative of many of your customers. An MVP should not deliver functionality that only a few people would like.

Determine the Must-Haves AND Exciting Perks

Determine the basic needs (not the wants) of that persona and then add some exciting perks. You want people to be eager to try your new product to get the feedback you need. It is ok to leave some Product Features incomplete if they are only nice-to-haves. However, do not skimp on the must-haves.

This will become an endless cycle of evaluating customer feedback and determining Minimum Viable Features for the following release. In the new world of Lean software development, there will never be a last version of your product.

We have come a lot closer to true business agility and achieved a long-held dream of the business community, namely quickly make major changes to existing products and release new features.

The Metrics That Matter for Your Business

What are Metrics?

Metrics are calculative measures that are used to track and evaluation the state of your business, and performance. It is how you determine whether or not your business is doing well. Different persons are involved in a business, so whatever the metric, they must address the workforce and the customers, the investors and the managers. Every aspect of a business has a specific performance metrics to it but generally, metrics are those quantifying measures with which you keep the status and performance of your business in check.

Lean helps your business grow and improve continuously, business metrics, on the other hand, helps you follow up on the growth and performance of your business.

It helps determine how much or how well your business is doing with all the Lean principles and practices in having been put in place.

Take for example, in marketing, marketers have a metric system to with which and through which they stay on the success of their marketing, the same thing applies to media advertisers and as well for politicians who do campaigns. Some questions will be asked, questions such as how many persons were, we able to reach, and how many persons responded, and then how many persons gave a positive response? The idea is to know what the success and the failure is, having a target result in mind with which they will judge the performance result.

A metric is more like a guide; it helps your business track and achieves target results. In that case, there are certain checkpoints or tracking measures. Let us take an athlete for example; they know they train against various factors. They have to train enough to get to the point where they can now beat the time. Time is probably the athlete's highest target.

Need for Metrics

- **It will help drive the strategy and direction of the organization:** When metrics are put in place, the path to take towards the organization's destination will be known.

- **Focus:** it will help put the organization, employees, and everyone involved in check and keep them constantly focused, with their eyes on the ball. If there is a target to meet in a month, with the right metrics, the numbers will be rolled up so that progress can be tracked

- **Decision:** In cases where decisions on certain matters need to be made, metrics are the best resort to turn to. It will help give out in clear terms, the need to make or not to make a move at a point

- **Performance**: It enables an organization to do better. Metrics monitor activities going on, when this is viewed by the head of an organization, the level of progress made is known and the organization knows how much effort should be put in

- **Change and evolve with the organization:** As metrics are being monitored, the organization changes and evolves as more progress is made, there is also an evolving of metrics as the organization strives to get better

- **Objective process:** The goal of every organization is to make a profit and at the same time satisfy the customers, in a bid to satisfy customers, quality services must be rendered, processes have to be organized to suit the customer's needs.

Metrics that you look at to know that Lean is affecting the health of your organization.

Success must be measurable; if not, you cannot tell whether this is a success or not. To know if you are successful, you would first have to have a defined perspective/vision. What did you want to achieve with this business you started? Where do you see this business in 50 years? All these are essential steps to know if one is along the path of success or not. With your vision in mind, you can quickly look at specific metrics to see if you are succeeding or not.

- **The cost that it would take to retain a customer:** as a business, you should have a strategy that you implement to maintain customers, and that strategy comes with a cost, that cost should be minimal as you engage in Lean methodologies; you should find more cost-effective ways to keep your customers.

- **How viral is your product?** The virality of your merchandise can be an excellent pointer to the health of your business. If you get more people to know you exist, you stand a better chance of getting engaged. Your viral reach can be measured by how many you have participated on Instagram, and Twitter.

- **Lead time:** the lead time is the amount of time it takes for a product to go through a Lean process to completion. To be able to track your progress, you need to know how fast your products are produced and how fast they get to the consumer.

- **How easily is work distributed among the team?** This question is fundamental. It answers the issue of the workflow. For a product to reach its final stage, it goes through many departments, and the rate at which this work gets executed is essential. Your company is healthy if your team members distribute well, have a strong team spirit, and deliver the task before or right on schedule.

- **Increased number of open issues:** it is only reasonable that mistakes would be made, and problems would arise but if these issues are becoming overwhelming, you must look into it before it ruins something. The state of work is essential for the quality of the product—it is garbage in, garbage out. What you invest in, would, in turn, affect you.

- **Customer feedback:** apart from internal evaluation, some external assessment is necessary as well. What your customer says about your product is the brand your product has in the mind of that customer.

Overview of Over-Production

The production cycle has inbuilt questions to start the following cycle. The first one is to please only the customer and stop when you reach the target. Have I achieved today's quota? If the answer is yes, then stop production. Until the customer places a new order, do not make anything.

This principle applies to all departments in the organization. The idea is to achieve the perfect value stream. Other than this, there is nothing you need to worry about. In Lean, we reduce the steps we use to help cut waste, while the Six Sigma principle checks for variation. The more variations there are in the process, the more chances there are for waste to accumulate. You need to follow only Lean principles of keeping the number of steps down.

Conclusions about LEAN

Lean businesses always identify ways to maximize the value for their customers, which is the core objective of lean thinking. Most people are under the notion that lean thinking can only be implemented in sales and marketing departments since those departments work directly with customers.

This is not true since lean thinking is now being used to deliver value products to stakeholders of all departments.

Most people view lean as a tool that can be used to eliminate waste from processes and internal mechanisms thereby maximizing the value for the customer. But lean is a business process and kaizen are its cultural center.

This is an important aspect to consider when a business wants to identify the value of long-term processes. Most businesses still believe that lean thinking is a way for the demand side since they are not looking at the value stream.

These businesses can make better profits since the demand for their products exceeds their supply. However, most businesses are in a market where supply exceeds demand. Take mobile phones for instance. Numerous companies have been set up in different parts of the world that develop new phone models every day. However, most people choose to purchase Apple products, because the business has catered to the demands of the product and has always tried to identify ways to maximize the value of the customer. Therefore, businesses must remember that lean is not only about removing waste from the process, but also about identifying ways to enhance the value stream to maximize the value of the product. There is no company in today's economy that rejects more prospects or refuses orders. The business must always look for ways to drive revenue. Therefore, a business must improve continually to enhance and improve the processes in the value stream. So, how does a business use lean thinking to identify value?

- *Understand the demands of stakeholders and customers*

- *Identify elements in the process that are waste contributors and those that affect the quality of the product*

If a business is implementing lean thinking, it must eliminate processes that contribute to waste and those that do not add any value to the product or service. A business will view every activity that it performs and views the steps to see if each of them adds value to the final product or service. An activity is defined as a waste contributor if it adds cost and takes time to complete but does not improve the final product that is delivered to the stakeholder or customer. Every business focuses on how to shorten the timeline and how the value flow between the business and customer can be improved. The value is identified by becoming a faster, cheaper and better business. In simpler words, a business must always change its processes to produce goods and services that a customer is willing to pay for. Another way to identify value is by defining the internal customers or stakeholders. These internal stakeholders are members of each department that use outputs of one department as input to achieve their business goals and objectives. Regardless of whether a business is working with internal or external customers, it must focus on how the customers are satisfied rather how well they are satisfied. The fundamental of lean thinking then changes to the following – *"if a process is improved, the value of the process is also improved."* Most businesses are product focused. These businesses cannot view the market or access the market to become the best. They also make the mistake of looking at the value of the product or service and how it will help the customer. Businesses must remember that the idea of value is abstract and there is no real definition. The business must always identify ways to create, identify and deliver value to its customers.

What is Agile Project Management

These days, it almost feels like agile project management is on everyone's lips. The term gets tossed around with so much ardor (among those who are for it and those who are against it) that we have almost lost its meaning altogether.

Agile is about a lot more than just hanging out in circles every day and playing little games when it comes to splitting larger tasks into smaller ones.

Agile was born with a reason — but even more than that, it was born in a time and for a time that needed a drastic change in approach.

Although agile methodologies (like Kanban, for example) have been practiced for many decades already, agile project management — in its raw, official format — was born a little under two decades ago.

In many ways, it feels like it's been ages already — and that is mostly due to the fact that agile has changed a lot. It's very foundation stays the same. But in terms of adaptability, agile has won the long-term game, and it is now one of the rulers in the world of project management.

How much of a ruler is it, really?

Studies show that about 30% of projects use a clear agile approach, while approximately 40% of them use a traditional/waterfall approach. The remaining 30% use a hybrid approach (Getapp, 2019) — which, contrary to what some may believe, doesn't show that waterfall has won the race, but that it needs agile adjustments to function in the modern world.

This is meant to be an introduction into the world of agile project management — what it is, where it comes from, and why it is so popular. We invite you on a journey of learning and discovery, at the end of which you will discover which version of agile works best for you and for your organization.

History of Agile

Agile project management was born out of sheer need. Together with the advent of modern technology and computers, a lot of things had to be done — and more importantly, they had to be done fast, accurately, and within the budget.

Agile methods started to take shape as early as the 1950s, but it wasn't until five decades later that the famous Agile Manifesto was laid on paper.

Sometime around the mid- '90s, most of what is now known as agile project management began to be contoured. At first, it was all dispersed — there was RAD (Rapid Application Development) in 1991, Scrum in 1995, and Feature-Driven Development two years later.

In 2001, it all came together, as if to offer clarity to a world that was getting ready to make a full jump into the one channel that rules them all today: the Internet. Sure, web connections had existed before, but it was at the turn of the millennia when things started to really take off.

On this background, seventeen brilliant software development minds got together in Snowbird, Utah. That meeting would go down in history, as this was when the actual concepts of agile project management took their official form.

We would be very curious to know exactly how that meeting went. We do know it didn't come out of the blue (you cannot simply expect the forward-thinkers in software development to just accidentally come together in Utah, can you?).

And we also know that the Snowbird meeting set the grounds for everything that followed in the world of agile project management. We would go as far as to assume that a lot of the amazing software tools we use today on a recurrent basis now would not have existed — they would have lingered somewhere, still in development.

Agile project management was born because there was a dire need to alter the project management landscape in software development. Back in the '90s, when the demand for software increased, traditional project management methods proved to be inefficient (at best) and downright disastrous (at worst).

In fact, it is frequently mentioned that most of the (major!) software development houses had (equally major!) lag when it came to their releases. On average, software development was lagging by approximately three years. For large projects, the lag extended further, up to 20 years.

It sounds preposterous, and it is.

But that's just what waterfall did to these projects. The very nature of software development is ever-changing, so it made no sense at all to stick to a management approach that focused on spreadsheets, more than the very core of what these projects did.

Agile project management has succeeded in removing those parts of waterfall that might have been bottlenecks in the development process.

Furthermore, as you will see the waterfall-agile hybrids have also ensured the streamlining of the waterfall processes, taking the best of the two worlds and providing organizations based on heavy documentation with an alternative to traditional project management.

Agile project management was born at the right time to become the backbone of the tech industry before it boomed completely. From the Silicon Valley to China, and from Iceland to Australia, agile has become a household name in project management. Even more, it has expanded well beyond the borders of software programming and is now used in pretty much every industry you could imagine. Hospitals, schools, governmental and non-governmental institutions, marketing, translations — everyone can embrace agile, precisely because it is so flexible and adaptable to multiple situations.

History is rarely written when we expect it. We don't know if those seventeen minds actually knew the kind of impact their meeting would have — but we do know that software development and agile are so intertwined these days that it seems almost impossible to completely separate them.

Advantages and Benefits

What makes agile project management so good, specifically?
There is a long list of benefits that bring agile project management to everyone's attention — specifically those in software project management, but most definitely not exclusively so.

Better Quality

One of the main tenets of agile project management is that it promises a better product quality.
To get things straight, it's not that products developed via waterfall project management lack in quality. It's just that it is far more likely for an agile-developed product to be qualitative by the point of its full release on the market.

There is very strong logic behind this.
On the one hand, waterfall project management tends to be too strict within its own limits. This means that it is far more likely for mistakes to:

- Be noticed too far out in the process (and waterfall will not allow the team to reiterate the same feature/part of the project)

- Be noticed when the product is already on the market/in review by client

Agile project management is very focused on continuous improvement. As such, a product has a much higher chance of actually getting better throughout the development process.

Or, in other words, instead of sweeping all those small (or not so small) mistakes under the rug (as you would do in waterfall project management because you have to follow the plan), you will just deal with them there and then.

Sounds much more feasible, right?

Better Customer Satisfaction

Another reason that makes agile so advantageous is related to the fact that, by the end of the project, customers tend to be far more satisfied.

How so?

There are a few verticals to consider when it comes to customer satisfaction, and agile makes sure that all of them are properly met. For instance:

- Agile will allow you to change the requirements as per client feedback.

- Agile will force you to release bits of the project as you move along, ergo, it will allow your customer to provide you with input that is easier to implement (due to the small size of the actual bit they are testing).

- Agile will help you deliver a better final product.

Given all these factors, it makes all the sense in the world that customers will be happier — throughout the project, as they will be able to request the modifications they need and, at the end of it, as they will receive a product that fits their requirements, purposes, and desires.

Do keep in mind that the same stands true in those cases when the "customer" is an internal stakeholder — such as, for example, when you are managing a software development project meant to be used internally.

Better Transparency

This agile benefit is very tightly connected to what has been mentioned already. When you can ensure better quality and better customer satisfaction, it all comes with greater transparency.

This transparency will manifest itself on all the verticals of project management. You will see better transparency in your team.

You will also see better transparency within the organization, regardless of whether or not the upper management uses the same project management approach as you do.

Finally, you will see better transparency between you and your customer (be it an internal one or an external one). When you constantly ask for feedback and continually improve the product to suit your customer's needs, you create a more genuine relationship with them. You start to truly communicate, rather than engaging in nothing more than ping-pong emails.

Better Control

For those of you used to the premises of waterfall or traditional project management, it might seem that agile is anything but control-focused.

In fact, it very much is.

Agile project management allows you to control your project at a granular level, precisely because it encourages (and downright forces) you to split your project into small, bite-sized bits and pieces.

Waterfall project management forces you to lay it all down on paper before everything begins. At the same time, though, it also forces you to stick to the plan even when things go south. And yes, they will eventually go south, one way or another: the client's requirements might change, you might realize something is taking longer than planned, your product might be bugged, or the costs might end up exceeding your expectations. There are a million things that could go wrong, especially in software project management (where things tend to be more experimental than, let's say, oil drilling, for example).

When you can manage all these things that could go wrong as they happen, you gain control over the entire process. Even more, you can use your (bad) experience to improve the process, as well.

Don't take this the wrong way. Control is not one and the same as micromanagement. You don't have to constantly look over your team's shoulders and manage each tiny detail every step of the way. That would just ruin the bridge of transparency, honesty, and self-discipline you are trying to build between yourself and your team.

Better Predictability

Again, this might seem like it's the exact opposite of what agile project management is all about.

But when you take a closer look, you will realize that agile projects can be better predicted precisely because they are managed step by step.

Let's compare this with baking a cake.

When you buy the boxed mix, you can easily and accurately predict what you are going to get — a decent cake batter you can then personalize according to your tastes. However, you don't know all the ingredients in that boxed mix — and, although the short-term result might be easy to foresee, it might be a bit more difficult to predict what will happen to your body if you continue eating boxed cake every week, for decades on end.

That would be the waterfall project management approach. You are using a mould and hoping that everything in your project will fit that ideal, very predictable format. However, long-term, you have no idea if your project plan won't go against you.

When you bake a cake from scratch and you know where each ingredient comes from, how many calories it has, and how many nutrients it provides your body with, you can predict its effects on your body if you eat the same type of cake for an extended period of time.

Plus, as long as you accurately measure each ingredient's quantity, you will be able to accurately predict how your cake is going to look and taste like. It might take a bit of practice until you learn how to do this correctly but, once you learn its tricks, the cake made from scratch will be more predictable in every single way!

That would be the agile project management approach. It might seem totally unpredictable at first, but the results will become more predictable once you have the right tools and the experience to accurately measure and approximate everything.

Better Risk Management

One of the major downfalls of waterfall project management is connected to the fact that it remains confined within its own tables and spreadsheets.

Waterfall project managers plan everything out at the beginning of the project. Agile project managers do the same. The main difference lies not in whether they plan, but in what happens when things don't go according to that plan.

As mentioned before, waterfall tends to sweep risks under the carpet — or, at least, estimate them poorly and through an idealistic point of view.

Agile, on the other hand, doesn't do that. It faces the problems head-on, tackles them, removes them from your path, and then allows you to draw honest conclusions.

As a result, your risk management will improve, as well. When you stop hiding your head in the sand, you can see things more clearly. As such, you can manage any potential risks with more accuracy, as well.

Better ROI

Better products + happier clients + better risk management cannot go wrong.

It's a universal formula for success. The more you can manage your money and put out better products, the more likely it is that customers will:

- Come back to you

- Pay on time

- Evangelize and recommend you to other potential customers

- Leave great reviews for your company on various channels

Sounds like a dream?
We prefer to call it agile.

Better Metrics

This advantage circles back to the fact that agile won't allow you to just sweep problems under the carpet. It will make you have a face-to-face conversation with these issues, get to know them in-depth, and then tackle them from a stance where you actually know what to do.

Plus, agile project management is a team effort in every respect. From the moment you start splitting your project into smaller chunks, your team will be involved in the process. They will be able to give you real-life estimations on how long everything takes.

Finally, agile project management will allow you to track what is genuinely going on, rather than what you idealistically projected to happen.

All of these aspects will eventually lead to better, more accurate, more realistic, and more useful metrics when it comes to team performance, ROI, and time management.

Better Collaboration

If there is one thing absolutely everyone loves about agile project management (aside from the apparent chaos, which, by the way, can become addictive) is the fact that teams just tend to work better when they are managed under an agile method.

Agile project management fosters an environment that focuses on self-discipline, honesty, and taking responsibility. When you have these three ingredients, you create true team spirit — the kind where people naturally understand and empathize with each other, where they genuinely want to help each other, and where various types of frustrations and bad feelings don't even take root.

Agile is all about collaboration. The way you collaborate with your team, the way your team members will collaborate among themselves, the way your product manager will collaborate with the client, and the way you will collaborate with other stakeholders and upper management within your company — this will all change for the better.

This is not an empty promise. It lies at the very foundation of what agile is and what this approach aims for.

Better Work-Life Balance

We won't lie.

Not all people who work in agile project management have a great work-life balance.

But, then again, not all people who work in anything have a great work-life balance.

It is generally believed that those who work in agile project management (meaning the project managers and the teams) tend to have a better work-life balance because they learn how to efficiently manage their time. Therefore, they are much less likely to slack off and prolong their workdays into work nights and work weekends.

They are more likely to get their job done in the time it is supposed to be done — so that in their off hours, they can go back to their families, hobbies, and spare time.

Overall, this can lead to nothing but better, happier, more productive employees.

And we all know how happy that makes management, HR, and every single part of your organization, right?

You don't have to take our word for it when it comes to all these benefits. You just have to look at those companies that have embraced agile as part of their structures — they have plenty to say about it and how it has drastically changed their entire way of doing business.

These are just some of the advantages. You might experience all of them, a few of them, or more. In any case, you will definitely enjoy a noticeable, realistic improvement in the way your projects are managed!

Main Principles

A deeper look into agile management reveals the fact that there are principles which govern how to run a project. In other words, it tells a lot about how an agile project should be handled. There are 12 principles of agile project management.

1. The highest priority is to meet customer requirements through rapid and continuous delivery.

2. Changes are acknowledged at any stage of product development.

3. A higher frequency of delivery of product or service is embraced.

4. Stakeholders and developers work together closely during the development of the product or service.

5. The project is built around a group of motivated people.

6. Face-to-face interactions are regarded as the most effective form of communication.

7. A working product is the primary measure of success.

8. Agile processes advocate for sustainable development.

9. Agility is enhanced through ongoing attention to detail, good design, and excellence.

10. Simplicity is a vital element.

11. The use of self-organizing teams leads to the development of ideal architectures and designs which aid in meeting requirements.

12. Regular intervals are utilized to inspect and adapt to guarantee effectiveness.

A look into these principles reveals that the principles act as guidance on how different people can collaborate and work toward a common goal. There are many topics that these principles touch on, including people interactions, management behavior, team behavior, continuous improvement, and measuring progress.

Understand the Principles of Agile

In real life, they translate into a variety of tactics and practices that make agile actually work. You can compare this with a car, to better visualize how this happens. If the Principles and the Manifesto are the theoretical laws of physics upon which agile is built, then the practices and specific tactics are the ways in which the different parts of a car are pulled together to make for a working vehicle.

Let's jump in!

Customer Satisfaction

At the end of the day, customer satisfaction is why agile works, why agile was created, and why project management itself exists.

Customer satisfaction is the ultimate goal, the final frontier, and the pot at the end of the rainbow. It is what you aim for — you, your entire team, and your entire organization, in the end.

As such, every single one of the 12 Principles correlates to customer satisfaction. Such as the fact that you will make your life as a project manager easier and the fact that you will help your team members grow harmoniously.

However, when it comes to boiling everything down to one main concept, it is all about customer satisfaction.

While all of the Principles are equally important when it comes to delivering a product that will ultimately satisfy your customer or internal stakeholders, the first four focus more on making clients happy, while the others come as a kind of support in your endeavor.

To make sure you make your customers happy, you will first have to define who they are. In outsourcing companies, for example, this specific matter is quite clear: your customer is the company who ordered the software or product.

When it comes to developing internal products (such as, for example, an exclusively internal messaging tool), things might be a little fuzzy. In essence, however, the customer is the person or group of persons that ordered the product and with whom you will maintain continuous communication throughout the development of said product.

It is worth mentioning that, in general, project managers in agile don't necessarily talk directly to the customer — or, at least, not on a recurrent basis. The product owner is the person who takes on this role, ensuring proper communication between the customer and the project manager (who will later relay the information to the team and ensure all tasks are correctly assigned, timed, and financially managed).

The specific role of the product manager is to translate the customer wants into actual product requirements.

Say, for example, that your customer has ordered a social media management tool. They want to:

- Be able to post on Facebook

- Be able to post photos on Instagram

- Be able to schedule their posts

- Be able to monitor all their social media channels in one place

In product requirement terms, this might sound different:

- Cross-channel posting and scheduling

- In-tool image editing capabilities

The first four bullet points are the ideas the customer will come up with. The latter two, however, are what the product manager will relay to the project manager, who will in turn conduct team meetings and ensure that those product requirements are accurately split into micro-projects. Together with the team, the project manager will also make sure that working software is delivered on a recurrent basis.

How do you know your customer is happy?
Simply put, customers are happy when:

- Their needs are understood (the product manager's job)

- They see actual progress by receiving working software on a recurrent basis

- They see their feedback is actually followed and the product improves from one iteration to the next

- Their final product matches their initial needs, even if the requirements have changed throughout the duration of the development process.

It sounds both simple and complicated at the same time (especially if you have tried to maintain customer expectations and satisfaction at high levels before). Agile can help, though. The structure of agile is, in itself, one of the main ways customers in a variety of fields (including, but not limited to software development) are happy these days (as opposed to how they were, let's say, two decades ago).

Making and Managing Changes

A famous Greek philosopher once said that change is the only thing constant in life.

We constantly change, even when we don't actually see it happening.

We change from the very moment we begin life as embryos to the moment we fade out and return to Mother Nature.

TRANSFORMATION

It makes all the sense in the world, then, that agile would embrace change. In fact, this is one of the main tenets that makes agile so different from waterfall project management. While traditional project management methods see change as a boogieman waiting to attack from the back of the closet, agile takes change by its horns and embraces it.

Agile-based project managers understand that change is inevitable. They understand that customer requirements change, team structures change, and, ultimately, initial time-related and financial assumptions change, as well.

For those of you exclusively familiar with a traditional project management approach, the whole "embrace the change" concept might sound like downright chaos.

It isn't.

Same as waterfall, agile has its own processes and procedures to handle a variety of situations. The difference is that agile expects the unexpected — and, as such, it has developed its own way of dealing with change.

Although there are different ways of addressing all sorts of changes, the most universal method includes the following steps:

1. Understand the change

Sometimes, the change might come from the client (e.g. they have decided they need to integrate LinkedIn among the social media channels they want to manage via the tool they ordered from you). Other times, the change might come from the functional requirements (you have realized you need to implement a picture upload feature before you implement the actual scheduling tool).

At this stage, you should understand what the change means for the entire project and what its business purpose is.

2. Understand the scope of implementing the change

Regardless of where the change comes from, you have to understand its ramifications across all aspects of the project. Discuss it with your team and determine exactly what it will mean for your entire process, for the timeline you have created, and for the budget you had on paper.

Do make sure you take everything into consideration here and ensure your team agrees on all levels. It is important for everyone to be on board with the plan you are making, so that you can all implement it later on.

3. Ask for approval

This stage might be skipped under certain circumstances — such as when the customer specifically requests not to ask for their approval, for example, or when you know that your higher management has given you leeway in terms of approving such changes.

Other times, however, you will need to ask for approval of the change. In these cases, it is quite likely you will have to bring forward the implications of the change, as well as what you discussed with your team regarding what it will mean time-wise, resource-wise, and budget-wise.

4. Implement the change

When you receive your approval, you can proceed with the actual implementation of the change. Most likely, it will involve a re-planning of all the tasks and everything adjacent to them.

Changes can feel like little panic attacks when they occur. However, when you have an agile methodology to employ in your project management endeavors, you will find it much easier to handle all sorts of changes — from those related to the customer to those related to the cohesion of your team.

Continuous Customer Input

Agile projects are usually split into multiple iterations. They might be referred to differently from one agile method to the other (e.g. they are called "sprints" in Scrum, for example), but their main point is the same throughout the entire agile spectrum: to ensure that working software is continuously delivered to the client.

Receiving ongoing customer input is extremely important in agile because it ties back to providing customers with actual satisfaction when it comes to the final product.

In other words, you absolutely need your customer's feedback to ensure their happiness throughout the duration of the project — and upon the final delivery, as well.

There is a very good reason they call it continuous customer input. In agile, it is not enough to ask for feedback when you deliver a piece of working software at the end of a sprint. It is actually recommended to seek input before the end of the sprint. This way, each sprint will include the implementation of the feedback and the delivering of the final version of the working software.

Some customers might not be completely used to this MO. That's okay, you can help them understand that continuous feedback is much more productive than giant lumps of feedback that come sporadically. The more often you receive their input, the easier it will be to implement it — and, as a result, the happier they will be in the end.

Implementing Agile

In theory, agile project management sounds really easy. It all boils down to:

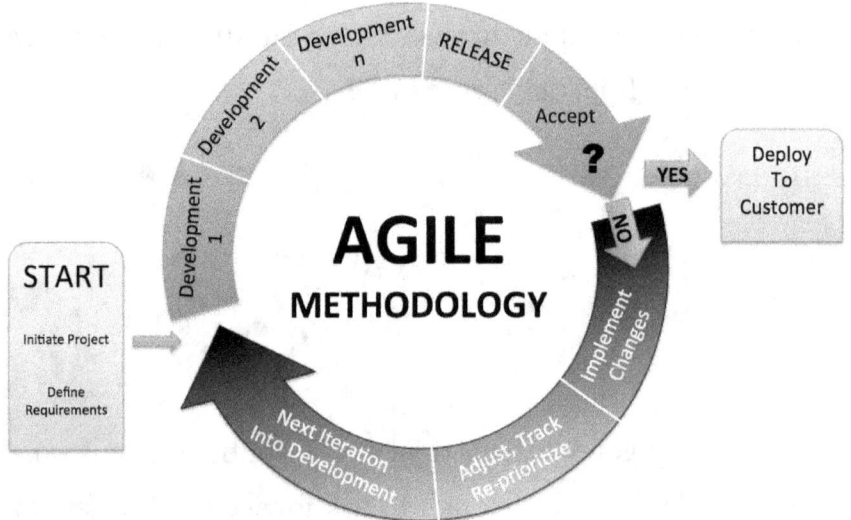

- Making sure all product requirements are understood

- Making sure product requirements are translated into stories

- Making sure each story is split into the appropriate number of tasks

- Making sure each task is properly prioritized

- Making sure you take the iterative process as an opportunity for continuous improvement

- Making sure working software is delivered at the end of each sprint

Doesn't sound so bad. Given that there is less emphasis put on documentation, it might even sound a lot more effortless to some of you.

However, what you do need to understand (and what we definitely need to be honest about) is that agile is not easy. Project management in general is not easy, regardless of how traditional or agile you decide to be.

It is quite important to acknowledge the fact that randomly applying the Agile Principles and Manifesto might help. But if you want real results, you should do so consistently, and you should make use of all the tools and techniques agile provides you.

Indeed, agile project management is all about being flexible — in terms of tasks, product requirements, changes, and the method itself. There is a reason there are so many types of "purebred" agile and hybrid agile methods: every organization has different needs, and agile project management understands that. As such, it has developed its own universal mechanisms while leaving plenty of leeway for adjustments as per the organization's needs, protocols, and goals.

The techniques and bits of advice we want to present in this will be equally useful regardless of which specific agile methodology and framework you might choose. Be it Scrum, Kanban, Lean, or any other agile methodology, you can rest assured that these tips will work at a universal level.

Define Your Vision

This is where it all begins, where the entire project is defined in terms of what you want to achieve with it. Of all the stages in the development of a project, this one will always feel the most motivational and inspiring.

Defining your vision is not about empty words, though — and you should definitely pay attention to this. Yes, it can be an inspiration and yes, it can definitely get quite creative, depending on the type of product you have to develop.

Furthermore, it is also important to mention that this is not a step to skip. No matter what type of agile project management methodology you might choose to follow, it is essential to take your time at the beginning of the project and define the vision. Why is this stage so important?

Simply put, it will outline everything you will aim for throughout the duration of the project. In some ways, you can look at your vision as the lighthouse that will guide you through the product development process. Whenever things go south, whenever you and your team get lost along the way, whenever you feel that it will never end, your vision will be there to lead you back to the right path.

Your vision doesn't have to be something larger than life. In fact, your vision definition should be quite succinct — not in the sense that you should speed up the process, but in the sense that you don't have to write an entire novella about the product you are planning.

There are multiple ways to tackle the vision definition stage of your agile project development. One of the simplest is to simply answer a handful of basic questions:

- Who is the product for?

- What do these people need or want?

- What is the product category?

- What are the key benefits the product brings forward?

- Who is the product's main competitor?

- What does the product do differently than its main competition?

When you answer all these questions, you will be able to write down your vision. For instance:

"AgileSocial is a social media management tool aimed at large agencies who need to manage tens of accounts in one place. The main benefit of AgileSocial is that it provides custom integration with more than just the basic social media channels (Facebook, Instagram, Twitter, and LinkedIn). Unlike Hootsuite (competitor), AgileSocial will provide more features in the free plan, such as the possibility to manage 20 accounts." This basic statement can do the trick, especially when you are developing your own product and you don't have a large team to work with. However, if you want to spend a little more time defining your product vision, you should consider the following steps:

1. Ask all the questions we have previously mentioned and draft the basic product vision, as per the example above.

2.   **Validate your vision by asking yourself a new series of questions:**

- Is your statement clear?
- Is your statement meant to be read by your team and other internal stakeholders?
- Is the description comprehensive and compelling enough when it comes to explaining the customer needs?
- Is the description describing the very best outcome the product development could lead to?
- Is the business objective clear?
- Is the vision congruent with the organization's vision and values?

3.   **Validate your vision with the following people:**

- Internal stakeholders
- Development team
- Scrum Master (in case you aren't the Scrum Master)

4.   **Rethink and rewrite your vision as per the input you have received after implementing the second and third points in this list.**

Regardless of whether you want to take the long way or the short one, this is a stage you simply shouldn't rush past. It might not sound like much, but you have no idea just how lost you can get when change occurs and your initial plans are turned upside down. In these situations, having a clear written vision statement can be a real-life saver from many points of view.

Tools and Methodologies

Agile Management has been around for years, if not decades. The idea that projects should be completed in a timely manner by achieving milestones is not a new phenomenon. The methodologies for this type of management have been advancing over the last few decades and have grown to include several different methodologies, each providing a different framework for the inner workings of a project. Having a deeper understanding of each available methodology will give you a better understanding of this management style and how you can use it with your own team on their projects.

Agile Scrum

Scrum is a simple way to provide a lightweight framework for a project using specific guidelines. They are an incremental part of the project and help to make serious decisions that will affect the overall end goal. By having the product owner involved, errors are reduced and flaws or unwanted parts of the project can be dropped without detrimental harm being done to later steps. Scrum allows for small or large projects and teams to be organized easily and deliver a project within a quick framework of time. Therefore, the fast iterations make this methodology the best for teams working on a project where customers and stakeholders expect an early release of the working product. This kind of participation helps the team make any necessary changes that may be pointed out by the stakeholders or product owners.

Kanban

This Agile methodology is focused on manufacturing. At its core, Kanban may be considered as an extensive to-do list. Not different to Scrum, the requirements of the Kanban methodology are monitored based on their current stage during the process.

Kanban can be a simple transition if you have the right team. To make sure that the transition is smooth, various people in the company including the stakeholders, testers, business analysts, and developers need to meet on a regular basis to discuss the project. When your business is shifting to Kanban, you must remember that this methodology is going to provide you with the fastest means of productivity for the code, but there are still some risks of the code going out with some errors.

Kanban is not time-sensitive, but it is dependent on priority. This means that anytime a developer wants to jump into the next task, he or she can do that very fast. This approach has a few meetings to help with the planning. It is not like Scrum. Kanban has a simple transition for the ideal teams. To ensure that the transition to Kanban is efficient and smooth - developers, business analysts, stakeholders, and testers have to meet regularly and discuss. While shifting to Kanban, one should remember that this type of methodology provides you with the fastest means of productivity in your code. However, chances are that the code might have some errors.

Kanban is the best for small teams or those teams that don't build features that should be released to the public. Besides that, it is a top-notch methodology used in different types of product or teams whose major goal is to remove bugs in a system.

Extreme Programming (XP)

Kent Beck is considered as the creator of XP. It is a popular and controversial Agile methodology. It focuses on the provision of high-quality software in a short period. It operates on customer participation, rapid feedback, subsequent planning, and testing. This methodology has been popular yet controversial since its introduction. XP allows for teams to deliver high quality work on a consistent and quick basis. It provides a framework for teams to help them work quickly and efficiently while still maintaining a very specific quality of work. With XP, software should be delivered within 1-3 weeks and involves constant testing, reviewing, and planning. This is great for smaller teams as collaboration and tight teamwork is needed to keep quality and speed up at the same time. Although this can work for larger teams and projects, they are more difficult to manage this way.

Crystal

This is one of the more adaptable methods of agile management. There are several different forms of crystal management but each focuses on size of the team and project priorities.
The team and how it works toward milestones is adjusted for each project to create a unique framework to work within.

Those who use the various Crystal methods often take on many different types of projects over a short period of time. This method allows for teams to easily adapt from one project to another one that is completely unique.

There are a few metrics that come with the idea of Crystal. These metrics are going to include things like simplicity, teamwork, and communication. Like with some of the other methodologies of Agile, Crystal embraces early and regular delivery of a working product. It can also promote things like eliminating bureaucracy, user participation, and adaptability. This is by far the most lightweight and easy-going approach. Crystal consists of a collection of Agile methodologies, some of which include Crystal orange, Crystal yellow, Crystal clear, and many more.

A few metrics of Crystal include communication, teamwork, and simplicity. Like other Agile methodologies, Crystal embraces early and regular delivery of a working product. In addition, it promotes adaptability, user participation, and elimination of bureaucracy.

The Dynamic Systems Development Methodology (DSDM)

The Dynamic Systems Development Methodology has processes that are refined over time to improve them.

The requirements, known as iterations, are defined and delivered within a short period of time and all of the tasks that are noted as important are done.

DSDM champions fitness in the business as the major focus in the delivery and acceptance of a given system.

In this methodology, requirements are listed early in the project and processes are refined to improve them. Requirements, often called iterations, are defined and delivered within a short time. All important tasks must be done in a DSDM project. In addition, not every requirement is highly prioritized.

Feature-Driven Development

Also known as FDD this method of development is meant to produce deliverables that are functional within a two-week period. It focuses on small teams and intense work with larger milestones and stages. FDD requires teams to meet often with the product owner or client and describes short phases that are done extremely quickly and put together in a limited time frame for delivery.

These are the current methodologies of software development. They each continue to grow and change with the years and evolve as the knowledge of development and software also grows. Picking the correct development method for your project and team is very important.

If not picked correctly, you may have very serious unintended consequences. Take a look at the project details and your team size to determine which of these development methods within Agile Management are best for you and your team.

Managing Risk in Agile Project Management

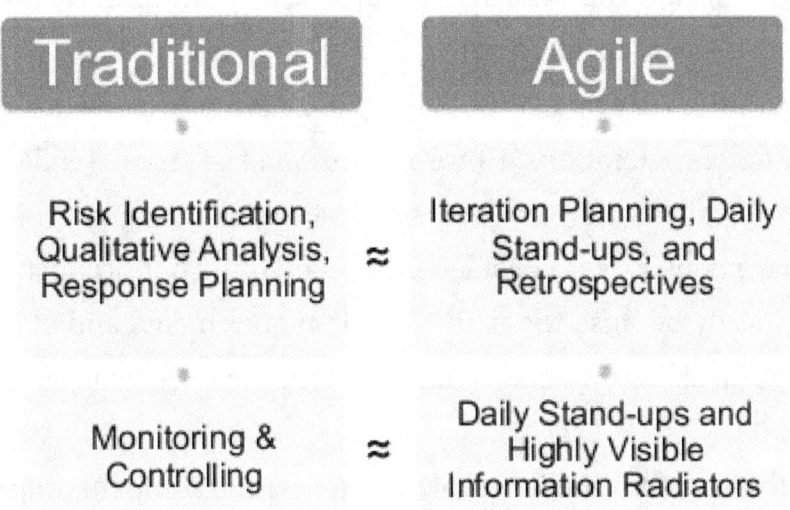

Risk management is a quintessential element of all types of project management. It is, ultimately, where real project management starts and where great project managers can show off their true value.

Managing risk in agile project management is tackled a bit differently than it is in the more traditional approaches. In waterfall, risk management is done based on the mega-plan created at the beginning of the project.

In agile, however, risk management is done iteratively, with each new release. The more sprints you go through, the more accurate a view you will have on what the risks are and what you can do to avoid them.

This is not to say that you will jump in headfirst when you start your first few iterations. However, you won't be able to (and you shouldn't) plan down to the smallest detail. In agile project management, this is considered to be anything but productive, specifically because the nature of the requirements and of the project itself can change — and, as such, the risks will change, as well.

For those of you who have only worked with traditional project management methods, agile risk management might sound like complete chaos.

However, it is just as organized and just as structured as any other project management method.

We will dedicate this chapter to teaching you the ins and outs of risk management in agile project management. While we may not dedicate as much space to any other individual aspect of agile project management, we feel that risk management is too crucial, too large, and too misunderstood. As such, we want to give it plenty of time and space, so that you fully understand how it is done.

Classify

Identifying risks in agile projects is all about discussing stories with your team and finding those parts that might prove troublesome along the road. The risk identification usually takes place in the third stage of the project development (once you have already understood the product requirements and the size of the stories).

The reason risk should be managed during the third stage is because by then, you will have a deeper understanding of the type of project you are dealing with and a specific idea of what you have to do.

Once identified, risks should be classified according to their nature. This step is important because it will help you see the risks you are facing more clearly — allowing you to plan preemptive actions to help you avoid those specific pitfalls.

Of course, since this is agile project management, you should accept the fact that risks might change over the course of the project development itself. This is precisely why risk management should be a part of each iteration planning — the more granular you can go, the more specific the risks you identify can be.

There are multiple ways to classify risks in agile project management, but we will discuss two of the most popular ones.

The Descriptive Method

This risk classification method is not prescriptive in the sense that it will allow you to alter the risk classes as you see fit. Some projects may meet all risk classes, others might be more limited (and, as such, they will only have to deal with specific classes of risks).

Some of the most important and common classes of risks you might encounter include the following:

- **Solution** — risks that affect whether or not the final product is an actual solution to your customer's needs.
- **Timeline** — risks that affect whether or not the project will be delivered on time.
- **Budget** — risks that affect whether or not the project will actually stick to its initial budget planning.

- **Privacy** — risks that affect whether or not the project can comply and abide to privacy regulations and legislation (such as GDPR, for example).
- **Security** — risks that affect whether or not the project and its contents are safe from potential hackers.
- **Resources** — risks correlated with whether or not you will have enough resources (human and non-human) to finish the project.
- **Scope** — risks that affect whether or not the project is contained correctly.

Depending on the type of project you are managing and its very specific implications, you might also want to take into consideration political, environmental, or reputational risks, for example.

Also, it is important to note that some risks might fall in multiple classes. For instance, lack of senior developers can be a resource-related risk, but it can also be a budget-related risk (as you will have to spend more money for good developers) and a time-related risk (as you will have to allocate time to source and recruit new developers).

The PESTLE Method

There isn't much to differentiate what we called the "descriptive" method and the PESTLE method, aside from the fact that the latter uses an acronym to make it easier for users to remember the main categories of risks to consider in the planning process.

PESTLE stands for:
- Political
- Environmental
- Social
- Technological
- Legal
- Economic

As you can see, these risks are more general and extrinsic to the project itself, so the method might be more suitable for projects that are actually related to the political, environmental, or social scene (but not exclusively so).

Same as with the other method, some risks might fall in multiple classes — it is important to discuss matters with your team and analyze these risks from every imaginable perspective.

You can't predict the future, yes. But you can definitely anticipate scenarios — and this is where risk identification and classification should occur.

Quantify

Identifying risks and classifying them according to their nature is obviously important. At the same time, it is also worth mentioning that quantifying each risk according to its level of importance and the impact it can have on the project is also crucial.

You may or may not like this, but numbers give meaning in project management — and although agile might be a more innovative way of dealing with the management of projects in general, it still abides to the same old-fashioned rules in terms of assigning numerical importance to various elements.

Same as classification, risk quantification can be done in multiple ways. Because it is relatively simple and because it can be just as good as any other technique, we have chosen to present you a method that uses a basic matrix to help you identify risk importance.

Basically, this method uses a matrix made up two axes: Impact and Probability. Each risk will be assigned a certain numerical value for the Impact axis and a certain numerical value for the Probability axis. When the two axes are brought together, each risk will be associated with a number that reveals just how critical that specific risk is to the project as a whole, and whether or not it should be tackled first.

When assigning numerical values for the Impact axis, follow this guide:

1) **Minimal** — the impact it will have on its class(es) is minimal and the risk impact should be reviewed every three months.
2) **Nominal** — the impact it will have on its class(es) does not exceed 5% (e.g. the project budget will be overrun by 5% if this risk occurs).
3) **Moderate** — the impact it will have on its class(es) can be somewhat significant, but the occurrence is unlikely and it will not affect the project by more than 10 percentage points (e.g. the project budget will be overrun by 10%).
4) **High** — the impact it will have on its class(es) can be significant and it can affect the project by 25% (e.g. the project budget will be overrun by 25%).
5) **Extreme** — the impact it will have on its class(es) is major and it can affect the project by 50 percentage points (e.g. the project budget will be overrun by 50%).

When assigning numerical value for the Probability axis, consider the following:
1) **0-10%** — quite unlikely to occur
2) **11-40%** — unlikely to occur
3) **41-60%** — may occur
4) **61-90%** — likely to occur
5) **91-100%** — very likely to occur

Once the matrix is filled in, you will multiply the numerical values assigned to each axis and get a number. Starting with that number (called Risk Value), you will be able to plan ahead and correctly prioritize the way in which you plan ahead to avoid major risks and to be as certain as possible that they will not affect the smooth progression of your project.

Skills and Software Development

A key component in implementing the agile methodology in your project is learning how you can do it. After all, a method is just as good as the tools and implements it offers at your disposal.

Fortunately for you, the agile method is not just about a fancy system of getting things done fast. In fact, you are all the better for the system if you identify what you can do and what you can use to implement the method in your own team.

What are the Key Agile Skills?

Aside from the agile methodology being dependent on the tools that you use, it is also dependent on the people implementing it. Project managers like you should possess certain qualities to make the method effective and sustainable.

A. Ability to Prioritize

At a glance, every task that could be involved in a project seems to be essential. Although this might be true, a project manager knows how tasks are to cut out so that everybody could focus on what is important now.

The project under the methodology, after all, is going to be divided into various iterations. This means that some tasks are not yet important until their corresponding phase arises or, due to the segmentation of the work, are deemed redundant. Your ability to identify what work matters and what is unnecessary will then be crucial for this method.

B. Calm Under Pressure

A project manager using the agile method should have the ability to keep calm under pressure and make crucial decisions even under tremendous stress.

You have to remember that changes are meant to be uncomfortable. Once everybody has settled into a pace or have mentally prepared themselves to do one thing, the last thing that they want to hear is that the rules have changed.

As a project manager, you should be able to handle changes, even last-minute ones, and adjust the work of your team accordingly. In this aspect, you might even have to develop your diplomacy skills to deal with the eventual dissent coming from your team.

C. Coaching Skills

One of the key principles of the agile method is to have a motivated team. The problem with motivation is that it does not exactly last long on its own. You as a leader should be able to keep your team motivated enough to finish each iteration of the development process. You should give them the assurance that everything is still according to plan and, if they are not, you are there to help them transition to the new status quo.

And aside from motivating your team, you should also be able to enhance their skills and guide them through their work without heavy hand-holding. In essence, your leadership should make sure that your team's skillsets and abilities are not the same at the end of an iteration. The more dynamic and expansive the team's combined skillsets are, the more capable it will be in handling challenges that might pop up in the process.

D. Organizational Skills

As a leader, it is your goal to make sure that everyone is doing their share of the entire workload. Aside from prioritizing what needs to be done, you need to be able to remind everyone of deadlines for each iteration.

A major flaw with the agile method, after all, is that it is easy to lose track of the overall goal especially if the iterations are long and numerous. It is your role, then, as a leader to remind everyone that everything that they do must not only contribute to the success of that iteration but to the overall project.

E. Quick Thinking

The ability to make important decisions is a major highlight in the agile method. Project managers then should be able to make rapid changes when the need arise without losing the momentum they have already built for the team.

This means that you should be able to drop strategies at a moment's notice no matter how strongly you feel for that tactic. You must understand that changes are there for a reason and you have to respond by making the necessary adjustments to your schedule. And keep in mind that some decisions have some time limit to them. If you take too long in mulling over your thoughts, you might lose valuable opportunities which results in some periods of inactivity for the rest of the team.

F. Adaptability

Accepting change should start from the leadership. As such, you should be the first to welcome the prospect of changing conditions in the development process.

When you are the first to adapt, you are actually helping the team adapt to the changes as well. This should reduce confusion in the implementation process while also preventing a further breakdown of communications.

But being adaptable is not going to help you if you relay the need for change as quickly as possible. You have to make your team understand why there is a need for changes and demonstrate to them that such changes do not negatively affect the entire iteration but, instead, would enhance the quality of their work.

Management Software

Anyone who wishes to use the Agile Method should also find the corresponding software for it. These programs come with features and systems that make implementation of the agile process possible and, in some cases, easier. Here are some of the Agile-optimized software that you could use for your project.

1. Planbox

One of the most important parts of the agile method cycle is what are called burndown charts (more on this later on). Planbox is a program that can track down these charts so everybody in the team has an accurate idea as to how far (or near) the team is in achieving a certain goal.

The program also integrates features like customer feedback, bug reports, fixes, and other user-generated content that can help you improve on your end product. It also comes with evaluation tools that should make your periodical reviews and retrospective more comprehensive.

Lastly, the program comes with an advanced reporting system that allows you to easily review the status of problem areas in each iteration. And the best part is that Planbox is absolutely free in the market right now.

2. LeanKit

If you are attempting to implement the Kanban variant of the agile method, then this program is the most suitable for you. One of the major features of this program is a live reporting feature where users can post work items and have the same addressed in real time.

This is ideal if your team is not physically together in one workplace. Perhaps you have remote teams working in other areas which makes daily meetings near impossible. But with LeanKit, in-team correspondence is easier which should make sure that everyone involved in the project is on the same page.

Aside from a live posting and reporting system, LeanKit is also optimized for cross-team platforms and is great for keeping track of dependencies. The program can also be made compatible for Scrum work frames.

The entire program can cost you in between $20.00 and $30.00 per month.

3. Jira

Built from the ground up for the Agile methodology, Jira is often considered to be one of the more dependable project management operating systems out there. It has a rather robust set of features that could help you track, monitor, and even communicate with the rest of your teams through each iteration of the process.

The only major flaw with Jira is that it can be intimidating for newcomers to the agile methodology. It can be complex to use at times and the act of merely setting it up for your workplace will require the help of an experienced developer.

Aside from this, Jira can be expensive. The solutions it offers and the services offered by the team can set up any company by at least thousands of dollars every year. If you are part of a small tech startup, then Jira might not be the best solution for you. Just yet.

Despite these flaws, Jira is rather excellent when it comes to tracking and addressing bugs, and inter-team correspondence. It also has various custom fields that allow you to make the program fit the specifications of your current projects.

4. GIthub Project Management

This program's main selling point is that it is the largest hosted GIt-based server in the market right now. So, you may ask, what does that do for your agile project management method? The answer is that the server allows all your developers to store all code done in projects that have been already finished.

This means that you don't have to rework code you've already done for new projects which can cut the development time by a considerable degree. And the best part is that it can record edits done in real time which means that work can continue where it was left in case of emergencies.

One of the great features of the GIthub program is that it can integrate many other tools for different people involved in the project. There is a panel dedicated to developers, another for product owners, another for project manage3rs, and so on and so forth. Your development team can even set up a private communication channel or a public one dedicated to improving code.

The end result is that your team will always have access to the best versions of codes that they have already worked with which should keep work momentum at a high. Pricing for this management program starts free with a $21.00 per user monthly subscription fee if you want access to more features.

5. Clickup

If you have been looking for the most ideal agile management program, then Clickup might be the answer for you. A core feature within Clickup is a feature-driven management program that allows teams to get on top of what needs to be done per iteration while making sure that their efforts contribute to the larger end goal.

Clickup gives users the ability to see an overview of tasks that were completed, yet to be completed, works in progress, and dependencies. With this, you can at the very least prevent tasks from bottlenecking your entire team.

Some of the other features provided by the program include the ability to create epics and set up story points, analyze iteration progress in real time, give users access to custom templates and statuses for process management, time tracking, and other tools that could help in daily meetings.

The best part with Clickup is that it has a Free Forever plan. What this means is that you can get a hold of a copy of the system for absolutely free. However, for access to even more comprehensive features as well as maintenance costs, the program will ask for a $9.00 per month subscription fee for every person that will use the program.

Identifying Organizational Problems

In order for the agile method to work, the entire team must adhere to its principles. This is why the biggest challenge that you would face in implementing the system in your organization is the organization itself. As a matter of fact, there are a number of inherent problems that could impede you from fully enjoying from the agile method if not properly addressed.

A. The Culture

Not every company and team culture out their support or is even compatible with the agile method. And even if your team is immediately on board to the process, there is the chance that the higher-ups are not so welcoming of it.

This is where a lot of diplomacy should come into play as you have to convince the people that you directly report to that there are benefits to be had from the agile system in order to support it. You have to see things from their perspective in order to do this.

Perhaps the management feels that they are giving away too much independence to your development team and are afraid that this would disrupt internal communications. Or perhaps they have mere misconceptions about the methodology.

Whatever the case, you can actually do a lot on your part to dispel their fears about the system so they would support your project across the different iterations.

B. Unclear Understanding of The System's Impact

In order to get the best results from the agile method, it is not enough that you just implement the systems and tools at your disposal. More often than not, blindly following the principles without reconciling it with the company's goals can result in you wasting time, effort, and money.

Aligning the system with the company's goals and values will still matter as this helps the rest of the company understand why you have to do your project in different iterations. If your team and the rest of the company understands how the Agile method can positively affect the entire organization, you can be certain that the system becomes sustainable in the long run.

C. A Tendency to Rush

One fatal flaw of the agile method is that it taps into man's annoying tendency to rush things through. In the hopes of getting things done fast and in massive quantities, the brain tends to overlook key details.

This results in teams getting focused on getting things done ASAP while missing the most simple and manageable aspects of the development process. This can lead to serious repercussions later on as problems set up in previous iterations can pop up in later ones.

As such, project managers must find a way to keep everyone focus while maintaining the pace of work. In essence, you serve as the first and last line of defense against your team becoming reckless in the development process.

Planning Your Projects

Experience accumulated all through enormous scale usage of Agile standards in programming improvement assignments instructs us that the directly well-known Agile programming improvement techniques (like Scrum http://www.scrumalliance.org/>) do now not scale to program, item and business endeavor level without change. The essentials for alterations to these strategies are seen in Lean standards, or: the eventual fate of Agile methods is found in its roots. This paper depicts an arranging structure that has been utilized effectively in enormous scale Agile errands and examines the effect of presenting this system on three center Lean standards http://www-personal.umich.edu/~liker/>: Muri, Mura and Muda.

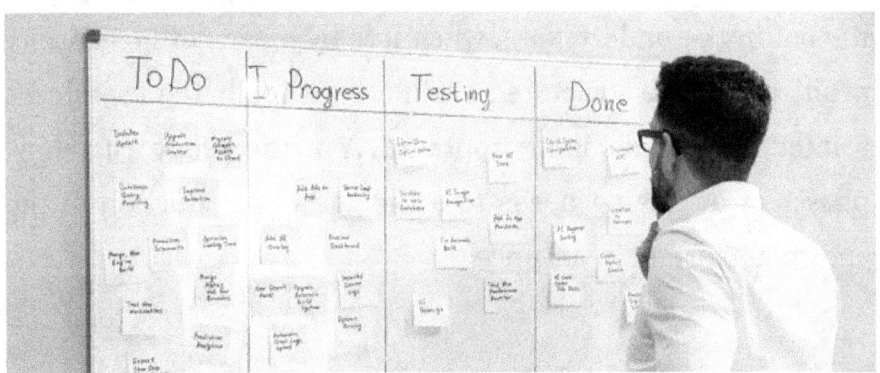

Arranging in Large Scale Agile Projects

In Agile http://www.agilemanifesto.org/> techniques, stacking a gathering with work is accomplished by means of age arranging. Because of the brevity of the new discharge (ordinarily one to about a month and a half) an organization decreases in hugeness and arranging helpful properties in significance. For little tasks, it might furthermore be sufficient to design exclusively a solitary age at once. The accomplished disadvantage of age arranging when used to errands that keep running for additional then a couple of emphases or with several groups is that the perspective on the more drawn out timespan ramifications of emphasis activities can be lost. At the end of the day: the perspective on "the entire" is lost. An answer is to add arranging degrees to include the present perspective on "the entirety".

In plan-driven and cascade philosophies, this issue is defeated through a huge forthright structure, planning to anticipate precisely how a dreadful parcel work is stressed in each challenge task. This prompts an enormous subsidizing right off the bat in the undertaking, when it is by means of no capacity positive that the structured usefulness is really the usefulness wanted through the item proprietor. A methodology with a few phases of arranging needs to avoid the reintroduction of the enormous format in advance.

Arranging activities for huge scale venture endeavors rely upon 5 levels:

- **Product Vision**
- **Product Roadmap**
- **Release Plan**
- **Sprint Plan**
- **Daily Commitment**

The basic assignment of test activities tended to in every one of the five degrees increments, and along these lines the amount of component tended to (cash contributed), the quantity of people concerned and the recurrence can intensify without strolling the danger of burning through cash on features that may also now not be constructed or may moreover be fabricated in an unexpected way. Every one of the five degrees of arranging tends to the essential arranging standards: needs, evaluations and duties.

Item Visioning

The broadest picture that one can paint of things to come is a dream of an item proprietor. In this innovative and judicious she clarifies how an enterprise or item should look. She proposes what segments of the framework need to exchange (need) and what endeavors can be utilized to gain this goal (assessments and duties).

Item Visioning - How To

Potential structures for a visioning practicing are to make a lift assertion or an item creative and farsighted box http://www.joelonsoftware.com/articles/JimHighsmithonProductVisi.html>. The statute of every exercise is to make a statement that depicts the future in expressions of wanted item includes, objective customers and key differentiators from going before or forceful items.

Geoffrey Moore http://en.wikipedia.org/wiki/Geoffrey_Moore utilizes the accompanying shape in his lift proclamation: "For (target client) who (articulation of the need) the (item name) is an (item class) that (item key advantage, convincing reason to purchase). In contrast to (essential aggressive option), our item (last presentation of essential separation)." The item innovative and insightful portrays an ideal nation that is a year or more later on. Further arranging (structure) exercises will detail the vision, and may furthermore occupy from the vision on the grounds that the future will pass on us a changed point of view available, the item and the necessary endeavors to make the inventive and judicious reality.

Monitoring and Tips for Success

There are currently numerous companies out there trying to leverage various metrics to measure the overall success of their organization. But, when it comes to leveraging the metrics of agile project management, things are a lot more complex than you would actually think it to be.

When you start an agile project, you already have to make plans on ways to measure success because without measuring success in the right manner, your project can't proceed forward. Furthermore, when it comes to agile, there's not a single method or metric that will be perfect for organizations of all sizes and kinds. Keeping those factors in mind, the following are some of the most important metrics by which you can measure the success of your business' agile project management implementation.

Timely Delivery

Timely delivery is one of the most important metrics that most organizations use to measure the success of agile project management. But since agile already relies on time management to finish projects within schedules - in this case, timely delivery is meant by the work that is done in accordance with the overall expectations of what is about to be delivered.

This helps in improving the visibility aspect of agile project management in regards to the work that is being done and delivered on a consistent basis over time. This helps team members to be more encouraged about their work and therefore deal with complex situations beforehand.

The Defects

When you take any project into consideration, you have to take care of its defects as well. Defects can be part of any project. But, with the help of agile project management, your team will be able to reduce or minimize the number of defects that largely occur. You can easily track the defect metrics and allow the development team to learn and know the way it can avoid such defects and also rectify the same as well.

The number of defects and the increase or decrease in such defects will help you know the overall progress of the project. It will help you to spark discussions with your development team, thereby improving the overall techniques during the sprint retrospectives.

The satisfaction of the Customer

This metric is used to measure how much the customer is satisfied with the overall progress of agile project management. Using this metric to measure agile projects is the real idea that lies behind the whole agile philosophy.

Agile relies on customer feedback to develop better and more efficient products by mainly focusing on the needs and requirements of the customers.

The agile methodology generally works to deliver the best value to the end-user through its working product or software. You can measure customer satisfaction in various different ways, which includes usage statistics, an increase in the number of sales, user opinions, and reviews and the likes.

The Quality of the Product

It can be a little more difficult to measure the quality of the product developed through agile procedures, with the help of such metrics. Like it was mentioned before, the methodology of agile relies upon the creation of value for the end-user. Therefore, it means that even though there is a greater emphasis on the quality of the product, the most challenging part is the way you can measure the obtained success.

You can do this by starting to look at the overall customer satisfaction along with the growth rates in terms of revenues and also the other technical aspects of the agile environment's testing phases. When it comes to agile practices and policies, the development team focuses on building software with the help of quality product integration right from the start.

When the development team allows for continuous testing methods throughout the lifecycle of the product, it ensures that the software or the product is being developed in the right manner, which will ensure the right kind of quality at the end of the product of software lifecycle.

The Value Created for the Business

It's essential to measure the business value which is being created through the help of the various agile policies and practices. It has been mentioned and recognized in the Agile Manifesto regarding the significance of business values in many agile principles. When you're planning to measure business value, the ambition should be very clear about what you need. This is because creating value for the business is all about knowing whether the requirements for compliance or contract has been fulfilled.

Therefore, if you can apply the metric of business value to measure the kind of features that are to be delivered by the development team, then it will help in measuring the whole project's success in an effective manner.

The Overall Product's Scope

The success of your agile project can also be measured with the help of the project's scope too.

The scope of the project will contain all the necessary requirements and features, as an integral part of the agile project management.

When you will be setting a goal regarding the developments that are to be made in the upcoming three months, then it can get quite rewarding when tracking the status of the project and also completing the relevant tasks related to it as well.

When you'll be receiving updates in real-time regarding the benefits of your project being completed, it will benefit everyone involved in the development of products or software. You will be easily visualizing the success of the project and also its overall progression towards the finishing line.

The Product's Visibility

Without a shadow of a doubt, visibility can be a massive factor and also an essential metric in various agile policies and practices. Good product visibility will also lead to better success in the overall project as well.

The product's visibility is based on the overall transparency of product development and transparency is very significant in building long-term trust as well.

In simpler terms, the plans of the project should be available to all and everyone should have access to the progress of the project, so that trust between team members could increase multi-folds. Following that method, everyone involved in the project's success, including the managers and stakeholders can provide their perspective on the project's success.

You have to make sure that the features of the project should be portrayed side by side with the current project plan in mind so that everyone could see the overall success. Moreover, with the help of visibility, the alignment of different teams becomes easy. When more than one team is working on the development of a particular project, then with the help of visibility, you can spark mutual understanding and cooperation between the team members and the teams as well. This will in-turn give a boost to the overall success of the project

The Return on Investment Or R.O.I

Return on investment can be defined as the income that is generated by the product or the software that is being developed. If the product costs less money to produce, which means that the company had to spend less money overall, then it can be said that the product's ROI is high.

In terms of agile projects, the concept of ROI is different than what is being used in traditional projects. With the help of agile projects, you can easily allow the product or software in hand to help you generate income from the first iteration or release itself. The revenue will continue to increase with every release version. ROI is indeed a great metric for a company to appreciate its development team and also the overall value of the project that is ongoing as well.

With the help of ROI metrics, organizations can decide whether to fund or scrap a project completely. The ROI potential is what most companies look at. The ROI of individual projects, as well as projects for the company as a whole, can be tracked by the company.

The Overall Productivity

When working in an agile environment, it is very essential that productivity is kept at an all-time high. It can also be a very useful metric to monitor and look after the overall success of the project as well. In an agile environment, productivity is measured in terms of overall output.

Thus, you can easily figure out the impact of productivity by looking at the requirements that are completed or done. If a team is high on productivity, then the requirements will be done fast and quick. If productivity is less, then more time will be required to complete the same requirements.

The Overall Predictability

Predictability is another one of the most important factors when measuring the success of agile project management. You can measure predictability with the help of the velocity trend. Velocity trend can be defined as the maximum amount of work that a scrum team or an agile team can pull off or complete in each agile sprint.

When you'll measure this trend for around three to four months, you'll come to know about the amount of the work that has been done or completed at a pace that is sustainable enough for the development team. In case the metric of velocity differs on a drastic basis, then it can mean that there are a number of factors that can be responsible for such behavior, including team changes, teams getting used to the new work and so on.

Success can also be measured on the number of user stories that are being completed on a regular basis per week, which will also be a nice indicator of predictability too.

The Duration of The Project

There's no doubt that the agile project is done much quicker than normal traditional waterfall projects. Thus, by allowing the project to start quicker and at a much faster rate will help you cut all the bloatware that is unnecessary.

Bloatware, in this case, is referred to as the requirements that are not significant and are not required.

In this way, the project teams following agile project management can deliver the project at a much faster rate than ever before.

You will need to measure the time duration required for the whole project to complete to know the success of the process.

The Overall Project Cost

The cost of the agile projects will depend on the actual duration of the project. The longer will be the duration, the greater the cost that will arise as well. But, since projects following agile methodologies take less time to complete than traditional policy-following projects, the cost will also be on the lesser side. Companies or organizations can use the various cost metrics to plan their budgets, determine the overall return on investment and also know the time to exercise the redeployment of capital to boost the working productivity. If the project cost stays within the budget, then it will be called a success.

The Process Improvement

Agile principles and policies depend on a crucial philosophy, which includes continuous improvement of the project development in hand. The development team should always strive to be better at all times. But measuring the process improvement will be not possible if the outcome of the project is not measured at all. Therefore, success needs to be measured at every sprint ending to know the current status of the project.

You need to use the combination of the above-mentioned steps, including predictability, productivity, and velocity to know whether the development team is putting in the hard work.

Finally, it should be kept in mind that keeping track of the various agile metrics is always beneficial to the organization or business entity. It will help the company to choose the right team and also the project for future success. You'll need an overview that is balanced in every field in order to make decisions which will work in favor of the development team following agile practices and policies, and also the project itself. You need to apply these metrics in the best possible manner to help in counting the overall success of the agile project management implementation.

The Agile Process

There are two things that should be achieved with the agile project management methodology: shorter production cycles (without sacrificing quality, of course) and more frequent product releases. By having shorter development iterations, a team should be able to react to changes from outside sources more effectively.

As was stated before, there is more than one way to do the Agile method. Scrum and Kanban, for example, feature fairly different work structures from the others. However, each agile methodology follows the basic process which is as follows:

1. Project Planning

Like with any method, you should make the team understand the end goal of the project before starting it. Here, you will explain to them the potential value that succeeding in the project will bring for the team and the company and how it should be achieved.

You may set up a scope for the project here but do not make it unchangeable. The whole premise of the agile method is to adapt to changes that may happen in the middle of the development process. As such, you should avoid getting your team stuck on achieving goals through a static work frame.

2. Creating the Product Roadmap

A roadmap maybe a buzzword for tech guys right now but it is a rather simple yet vital concept to software development. To put it simply, it is a breakdown of what features will make up the final product.

What makes it crucial to the development process as the roadmap tells your team what to focus on in each phase. Also, at this point, you will set up the product backlog which will list all the features and deliverables that will be included in the final product. When you plan for iterations in the future, your team can refer to this backlog to identify what to focus on.

3. Planning Releases

In traditional project management methodologies, there is only one implementation date that comes after the entire project has been developed. However, in the agile method, your project will have a shorter development cycle with features released at their ends.

Before you start the project, you should make a high-level plan for feature releases. And when beginning a new cycle, you shall revisit and re-assess the release plan for those new features.

A high-level plan is basically one that provides a manager's view of the project in its entirety. It's not just a detailed plan where all the tasks required for project completion are indicated. A high-level plan includes information on what needs to be done, who is supposed to do the task that needs to be done, how it is done, and when things are expected to be done. This plan is developed with the goal of making sure that progress can be tracked over time.

4. Planning Cycles

Before starting each cycle or iteration, the shareholders need to plan with your team on what shall be accomplished in each segment. Of course, this will also include how such things shall be achieved and how much of a task load should each member of the development carry.

At this point of the process, it is important that you make sure that the load is shared evenly amongst members. This way, they can efficiently accomplish each of their assigned tasks per iteration.

Also, you will need to document your workflow visually. This is to make the task assignment process as transparent as possible to your team and to prevent bottlenecking from occurring when implementing the schedule.

5. Regular (Ideally Daily) Meetings and Correspondence

In order to make your teams accomplish their tasks more efficiently in each cycle, or assess what needs to be improved on, you have to make a habit out of holding short meetings every day. During these meetings, every member will be given the chance to talk briefly as to what they have accomplished for that day and will they be working on in the next.

But it is important that you keep this meeting short. Spend no more than 15 minutes in talking with your team as these meetings are not meant for extensive problem solving or chances to talk about things that everybody else has already settled or know of. In fact, you can even do these meetings standing up.

6. Cycle Reviews and Retrospectives

At the end of each iteration, the team will hold two major meetings. In the first major meeting, you will do a cycle review with the client and the shareholders to present to them what has been achieved. And not only are you going to present a sustainable feature, you are going to show to these people a working product.

This is a rather important meeting as it bolsters the communication lines between your team, the shareholders, and the clients as well as allowing them to give an input which could help in the next iterations.

The second major meeting is the Cycle Retrospective. Here, you and the shareholders will discuss the things that went well during that cycle, what didn't, and whether the work load may have been too heavy or too small for the team. Of course, this meeting will also focus on identifying recurring problems that should be dealt with in the next few iterations, if any.

If you and your team is relatively new to the whole agile project management concept, it is important that you do not skip on these meetings. These meeting would help you determine the task load that your team can handle in each iteration as well as the most effective length for each.

What is the Agile Mindset?

In order to properly implement this methodology, it is important that you and your team have to change your mindset. To do this, you must adopt some values that are necessary for the success of the methodology:

- **Client Satisfaction is at the Top**

The needs of the client must be put first. As such, you must make it a goal to regularly produce content that is functional and of good quality in a timely manner.

When you present progress to a client, they must be able to test it for themselves and come to the conclusion that it is good. They must also be given the chance to air out their concerns and input for the project while also being assured that their concerns are duly noted and will be applied to the best of your abilities.

- **Adaptiveness and Improvisation**

Changes can happen at any time during the process. Even last-minute changes can occur which would ultimately affect the quality of the product. Despite this, you and your team must be accepting of change in any form it takes and adjust your efforts to meet the new goals and conditions.

For leaders, this comes with the extra requirements of being fast enough to act on sudden changes and make important decisions as quickly as possible. The less they mull over what to do next, the more responsive the team will be in addressing sudden shifts in project conditions and goals.

- **Fast Development Cycle**

The ultimate goal of the agile method is to optimize your time. In essence, you and your team should make it a point not to waste time by focusing on the most important goals for each iteration.

Of course, this should mean that each stage of iteration of the development process should be as short as possible. However, you must be always ready to show results and the progress you have made when clients, shareholders, and management would demand of them in the end of each iteration.

If you have noticed, these three qualities basically summarize the Agile Project Management methodology. They are not exactly written in stone but, as the method itself states, this is the best strategy that you can use to adapt to changes instantly without losing sight of the overall goal.

Also, if certain aspects of your methodology do not work out as planned, you can always make improvements until you see the desired results.

All in all, with the methodology, you should produce three things: a good product, a timely delivery of the same, and a really satisfied client.

What Are the Reasons Why Agile Project Management Could Fail?

There's no doubt that the methods of agile project management have been gaining popularity for some time now. But even the best policies in the world can fail due to a number of reasons. Therefore, if you want your project team to succeed using agile methodologies, then you need to keep in mind about these following potholes that can render your plans ineffective.

The following factors are some of the reasons why you should always keep an eye out for your agile policies so that you can avoid these loopholes.

- **The Lack of Experience**

It was reported at the 9th annual State of Agile Survey that almost 44 percent of people who voted in the survey complained about lack of experience, affirming that is one of the key reasons for the failure of agile methodologies. Agile is not only about the way you think, but also what you do and the way you do it as well.

The team members who have the deficiency to apply agile practices that are basic in nature will always run into trouble in the later stages of the project when more complex strategies will be involved. Therefore, it is very important that you invest in solid foundations by training your team members in techniques that are agile related and also perform proper coaching for their best use case scenarios. That's only when your money will be better invested.

- **Clashes in Company Philosophies versus the Core Values of Agile**

Lack of any support for cultural transition and the differences in company philosophies versus the agile values are two of the most popular reasons why agile methodologies fail so often. Agile policies are all about the way you think and what you do according to that thinking. In case the organization's culture is hostile or ignorant to the values and principles of agile, then the success of the in-house team members following agile policies will be very slim indeed.

It should be kept in mind that agile also impacts organizational values as well, and in order to facilitate that transformation, agile policies should be adopted on a wider spectrum. It will allow you to enjoy more success in the long-term.

- **No Support from The Management**

Sometimes, when an agile transformation is poorly planned, it reduces the massive enthusiasm of the project team and managers, thereby reducing their morale and working capabilities. If the executive guidance is not strong enough, the management department will feel disjointed from the development team.

When an agile transformation takes place, the executives of an organization need to change their behavior in such a way that it will encourage the project team to live the values they want and also help them to understand and adapt to the changing agile values of the organization.

- **The External Pressure to Follow Traditional Procedures**

This problem is very common in large-sized enterprises, mainly where teams following both agile and traditional methods, work under the same umbrella department. This means that agile policies have to work in tandem with traditional procedures, as opposed to traditional procedures working in tandem with agile policies.

Thus, agile has to co-exist with traditional methodologies, which will ultimately affect the organization's planning, retrospectives, reviews and also agreement on organizational interfaces that are mutual to each other.

- **The Team's Unwillingness to Follow Agile Methodologies**

Such situations arise when the members of a certain team continue to identify themselves through the use of a different function. Therefore, this leads to the formation of a strong personality between the team members and therefore affects his or her position at the pecking order as well.

Thus, there is a certain disparity and difference in focus and behavior that develops between the team members, according to their pecking order. Capable coaching and training of the tam by the management executives are required to overcome these differences in ideologies.

- **The Training Received by the Team is Insufficient**

Training can be broken down into three parts:

- *The training was received by no one.*

- *The training was done selectively.*

- *The training was not up to the mark.*

It's not at all a very good idea to skimp on the overall training, because it can never lead to a successful organization. You have to make sure that all your efforts in the implementation of agile policies receive training in the best possible manner, including the management executives as well.

- **Unreliability of the Team**

If you want your agile project to be successful, the members of the whole organization working on it should be on the exact same wavelength as others. If half of your project team members or even your stakeholders do not attend important meetings - the project will simply fail. The best way to avoid this issue to make sure that your team is efficient enough and is dependable on each other to avoid this common problem.

- **The Leaders of the Team Are Weak**

Before you choose the best scrum master in your agile project team, you have to make sure that the person is a very strong leader and has commendable leadership qualities as well. But not every person out there has the perfect leadership qualities to make the team work together in unity.

When leaders are weak, the same precedent will be set before the team members too. The scrum master or the project lead should have the capabilities to oversee, lead and also perform any decision or action that is to be undertaken.

- **Lack of Any Communication with the Stakeholders**

Any deterioration or lack of communication between the stakeholders can easily be the downfall of any agile related project. There can be times when stakeholders will not be fully transparent about their expectations from the team members as well as the project offerings. You have to set up good communication channels with your organization to ensure that such things do not happen and stakeholders are fully able to express and present their necessities to the agile project team members.

- **Specifications of the Project is Incomplete**

Sometimes projects can fail due to the requirements of the project not being defined in the right manner. Agile projects always focus on the important deliverables and actions of a project and then deals with any possibilities that may come up during the overall implementation of the process. Having a project with requirements that are almost incomplete will prevent the project to go into the actionable mode - which is very important to make the project a success.

- **Implementation of the Retrospective is Not Effective**

One of the main goals of carrying out agile projects is to perform retrospectives and discuss the same with your team members. A retrospective is all about learning from the process - the positives and negatives. It will help you to know how well the team is performing and how the performance could be made better as well. If you're not carrying out retrospectives, then your team will not come to know about their faults.

It will be much more difficult to know the current stance of each person and collaborative efforts within each other will be difficult. Therefore, retrospective meetings should be taken at regular intervals.

- **Team Is Focused on Success and Not the Art of Learning**

One of the huge reasons for the failure of agile projects is the lack of ambition to learn first rather than to succeed at first. Team members become focused too much on project success and forget the opportunities to learn the various values and methods of agile project management. Mistakes should always be seen as a way to improve and learn something new. For example, if a software doesn't work as you would have expected it to be, you have to see it as an opportunity to learn something new rather than seeing it as a failure.

- **Lack of a Set of Best Methods in Agile Project Management**

When you compare agile with policies such as Six Sigma, it

doesn't have it set of best practices or methods that one could follow. Due to this reason, the agile policies of two different organizations may vary hugely. You have to let your team know clearly about your expectations.

If some policies don't work, you need to strike it off the list as fast as you can. And when some policies will work, you have to add to the list. The trial and error method should be used in this case because agile project management doesn't give you the framework of the best procedures or methods.

- **Time is Used Inefficiently**

It's quite impossible to complete a project successfully without the following time in the right manner. Time management skills are very important if you want to succeed in any given field or industry. If you spend too much time on developing a single feature, the other features of the project will suffer. Similarly, spending less than the required time will make the feature half-baked or buggy. Time management should not be underestimated and with agile methods, you always need to keep on your toes to achieve the best results.

Tools for Greater Team Effectiveness in Agile Project Management

The Team

Your team is your single greatest asset and tool for effective Agile Project Management. Because of this, you want to ensure that your team is running in the best way possible.

Team Mission Statement

Just like the greatest companies have their mission statement, the best teams have their own mission statement. This is something that will allow the team to reference and serve as a guide for how the team functions. The mission statement doesn't need to be long, but it does need to embody what the team is about and what their overall goals are. Make sure to take some time to really think through what your team's mission is and also make sure that everyone on the team agrees with this mission statement. One way to solidify their agreement is to have each individual sign the mission statement and receive a copy of the signed document.

Keep meetings and interactions brief

Throughout the course of your project, you will have many meetings on various topics. Another way to keep your team efficient is to ensure that meetings that are set up are only long enough to accomplish the goal of the meeting. Try to keep your meetings short and finish your topics in 20 minutes.

Quick Conflict Resolution Agreement

One thing to consider as part of your mission statement is to add an agreement for a quick conflict resolution. As you've probably experienced throughout your life, conflicts will happen, however, if dealt with quickly, the conflict does not have to cause delay or derailment in your project. One of the things to consider for this type of agreement is to set up a time limit for any disagreement and after that time another member of the team is brought in to help resolve the conflict

Celebrate success

As you bond as a team and start to get better, you will start to achieve success. One thing that is often missing in many companies is taking the time to celebrate successes. You are probably motivated by personal achievement as your reward.

However, I encourage you to take the time to celebrate your success as a team. This does several things. One of these is it allows your team to bond at a deeper level. When you're able to get your team out of the office and into an environment where they can be a little freer to speak their mind, deeper relationships are built, and this translates into greater trust in the work environment.

Understanding Yourself

If you're going to be effective with any type of soft skills or be in a leadership role, you will need to first understand yourself. Knowing what your strengths and your weaknesses are is critical to your success.

Communication skills

While working on an Agile project, the majority of your interaction will come face-to-face with your team on a daily basis. In addition, as the scrum master, your role is to remove anything that is blocking the progress of your team. This may mean that you have to go to leadership or other individuals and be able to negotiate on their behalf. Your ability to communicate in the written word and be clear about your intentions will go a long way to making you a good Agile project manager.

You must go far beyond written and verbal forms of communication and be skilled in nonverbal communication.

Confidence

One of the key components of leadership is confidence. Having confidence is as much a state of mind as it is a skill. Like any skill, confidence can be learned and developed. Going back to body language, one of the things you can do to increase your confidence has to do with the way to sit and stand.

You will need to show confidence. Your posture will need to show that you are in control or at least that you have things under control. One thing you need to remember is that most of the team members have no desire to be in a position of leadership and if you are in a leadership position, then you must belong there.

Delegation

Delegation is as much an art as it is a skill. If you are going to accomplish the most you possibly can you must learn to delegate to those you know you can trust effectively. By doing this, the amount you can accomplish will be far greater than what you can do on your own. One of the keys to delegation is another soft skill, and that is to have patience.

Patience

You should have the patience to allow others to take things away from you and help them if they fall. For those of you that are real go-getters, and if you're reading this you probably are, giving up work to someone else is very difficult.

After all, if you want something done right then you know you need to do it yourself. However, learning the skill of patience will help you in all areas of your career and personal life. Specifically, this will help you to be a more effective and influential project manager.

Adaptability and Creativity

If you're going to succeed in any aspect of your career, you will need to be able to adapt to your environment and be flexible. Being too rigid, especially in an Agile environment, will not work. You will ensure your failure if you are not able to be flexible in your actions and thinking. The entire premise behind the Agile methodology is adaptability. So, for you as the project manager or the scrum master, you need to make sure that you adapt to the environment, the team, and the needs of the project.

Mentorship

As a project manager you will be in a position of authority and leadership. Because of that, you will have people coming to you with questions and advice. The other thing that you'll find is that people are thirsty for knowledge and looking for somebody that can help them get ahead. Through your interaction, if they sense that you may be that person, they may start asking you questions and come to you for mentorship.

The Agile Development Process

There is actually no single methodology out there that can work for every project. However, there is no doubt that many development teams and companies are slowly doing away with the more predictive and restrictive methodologies like Waterfall and embracing something more adaptive like Agile.

In fact, you might be surprised that methodologies like Agile were born primarily out of a frustration on how things were used to be done back then. By giving the team much more control over how things are done and for how long, the theory is that the end product will be a far more comprehensive software while still staying true to the client's original vision.

With that, you can easily understand that the Agile process will follow a considerably different development path than conventional and traditional methodologies.

How Development was Done Before

The conventional software development process will involve six phases which are as follows:

1. Planning

Obviously, every development process starts with you laying down the specifications of the project. Here, the flow of work will be identified and segmented into smaller and more manageable parts.

The functionalities of each segment and element will also be identified as well as the schedule for each phase of the project. Lastly, workload will be identified here as well as the roles that each member of the development team would perform.

2. Analysis

This part will involve the identifying of goals as well as setting the scope for the entire project. This is a far more detailed process than the planning phase as each stage of the project will be scrutinized.

A major focus on this phase is identifying the allocation of resources for each part of the project. What is the budget for each phase? What are the tools and programs needed? Is there a need to outsource work or hire entirely new people for the job (even temporarily)? These questions need to be sufficiently answered at this part of the process.

Of course, this process will also involve identifying potential issues that might pop up in the middle of the project. In turn, this allows managers to come up with solutions to prevent such from happening.

3. Design

Once planning and analysis have been completed, the team can move on to designing the product. This is a purely conceptual phase as you and your team would visualize what the project looks like by setting up its framework.

Here, the standards for each phase of the project will be established. As such, the team knows what they have to do in order to produce the desired software while also eliminating flaws.

4. Development and Implementation

This is the phase where the product is actually being built. Depending on the chosen methodology, this phase will involve multiple processes which include code writing and the implementation of programming tools and languages.

Once the software is developed, the implementation process kicks in where it goes through various studies and experimentations to see if it, at the very least, functions without crashing.

5. Testing

Once the basic structure of the software is finished, it will then go through a series of tests. Here, the goal is to identify bugs and glitches embedded into the code through the development process and then to fix them.

Like the development process, this is a rather extensive phase as the program has to be scrutinized in all of its aspects and functions to see if it is fit for mass production and distribution. The most important aspect to be tackled here is determining whether or not the product meets the criteria set in the initial phases of the project. In some cases, the overall layout of your program would be changed in order to address inherent flaws.

6. **Maintenance**

Prior to mass production, the team should then systematically scour the code for any bugs or glitches that were not identified and addressed in the previous phases.

This part also includes updates that would be introduced way after the product has been released. Patches to the code to address issues or enhance the functionality of the base product.

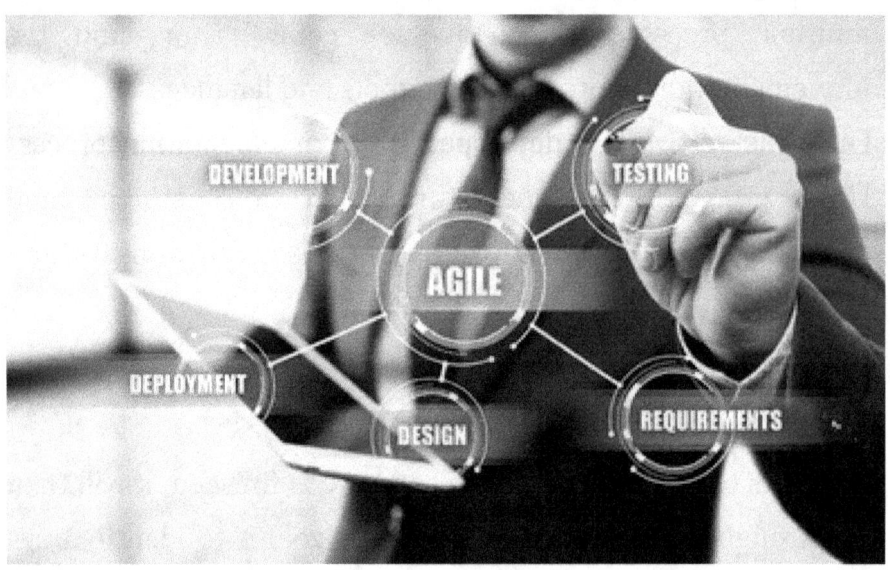

Flaws in the Conventional Method

Almost all predictive methodologies follow the sequence as laid out above. However, some methods like Waterfall would like to add a few more steps in between such as Research and Feedback.

Whatever the case, predictive methodologies tend to follow a strict sequence in order to create a product that works. However, that does not mean that it is applicable in all cases.

As a matter of fact, there are flaws inherent to these methodologies which may make them inapplicable to your project or, better yet, inferior to other more adaptive methodologies.

1. Restrictive Nature

At a glance, predictive methodologies are so rigid that you have no other option but to follow the plan as was established in the earlier phases. Of course, this means that you are not exactly responsive to changes as they occur in the middle of the project. In the end, you will produce something that might meet the criteria of the project but does not take into consideration developments that newly occurred. In short, the product might be good if made in restrictive methods but it could have been better.

2. Late Testing

These methods often put the testing process late in the project. This means that the identifying and fixing of bugs is not as comprehensive as you would like them to be. After all, if everything has a set deadline and follows set protocols, you are merely finding and fixing surface-level problems; not inherent, program-breaking ones.

This is where adaptive methods are superior as the testing phase is evenly spread out across all iterations. Simply put, you are correcting your mistakes as you are building the base product.

3. Client Feedback Not Impactful

In most restrictive methodologies, client feedback is often ignored. And if they do acknowledge client feedback, these do not have much of an impact in the development process.

For instance, a client might want to add something to the product during the Feedback and Testing portion. Depending on how big that change is, it may be ultimately ignored so as not to change the structure of the product or haphazardly applied that it ultimately ruins the quality of the software.

4. High Risk

Since these methodologies are so rigid in their application, you run the risk of not addressing major problems in the coding or add enhancing features until it is too late.

Also, there is a chance that you would have to deal with constant crunch periods as deadlines for each phase are tightly set one after another. As a result, the workload of your team increases along with the pace of work. As such, you run the risk of bottlenecking your project to the point that that end product is haphazardly completed.

The Agile Process Cycle

The process of implementing the agile method differs from one strategy to another. However, they all follow roughly the same sequence, which is:

1. **Conceptualization** – Here, the product is being visualized and designed. The framework for the project will be set up and segmented which helps in prioritizing what needs to be done. Issues like the allocation of resources and the distribution of workload will also be tackled here.

2. **Inception** – Once the project has been conceptualized, the manager must then focus on building the team (if it does not exist yet, of course). Here, the roles of each team member will be identified while the initial workloads and requirements will be designated to them.

3. **Iteration and Construction** – The most extensive part of the project, this process involves the teams going through each "sprint" or iteration as they build the product. The goal here is to present something that meets the criteria established in each iteration to upper management, shareholders, and the client.

Since the agile method is iterative by nature, it is necessary that the team goes through each of the set iterations and finish them according to the set time. At the same time, the product that they are building on must grow and develop to meet new standards and other last-minute changes per cycle.

4. **Release** – Once the base product is ready, it will undergo further Quality Assurance checks. This is where major bugs are fixed while the overall layout and user experience of the product will be revamped or enhanced.

This process will also internal and external testing, documentation of what has been fixed, and the final release of the iteration into mass production.

5. **Production** – At this phase, the developers should provide ongoing support for the software. This includes further testing and maintenance as well as the introduction of patches to the code, if need be.

This should serve as an extra "cycle" to the process where the product is enhanced even if it has already passed the mass distribution phase. Your team can even build on the product's base features by adding more while keeping the code as functional as possible.

6. **Retirement** – Eventually, that product will reach the end of its lifespan, which lasts a year or a few

after release. At this phase, the team should initiate some end of product life activities like notifying users of what is to come next and preparing them to migrate to the new product.

The sequence above presents the entire life cycle of products made using the agile model. In fact, there can be more than one agile-centric projects occurring in the same company or multiple iterations being logged in on different product lines. Better yet, the model allows a company to cater to different customers, internal or external, with their own range of needs that need to be met.

The Iteration Workflow

The agile process is dominating by cycles and iterations. Each segment of the project that is completed will actually build on the end product. In essence, with the agile method, you not only have a functional program in each iteration but also supporting features, documentation, and a code that can be used for future projects.

Iterations usually last between 2 weeks and a full month with a fixed period for completion. Since it is time-bound, the process is meant to be methodical and the scope is limited to what must be done in each iteration.

It is not uncommon for a project to have 3 to 10 iterations, depending on its size and type. Each iteration will also follow its own workflow, which can be visualized as follows:

A. **Requirements** – Here, the specifications of the iteration will be set. These must be based on the backlog for the product, the backlog for each cycle, and the feedback of customers and shareholders, if any.

B. **Development** – At this phase, the team develops or builds upon the software based on the goals set for that segment.

C. **Testing** – This phase will include Quality Assurance tests, internal and external training, and documentation of what has been improved or developed.

D. **Delivery** – Once the product is functional, it will then be integrated to make it cohesive. After this, the iteration of the product will then be sent for mass production.

E. **Feedback** – Once it is in the market, the development team will then monitor how the software is being received by the end users. Are there major flaws that need addressing? What bugs did the team miss but the customers noticed? Is there are a way to improve on the user experience? These questions can be answered at this point of the cycle.

Once the feedback phase is completed, the cycle begins anew with the team conceptualizing on what needs to be done next for the new iteration. The beauty of the method is that you can come up with a better product or an entirely new offshoot in a short period of time.

What are Product Backlogs?

The most basic definition of product backlogs is that they are a list of features that can be added to an existing software created in a previous iteration. And aside from new features, backlogs can include infrastructure changes, bug fixes, and other activities that is necessary to deliver a specific outcome in a current iteration.

In other words, a product backlog answers this question:

"What can we do to make this software Better?"

Aside from the project manager, the product backlog functions as an authoritative source of what needs to be done per iteration. This means that if a task, a feature, or a fix is not on the backlog, then the development team should not even think about investing an iota of effort in performing such a task.

However, the presence of a task on a backlog does not give the assurance that the same can be delivered exactly at the end of that iteration. It only presents the team with an option on how to deliver something that was already promised at the start of the project. It is not a mandatory task that you and your team should commit to.

For example, you and your team might be working on a videogame like, say, a massive multiplayer online role-playing game (or an MMORPG for the sake of convenience). Perhaps your product backlog would include the following:

- Increase item and weapon drops
- Expand on existing world maps
- Add new maps
- Balance skills and classes players discovered to be over-powered
- Fix game-crashing bug on Zones X3 and F10
- Improve chat-based communications
- Introduce Player vs. Player mode

Now, at a glance, you can determine for yourself which of the items must be added ASAP and what could be put off for the next few iterations. The point is that the backlog gives your team an idea as to what should be improved in the next iterations so the overall product is better.

The best part about product backlogs is that you can add on them the more the product is expanded on. The addition of new features to a software gives rise to new opportunities and problems.

However, do rein in your team a bit when it comes to finishing the backlog. There is no rule that your team should clear off that backlog in each iteration. In fact, some of the items in that backlog can be introduced as entirely new features in the next project, depending on the situation.

Burndowns

Arguably, the thing that you have to deal with the most in any project is time. To be specific, you have to make sure that the progress your team is making is sufficient enough to cover the entire time period for that iteration.

And there is this fact that people outside of the development team that want you to finish your tasks yesterday. Their intention, after all, is always this: get things done and fast.

As such, it is the job of project managers to understand that time is an element that they must proficiently control in every project that they take. The better data they have when it comes to time in relation to the work that needs to be done, the better a manager can make sure that their team sticks to the approved schedule.

This is where a burndown chart comes into play as it tells how much needs to be done and how much of time has been consumed by the team so far. A burndown chart is simply a graphical representation of how quickly your team is working through a customer's project.

How each agile tool comes up with a burndown chart varies but it often draws information from "stories", detailed descriptions of features of a program as provided by an end-user or the project manager.

So, how do You Read It?

Burndown charts are actually rather simple graphs. The amount of work remaining is always shown on a vertical axis while the time that has elapsed since the start and the projected end of an iteration is drawn horizontally.

The X-axis, the one that represents the timeline is always at a straight line since the period is set. However, the y-axis representing the work that has been done or needs to be completed might fluctuate from day to day. As such, you only need to read the graph from left to right.

But, of course, the more pressing question that you might have with the chart is "what is the ideal burndown trend?" To answer that question, you have to look for certain elements in your reading.

- **Ideal Work Remaining** – The ideal trend for this part should be a straight line connecting from the starting point to the current one. This is a telltale sign that each task has been sufficiently performed and there are no goals that have been untouched as of that iteration.

Also, at the end point, the y-axis line should cross with the x-axis. This indicates that no work is left undone.

- **Actual Work Remaining** – But, of course, it is not exactly easy to pull off a flat line when it comes to graphs. Changes in your work plan can cause some shifts in that graph, resulting in spikes of activity in every point of the chart.

So how are you going to make this work? The best actual trend in this situation is for the actual work line to never go above the ideal work line. If the actual work line does go above the ideal, it is an indication that more work is left undone than originally planned. To put it simply, your team is way behind schedule.

Benefits of Agile Methodology

Is it possible that there are clear-cut benefits from a philosophy without processes or tools? Although you could read through the manifesto in an almost Doctor Seuss like fashion, it's a very serious document. The Agile Alliance didn't craft the manifesto to put some ideas out into the world without knowing that a few results would happen nearly every time. The ideas, values, and principles, which make up Agile do set the stage for many great things. Of course, you'll want to ensure that you're using Agile properly. Don't try to implement Agile and expect all of these benefits if you're not working in software development. Compliance departments would not be happy if their team turned in a half-finished report, with working increments. In most departments, you need to deliver finalized versions of whatever you're working on, not just a functional version of the deliverable. There are times also when Agile isn't right for your approach because of limited access to customers or clients. If you're developing blind, then it's best to release your absolute best, rather than to release the functional version and then improving it.

The many benefits of Agile hit home for software developers, and they include:

- ***Predictable delivery of milestones***
- ***Opportunity to implement change***
- ***Focuses on customers or users***

- *Transparency*
- *Risk Reduction*

Predictable Delivery of Milestones

About the only predictable aspect of Agile is the increments, or in Scrum the sprints. It's not difficult to keep track of various tasks and goals within the project either which is a little bonus of this benefit. The delivery of milestones in one to four-week periods helps everyone, even those not involved in the development team, know that they're on track. It means that they can release or test the software well ahead of time. It also means that each smaller division of the software is known to work and work well before moving forward. There is no giant risk for companies to put in months of work to learn that something is causing the entire thing to fail repeatedly.

This benefit comes from face-to-face communication and the high-frequency of communication. It is possible to implement predictable milestones without Agile; however, you've probably seen first-hand the requests for extensions or blatantly missed deadlines. The reason why milestones work so well in Agile is because the methods involved break down the tasks and small goals for the team rather than for each person.

To see this in action, we'll present this example. In a Scrum meeting, the sprint goal could be something like, "map out user interactions for registration feature on paper, begin drafting design." Whereas in a normal project management meeting, that same goal might sound more like, "Jim, work on the user story and preferred interactions. Anette gets back to us with feedback from last week's milestone. Jody, test the user design when it's ready." See the disconnection here? When the managers in charge assign tasks to people rather than to the team, there's no guarantee that each person is using their skills correctly. From the above example, Jody, or Jim may have better connections to obtain feedback, but because the task was assigned to Anette, those resources will go unused.

Delivery of milestones largely rests on the structure of a self-organized team. The team identifies what work they're capable of delivering, and then figures out the best way to do that work. With all of this in mind, the milestones become much more predictable.

Opportunity to implement change

Change adaptation was the onset for the Agile Alliance formation and the drafting of the Agile Manifesto. The crisis, which plagued the software development community throughout the late 1990s, came from the inability to pivot and adapt to change in internal and external conditions. Agile allows that to happen, and this benefit is the leading reason for adopting Agile values. Through each iteration, it's possible for the entire team to recognize the need for change and alter their plan accordingly. It's also important to note there that documentation does play a key role in realizing many of the benefits of Agile methodologies. Where may teams only rely on a backlog, that one bit of documentation allows the entire team to reprioritize primary concerns when faced with change. It also allows them to implement changes to the backlog items that are set for the next sprint or iteration. That means that changes can happen in days or weeks rather than months.

Focuses on customers or users

The ability to focus on customer satisfaction is a huge payoff for many companies. When working with an Agile team, the focus on working software and improvement with every release or sprint. It can extend the product lifecycle by releasing the product earlier and keeping the product relevant for longer.

It's also possible to keep customers more engaged throughout the process. The focus on customer or user satisfaction is something that stems from traditional product development expectations.

A side-effect of this benefit is that your clients have access to the functional parts of the software earlier. So, when the customer can use and begin developing training for the software earlier, it means that the release will come in tandem with comprehensive training materials or troubleshooting. Ultimately the product is of higher quality and improved usefulness for the end-users.

Transparency

Saying that transparency is a benefit is a bit of a risk because it only works as a benefit if the members of the team exercise it properly. Essentially, it only works if the team makes it work. However, if the team members are working with an understanding of the Agile principles, then it should go without saying.

Transparency isn't just about communicating openly, though; it's about making sure that the goals are obvious and making it difficult to stray from those original goals.

Working with transparency will also require different levels of communication.

In one example successful transparency would include the communication between the Product Owner and the administrators in the company, while the Scrum Master must ensure that the Product Owner knows the progress of the project and help the team stay on task with their goals. It's a very difficult aspect of project management to manage, but it has a huge payoff. With transparency, everyone has realistic expectations, everyone is on the same page, and when it's necessary, people can ask for help. Without a doubt, transparency is a huge issue in traditional software development methods. In the waterfall method, it was common for no one to know what was going on with the development unit the development team believed that they were ready for testing. Then that often led to many people involved feeling as if they were misled or that the team failed in one way or another. Agile transparency starts with contract negotiation, customer collaborating and bringing together the team. Ideally, the concepts of transparency would be on the mind of anyone assembling the development team. Then, the team would work with the contract negotiations in an open and honest manner. They would provide what information or insight they could and be forthcoming when it was unrealistic or when the team wasn't sure of the information. Agile isn't about following a plan; it's about communicating what the product and the customer's need. Transparency is a must if you want Agile to work, and the presence of transparency makes the entire project more satisfying for everyone involved. In fact, it's so important that transparency is the one area of Agile that has tools in every methodology.

In Scrum, the task-board is the presence of transparency in that anyone could walk up to the board and see the stories, work in progress, and finished task. A Kanban board shows the backlog tasks, their status, and what is in testing or finished. Scrum meetings and sprint retrospectives also boost transparency. These meetings and face-to-face communication are built-in aspects of Agile that people often overlook. There are many methodologies, but each of them centers upon making sure that each member of the team can access what they need and communicate where they're at with their work.

Risk Reduction

Risk reduction is a huge deal for businesses in any department. Agile confronts the issues of risk head one by insisting that teams act transparently. But other aspects of Agile methodologies help reduce risk as well. For example, working in sprints such as with Kanban or Scrum, the small batches make it easy to identify and mitigate risk in real-time. Rather than working on a giant chunk of the development to learn of a gap in security or progress.

The small batches reduce the risk of outrageous costs, while the work in progress reduces the risk of wasted time. Transparency helps reduce the risk of low-quality, and the prioritization of the backlog reduced the risk of lost value for the company. The risk reduction for Agile methodology is outstanding, and it makes it imperative for software developers to understand how to implement Agile whenever possible. Using Agile can help you protect your relationship with your customers as well.

When deciding if Agile is right for you, make sure that you look at the big pictures. Are you using agile to accomplish one specific thing, or are you looking for a development method that looks out for your customers? The benefits of Agile are big-picture aspects because Agile operates on the big-picture level. It helps companies ensure that the final product is something that their customers want, and something that they need.

Disadvantages of Agile Methodology

Having an Agile approach to software development is hardly any terrible thing. However, there are a few disadvantages to many of the Agile methodologies. They can impact developers, the business people involved, and even the customers at times. Ultimately it comes down to the management of the project and the team, and how you accept various trade-offs of using different methods. For example, using Kanban when there are few members of the team who understand Kanban will likely lead to a severe loss of time to adjust for the learning curve. The disadvantages of Agile are many, but nearly all of them are avoidable or preventable, and it depends solely on the team's approach and understanding.

Major drawbacks of Agile can include:
- *Longer projects*
- *Many demands on clients and developers*
- *Lack of design effort*
- *Resource planning*
- *Done and finished are different things*
- *People get sidetracked*
- *Technical debt*

Too Long Projects

The sprints are short, but the projects are long. That extent of commitment, the many face-to-face meetings, and close cooperation makes for long projects. While a sprint surely won't run longer than one month, a two-month project can quickly become a six-month project. However, it's not just meetings, which extend the projects out. Remember that these meetings are vital for the software to meet user needs. The issue is that the close cooperation and the agreeable nature towards change make it so that the developers will often add numerous features or aspects to the software. The goal here is to ensure that the user expectations are met and that the team creates the best software that they can. However, the time and energy involved aren't always necessary. Teams need to take a step back and identify if what they're doing is necessary. Refer back to principle seven, "Working software is the primary measure of progress." Many teams lose sight that there's a focus within Agile on the goal of working software. Adding in the unnecessary can make a better product, but it can also lead to a much longer project. Working in increments, which is standard for nearly all Agile methodologies including XP, Scrum, and even Lean, can make it easy for a project to feel short when in actuality it's gone long past its completion date.

To avoid doing projects unnecessarily long, ensure that everyone on the team avoids adding aspects to the project, which aren't necessary. It's entirely possible for the development team, which stays on for updates and new rollouts to bring in advanced features and ideas in the months following the initial release. Then it frees up the rest of the team to work on other projects.

Too Demanding

Is it possible for any development project to be too demanding? Yes and no. This problem is not limited to software development, and it is specifically a problem for any team responsible for creation. It's also a problem of perception. What is too demanding for one person is a normal amount of work volume for another. The underlying root of this issue comes from one or two-person Agile teams. If there is more work than people, then it's not fair on anyone and the purposes of Agile will extend the life of the project, put more strain on the developers, and more strain on the clients as they rush towards a release. Clients then must learn the software and determine if it's of a quality that they can support.

The best way to mitigate this issue is to focus on collaboration early into the project. Scrum is one of the top methodologies in Agile because of this issue.

When working with Scrum, the team meets at the beginning of the project to design the scope of the project. Then the development team breaks that into sprints, and the full team meets at the end of every sprint. Even with very small teams, Scrum can help Product Owners and clients understand what they're getting and what their team is working with in terms of staff.

Lack of Design

This perceived problem does come with a set of disadvantages for the Product Owner and the clients. Although the foundation of Agile is trust, it is very difficult to execute. Asking your client's to trust a team they've never worked with before is hard for anyone. The Product Owner must also trust the team and for them working with the administrative side of the project can be difficult. Before Agile, with heavyweight software development, teams used the waterfall method. With that method, the administrative side was able to see the complete design before the work started. They knew exactly what they were getting, and they had an idea of what the final product would look like. However, when it comes down to Agile development that is not the case. The design is done per sprint, although the development team will often have a very rough sketch of the final product.

The solution to this issue is communication. When the administrative side of the Agile process worries, they should convey that to their development team. Make requests, ask questions, but mostly, ask if they're confident in their product. Trust is vital, but that doesn't mean that you can't communicate. As a client or Product Owner, Agile allows you to have a level of involvement. However, that doesn't mean that you can't communicate, and many Product Owners or clients involved in an Agile project don't understand that aspect. There is not a lack of design, but often a lack of communication about the design as it unfolds.

Resource Planning

Where other disadvantages are just veiled minor issues, resource planning is a major issue. Imagine if someone in the Marketing department approached their managers and said that they could develop a winning marketing strategy. But they had no idea what it would cost in terms of acquiring sales copy, ads costs, or the time to complete it. That is essentially Agile. While Agile's flexibility makes way for many opportunities, the primary issue that teams face is resources planning. Companies do not like operating this way, it makes executives uneasy, and essentially, only big businesses can get away with it.

What is worse is that the bigger the project, the more unknown the needs for resources. There is very little to do to prevent or mitigate this problem other than to go with the flow. If you're working with an Agile team, you will need to trust that they are doing their best with the resources available. However, if you are part of the Agile team, you need to ensure that you're using the available resources wisely carefully. It's on every team member to not waste resources. If you're looking for ways to sharpen your resource handling skills, consider opting for a course or two in Lean processes. There are many overlaps between Lean and Agile, and learning both could be useful for everyone on your team.

Done and Finished are Different Things

The phrase "Definition of Done" or DoD gets thrown around a lot in Agile discussions because it presents a unique problem. There is no such thing as finished. Because these teams release software in increments, customers or end-users are likely using the product well before it's actually "done." Most users don't mind or care, or sometimes even notice because they have a working software, which just keeps improving.

Often improving at a rapid rate, releases of patches, updates, and additional features make it so that these projects can last forever.

The fragmented output approach makes it extremely difficult to know when to throw in the towel. Then you have the aspects of keeping the software up to date with other software and the hardware that users rely on daily. For example, the release of the Microsoft Office 2019 suite happened on April 9th with version number 1903. However, on May 14th, barely a month later, another rollout happened with version number 1904. The system was available, functioning, and users were happy. However, developers weren't done, so they kept working. Updates on 2019 continue, and with Microsoft track, record developers will likely continue refining the coding and tweaking small things until the next Microsoft Office suite release. Essentially, a Microsoft Suite will never be finished. It's largely on the development team and Product Owner to know when to decide that a project is done. This method of working is one of the things that comes up repeatedly as a disadvantage. If you're looking for a way around this, then consider using Kanban. With Kanban, you'll have a visual representation of the many moving parts of the project and the initial aspects as well as the added features, which came up at various moments during development.

People Get Sidetracked

This problem is present in nearly everyone's workday, but for software developers, getting sidetracked can cost the company a fortune.

It can derail the team, the timeline, and on a small scale, it can derail the sprint. The problem comes from the combination of welcoming change, a core Agile outlook and having a minimalistic plan. Many blame the high-availability of getting sidetracked on a lack of processes. However, when you look at the many methodologies involved, Scrum offers a lot of structure for teams and does help them stay on track. It even gives some window of involvement for a horizontal check-and-balance with the Scrum Master and the Product Owner. If you're on a team that gets sidetracked easily, then resort back to the Agile principles and meet with everyone face-to-face. Focus in on the aspects that are sidetracking the team and identify why the team is getting off-track. Now, if you're the Product Owner or Scrum Master, then ensure that your team is working productively. Bring the focus back to the customer, not just what changing elements within the tech environment make it possible in term so features. Don't allow the surrounding environment to rule over the productivity of the team. Always come back to principle seven; the proof of progress is in working software. That is the goal, working software.

Technical Debt

Technical debt is a hot topic because although it is a

disadvantage, it is not inherently a bad thing. There are times when technical debt is necessary to prove that the team should make a change or just to move the project forward. Technical debt is comparable to monetary debt and often cannot be repaid. Essentially, it's feeding into software entropy to accomplish a more urgent goal or solve a more urgent problem. There are two types of technical debt, and both are drawbacks, but at certain times, both are necessary parts of Agile software development. The two types include deliberate and inadvertent. Deliberate technical debt is almost always taken because of release date constraints or due dates. Often the tagline is, "We'll release now and deal with the consequences later." While inadvertent technical debt, is well, inadvertent. Often it goes unnoticed until someone on the team can identify the software entropy. Often if a team has to ask which team member is taking care of something, then they already have inadvertent technical debt. For example, if someone asks, "Who's layering?" then it's clear that something was missed or not planned for during the Sprint Planning. The best way to avoid inadvertent technical debt is to use Kanban or Scrum, although neither will guarantee that there is no opportunity for inadvertent technical debt.

Although Agile does have its drawbacks, they're not anything that is more or less noteworthy than the disadvantages of other project managing methods. As a philosophy, of course, there is a lot of room for error. It all depends on the application, and in true Agile form, it depends on the people involved. It's easy for anyone to step in and say that Agile leads to waste, or that Agile projects take too long. However, there are many Agile teams, which are waste-conscious and choose to work with the Lean-Agile methodology. There are also many teams who reach their definition of done on time, or even ahead of time. Whenever you're looking at disadvantages of Agile, it's vital that you look at the human elements of that team. Then you can decide for yourself if the team was responsible for the project failure of if the project failed because Agile doesn't have strict processes.

How to Agile: The Work Ethic and Values

Agile is more than a way to organize the different tasks comprising a project.

In many ways, agile is a way of living. It is a standard you set as the project manager and inspire your team members to follow your lead.

Nothing in agile can happen without a proper work ethic and values that coordinate with the main goal of this project management approach: to deliver timely, cost-savvy quality regardless of what you are building.

We believe it is very important for you to get acquainted with the basic values behind agile project management. So, the last section of the chapter explaining agile fundamentals is precisely this: one dedicated entirely to work ethic and values you must embrace and then transfer to your team.

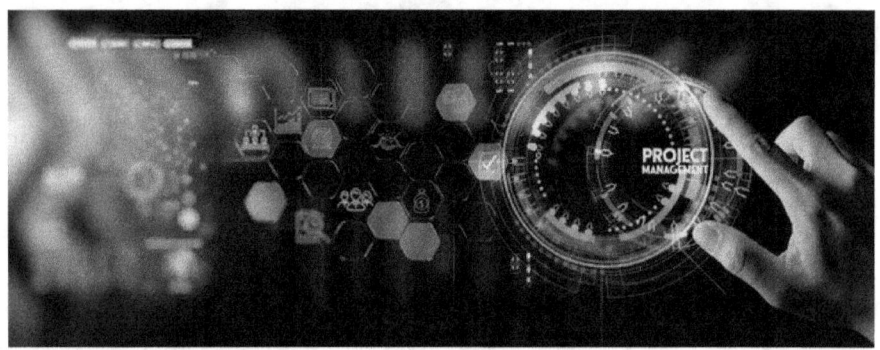

Plan Just in Time

In a nutshell, planning is what project managers do. Of course, anyone working outside of the project management spectrum will be tempted to believe all their PM does is mumble, fumble, and then fill in some spreadsheets.

Reality is quite far from that, actually. Sure, good planning is the brick and mortar of any project manager worth their salt. But beyond that, PMs have to be great psychologists, they have to understand products, they have to have business acumen, and about a hundred and one different qualities that make them and their teams function at peak efficiency.

Agile project management understands the difficult job a PM has and just how many different things they juggle every day. As such, the concept of just in time (and its brother, just enough) was born.

Just in time planning comes to serve both the PM and the team. On the one hand, it saves the PM precious time they can use doing a million other things (instead of over-planning things that are perceived to be inherently unstable in agile). As an agile project manager/Scrum Master, you have to plan just enough for the team to be able to do their job and for the customer to receive regular deliverables.

On the other hand, this concept is also useful for teams. When their PM doesn't over plan (and potentially micro-manage), team members can focus on doing what they know best, how they know best, in the least amount of time possible.

It's a win-win situation, really!

Don't Waste

In the modern world, waste is a massive issue. We waste food, we release toxic waste in the water, and we waste plastic like it's the healthiest and most environmentally-friendly thing since apples.

Agile project management understands that waste is a massive problem when it comes to developing products as well.

The concept of not wasting is tightly connected to Kanban - and, as such, it is tightly connected to Japanese factories. However, it can be applied to everything agile as well.

In project management, waste can come in a thousand shapes. It can be all about creating more products than needed (such as in manufacturing industries). It can also be about over-planning and creating more features than are actually needed (which circles back to the first rule of work ethic described in this section). And it can very much be about wasting time watching cat videos at work.

After all, who needs to create a thousand car wheels when the client has requested a specific nine hundred of them? And who needs a social media management platform that allows you to change the color of the background?

From "let's get cute" to "let's overdo it" and "I'll scroll down on Facebook for one more minute," waste is a multifaceted issue in business. One that agile promises to deter and eliminate step by step, minute by minute.

Display Leadership Skills

Agile project management is not a hierarchy of any kind. Yes, some of the titles given by some agile frameworks to PMs might sound pompous (we're looking at you, Scrum Master!). Ultimately though, they are just that: titles.

What matters more is that every single member of the team (project manager included) does their job, and inspires others to do theirs as well. Even more, it is absolutely essential that the project manager helps every single member of the team grow. It benefits all to do so: it gives the team members new perspectives and helps them feel useful, it definitely helps the business, and it helps the project manager gain a new sense of satisfaction as well.

That's where leadership comes into play. You can't inspire and promote a spirit of growth if your leadership skills are down in the dumps. Work on that - continuously, regularly, and actively. Become the leader you always wished you had (if you didn't have one).

Become the person people look up to and ask for advice. But most importantly, encourage each and every single member of the team to be a leader as well - to help others, to inspire them, to help them grow.

Leadership is like kindness - it is a transferable, nearly contagious value. Once you pass it on, it becomes an endless cycle of success on all levels.

Be Honest

What we love most about agile is that it fosters an environment of trust. It builds the kind of teams that actually like working together. Even more, in many cases, the trust between the members of agile teams expands beyond the limits of the office and grows into actual friendships.

It's wonderful to see this happen. And yes, we know just how much of a utopia it sounds to have a team that genuinely knows how to function together.

None of this would be possible without honesty, though. This value works on all levels of the agile project management approach, like glue meant to keep everything together: PMs, team members, tasks, and stakeholders alike.

From being honest with your estimations as part of the team to daily standups that are all about straightforwardness and honesty, this value expands into everything agile stands for.

And oh, how much it can benefit everyone!

Commit

In some ways, it is quite unapt to say that agile PMs manage teams.

The teams manage themselves - and that is the magic of agile project management in itself.

Aside from honesty, each and every team member must display commitment to the project, to the team, to the goals of the project, and to the values of agile in itself.

You can't be self-motivated, self-managed, and proactive if you cannot commit to values you genuinely believe in, if you cannot commit to doing what you say you're doing, if you cannot commit to self-growth.

Keep It Simple

Both a rule of work ethic and an actual core principle of agile, simplicity is where it all begins.

Back when agile was still in its infancy, smart people realized that complicating everything tends to be, well, complicated. It tends to absorb energy, time, and money. Worse even, it tends to lead to lengthy, nearly endless development processes that end in an anticlimactic way: poorly-built products.

On the other hand, simplicity overflows and reverberates into everything, and it allows everything to respond in the same way: by making things easier.

We have already talked about simplifying user stories and tasks, so we won't dwell on that. What we do want to emphasize, however, is that the same concept of simplicity should be applied in everything you do: how you speak to your team members, what you expect of them, and ultimately, how direct you are about what you genuinely want from them when things go wrong.

Prioritize

OK, this might be a bit ambiguous. All project managers prioritize, it's part of the Job Description.

In agile, however, prioritizing tasks becomes even more important because doing it poorly might mean you won't be able to deliver workable software.

Beyond the actual application of "prioritization" in how you assign tasks, the term should be included in your set of values as well.

What is more important, to place the blame, or find a solution? To get angry or find the root of the issue? To make spreadsheets in a thousand colors, or to create seamless processes that enable people to communicate and deliver?

We bet you know the agile answers to these questions by now.

Respect

None of the values mentioned until now mean anything without respect.

You can't have honesty, you can't avoid waste, and you can't project leadership skills if you don't have respect for:

- Each and every single member of your team, from the youngest to the most senior one.
- Your project and the goals it aim to achieve.
- Your customer/stakeholder.
- Your organization and its money.

If honesty is the glue of your agile project management approach, respect is the polish that makes everything shine and flow smoothly.

Obviously, these are just some of the values we believe you should incorporate into your work life as an agile PM. When you project these values out in the world, good things happen - professionally and even at a personal level. You become better, you grow, you push things further, and you help the entire world be a little better by delivering a product that will ultimately help others, one way or another.

Take these values with you at night when you go to sleep and rewind your work day. Adjust and change as needed. Nobody gets it right the first time, or even the first one hundred times. And nobody is spotless.

But as long as you have something to aim for, your agile project management skills will be on a continuous path to true success.

The Authenticity of Agile Management

The hallmarks of Agile Project Management are the driving forces behind having a team of people that are agile and can successfully put into practice this technique for management.

Fixed Length Iterations

The methodologies of Agile Management are structured around iterations (also known as milestones) that are a fixed length of time and are made up of features that must be completed.

Iterations should last anywhere from 2 to 4 weeks and the result of each iteration should be software that is ready to be tested, is currently working, and is ready for release to the client. An iteration should be a constant stream of tasks being put together to create features that are made into top-quality software. Iterations help a Scrum Team feel that every single hour and day counts toward the final project goal.

Tested Software

Agile teams never deliver software that is less than the best. Any bit of software that leaves an agile team's office should work to the best of their ability and should have been tested.

Software should never be released if it has not been tested first. In fact, it should have been tested through every phase of development. Consistent testing allows a team to know that their software works and creates confidence, focus, and engaged team members; from managers to programmers and everyone in between.

Value-Driven

Projects an Agile team takes on should always be value-driven. If it will not provide value for the client, it is not a feature that should be included in a program. Not only should the product be of value but it should also be delivered on a consistent basis.

An iteration should never occur where the quality of value deliverables is not realized by a client. Even if an adjustment has to be made, valuable deliverables should always be leaving a team on a consistent basis.

Adaptive Planning

That plan is not the end all be all, and as circumstances change, so should the plan. An outdated plan is never good especially in software development. Teams should be receiving planning updates on a consistent basis so they can delegate properly and release the correct features for each iteration.

Multi-Level Planning

Planning should never take place simply for what is happening at the current time. It should take place on two levels: what we are doing now and what we will be doing in the future. However, you should also be planning for the next iteration as you go. You should be thinking ahead for what features will be top priority next. The short term may be important but you should never plan only for what is in the short term. Your next iteration will sneak up on you quickly and you should be ready or at least have some ideas that you can bounce around. Agile Management projects are quick, and advanced planning is necessary to meet rigid deadlines.

Relative Estimation

Estimations can help keep a team on track and show which features may need to be broken down into further tasks. For example, the average feature should take 1 day to complete and can be completed in anywhere from 4 hours to 2 days. If you estimate that a feature will take longer than 2 days, it may need to be broken down into smaller more manageable tasks.

Continuous Testing

Defects, errors, and glitches can be readily avoided at every stage with testing. Many traditional waterfall management projects have a "test and fix" phase.

This is where before release, a team must go through and test their program and fix any glitches or errors. However, Agile Management allows for testing to happen at every stage of development so that errors are caught in a timely fashion instead of at the very end of a project. This speed up the testing process and can be more efficient than the "test and fix" method that is so popular in the software world.

Conclusions about Agile

A huge demand for Agile Project Management roses in the marketplace a few years back when it emerged. There was an urgency to adopt it as soon as possible for those organizations which used it as a test and were successful at achieving their projects more effectively than their competitors. As technology advances, there are changes that are meant to come into the processes and the entire organization has to go through these changes which some people may resist. Changing processes in an organization can make some people leave their job, but if they wish to accept the challenges there is nothing that a person cannot learn.

The techniques and methods that are included in this book will help you go through a project with Agile management even if you are trying it for the first time. All of the more successful companies in the market are currently following Agile Project Management, depending upon their own genres which they excel in.

If organizations do not adopt changes then it can be hard for them to survive, due to the customer demands which change every day. An organization must modify itself to meet these demands as the market has become customer driven and it is necessary that the client is satisfied with your service. Meeting a customer's needs is a critical factor for success in a competitive market. If you are not offering something which the client needs, then there will be some other similar company which will be doing so and the client will shift to them to get the services they want and need.

The next step is to figure out how to implement this methodology in your own business. We discussed many of the benefits of using the Agile method and even some of the challenges that you may face along the way. The first thing that you will need to concentrate on is looking at management and making sure they are onboard and ready to work with this system. Once you have everyone in agreement and ready to use it, it becomes infinitely easier to implement this methodology in your business as well.

On the surface Agile Project Management may seem confusing. It may seem as if it demands that you throw out all of your old management skills and adopt new ones. But once you dig deeper you learn that that is not what Agile Management is about.

By embracing Agile Management, you make a declaration of care and commitment to not only your employees but to your clients as well. By adopting Agile practices, you tell a client that the value and quality of their work matter. You show them that their input matters and that what they want ultimately trumps what a team may want to do. Employees in an agile team will see that you are taking their ideas into consideration and tasks and instructions will no longer be "passed down the grapevine." Instead, team members will be a part of small teams that delegate tasks delivered directly from the client. They will learn to trust their team members and they will form a bond that allows them to work diligently, efficiently, and quickly; providing high quality work in a fraction of the time a waterfall management system would.

Agile Management is the management style of the future. Although it does not work for every company, many that put it into practice are successful. With this guide, you know have all that you need to implement it at your business and with your team.

What is Scrum?

We can say that the accepted attitude about system development is that these processes are highly understood. The philosophy behind this is that every approach can and should be planned. Every act can be calculated, structured and efficiently implemented. Still, the practice says otherwise. On the other hand, the basic belief behind Scrum is that the system is unpredictable and that development is complicated. That is why Scrum is generally based on their definition of the system on overall progression rather than a predictable process. According to Scrum, the development of the system is a set of activities that are loose. The development combines workable techniques that we know of and tools that can be used by development teams. Furthermore, these tools are devised by teams to build the desired systems. Scrum suggests that loose activities disable precise management. That is why teams need to be ready to take some amount of risk. This being said, Scrum represents a kind of enhancement for development cycles that are oriented on objects.

History of Scrum

Practices that are considered to be the best of Scrum have evolved over the decades. They have also changed. In early papers, Scrum was simplified and some companies like Patient Keeper didn't have the closing phase of the project at the end of the 20th century. At first, Scrum had to pass many tests in order to achieve acceptance. These tests along with training and other documentation were all a part of the so-called Sprint which is one of the sections in Scrum. Afterward, the Scrum framework was produced and sold to many companies.

At that moment, Scrum's demo became an advanced framework with a large network of users. Some say that it became a live system that implemented advanced Sprint variations. Advanced Scrum principles and practices have been put into one course.

This course is called the Certified Scrum Master and it is one of the core training tools. It was developed by the first team in Easel Corporation that ever used this framework. Certified Scrum Master became official in 1993. It consists of several categories such as monthly iterations, sprints, meetings with three questions daily, etc. This first Scrum Master not only had additional backlogs and impediments, but it also implemented engineering principles of eXtreme Programming a few years before well-known Kent Becks' codified XP.

The first official paper on Scrum was written in 1995 by Jeff Sutherland. He was one of the lecturers at OOPSLA conferences. Sutherland was organizing a series of workshops about Business Object design, and he was the main lecturer on Ken Schwaber's implementations of those designs between 1995 and 2000.

The first paper about Scrum was published for the OOPSLA'95 annual conference. Jeff Sutherland had the opportunity to observe how the first Scrum works. Later, he set the basic principles for its operations.

Even now, Sutherlands' writing remains one of the most important and most popular papers from OOPSLA workshops. The original paper about Scrum can be found on Jeff Sutherlands' website: http://jeffsutherland.com/Scrum.

The complex theory of Scrum is introduced together with the difference between the empirical process and prediction. This distinction is important because business enterprises are complex. They represent adaptive systems, and so are the software programs that run them. Some experts compare business enterprises to biological systems. Complexity and speed of change and adaptations are similar. It's like an evolution of a live system. However, artificial existence is more flexible and faster to adapt. Its flexibility increases proportionally with chaos. We need empirical processes to prevent and control chaotic and unwanted behavior. Sutherland believes that this is the essence of Scrum. The leader of this first empirical process in real Scrum practice was Mike Beedle. He set elaboration and organization patterns along with the Jeff Sutherland – the author of the paper, and Ken Schwaber

Additional information about Scrum's core principles was described in the later papers of Mike Beedle and Ken Schwaber. These papers are called "Agile Development with Scrum.' Jeff Sutherland's contributions were added in a volume called "Agile Can Scale: Inventing and Reinventing Scrum in Five Companies" In the last 15 years, Ken Schwaber worked as a Scrum consultant in several companies, while Sutherland was conducting research in at least five.

The biggest business enterprises he used for his Scrum research are IDX, Easel, Patient Keeper, VMARK and Individual. Schwaber and Sutherland continued testing and evolving Scrum together over the years. One of the things that they were interested in the most was the hyper-production of teams. This happened with the first Scrum too. They believed that hyper-productivity is connected to the structure of deployment in Scrum teams. It also depends on the maturity of the stages that are implemented in the team structure.

Advantage and Benefits

If Scrum is applied correctly using the appropriate processes and rules, it can bring a lot of benefits to a project and result in delivering a high-quality product in an acceptable time frame. Scrum's Key Benefits

- Better team morale.

- Better client relations.

- Higher quality systems and products.

- Greater rate of productivity means customers see results quicker.

- Costs are kept down

- Faster product adaptability to change requirements.

- Better scope for product or system upgrades and continuous improvements.

- Less risk of project failure than conventional frameworks.

Framework and Principles

1. Focuses on the Needs of the Customer

Scrum focuses on the needs of the business, the users, and customers. The products or systems are built around information that is gathered from the stakeholders. Involving customers from the beginning of a project makes them feel involved and gives them a reason to be invested in it.

For instance, if a person is told — "This is what you are getting" — they feel like something is being shoved at them.

The system or software will not get the same response as it would if they were included from the start and before the system was introduced — "We are looking to introduce a system for… or how can we improve upon the current system?"

Giving the audience knowledge of the system is aimed at the chance to incorporate their ideas, needs, and wants and shows them that their opinion matters. People who are going to use the product feel more invested in it and therefore will be more open and accommodating to it when it is rolled-out for operation.

This also leads to more satisfied customers as they get to watch the product unfold as they are asked to test and give feedback on each iteration as it is finished.

2. Dedicated Product Owner

The Scrum Product Owner is constantly involved with both the stakeholders and the Scrum team. Proactively making sure there are no last-minute changes to the wish list, and if there are, making sure that they reach the Product Backlog in time for the Daily Scrum.

3. Roles and Responsibilities

The teams are smaller and are encouraged to take ownership of and responsibility for their part of the development. They have to self-manage and make sure that their day is planned accordingly in order to be able to report on their progress at each Daily Scrum. They also get to choose which part of the project or 'user stories' they work on.

As each hour of the day is well managed and 'timeboxed', it ensures that the project stays on track and there is no team member burn out due to having to work extra hours to catch up. If a Sprint is not on track, the daily workload is readjusted, and if a member of the team is struggling, other team members will pitch in to ensure they complete their task.

They have a dedicated Scrum Master who is the project manager that ensures all his project teams' needs are being met.

He is responsible for making sure their work is on track, sorting out any problems, and providing the Scrum team with the necessary tools and information they need to succeed in their assigned tasks.

4. Daily Scrum

The Daily Scrum is a 15-minute daily meeting where the team gets to update the Scrum Master, Product Owner, and at times Stakeholders on the previous days' progress. This is where they get to report on everything that went right and everything that went wrong, their concerns, problems, and so on.

It is the Scrum Master's duty to ensure all these issues are addressed efficiently and appropriately in order to ensure the project stays on track and the team is happy.

5. Sprints

The Product Owner gathers all the customer requirements and produces a Backlog which is prioritized and broken down into what are called Sprints. Sprints are pieces of the project made up of features that work together to form a section of the system.

For instance, in an ERP system, it could be the customer database section whereby the company would like to see a gathering of all their customer's credentials, payment details, and to keep a history of the payments. The development team sees this as an important part of the software as it is the information the company needs in order to get paid. Therefore, this may be the first module of work they start on.

The team will look at all the work required to create this module, the features, how it integrates with other parts of the software, etc. From there, they may even break the module down into smaller sprints if the work required will take longer than 30 days to complete.

Sprints are timeboxed which means they have a set number of days in which they need to be completed. This distributed method means that a project can easily be measured to ensure it stays on track if it has deviated, it is easier to fix per Sprint than it is to fix as a whole.

This also cuts down on the chances of developers having to put in long after hours to ensure they are caught up and any or all changes have been made.

Scrum Framework falls under the Agile project management methods umbrella. It can function effectively on its own or can be combined with other Agile frameworks such as XP, Lean, Kanban, and so on to be adapted for various business needs.

Understand Scrum

So, what exactly is Scrum good for? What can it be used for, and why even use it? What is the purpose, and is it even worth using it?

There are several reasons to use Scrum and implementing it into your business is definitely a smart idea. Think about the competitiveness factor. The market changes faster and faster every day, and only those who are flexible and contemporary can keep up with it. Using Scrum, a person can stay competitive and create a unique advantage for themselves. And the best part is that it's not some unproven fad! It's a solid and successful Agile Framework that has been proven again and again across various projects and teams. College universities use it to deliver projects to clients. Militaries rely on Scrum to prepare their ships for deployment. Even in the automotive world, a car is being built by using Scrum! And not just any car; one that is fast, affordable, efficient, safe, and should sell for less than $20,000!

Scrum also allows the development of features and gives the customer the ability to stay involved. The customer is able to receive working versions throughout the process, see the progress that is being made, and even add new ideas if necessary.

All of that is important because waiting until the end of the project to show the customer could potentially be a huge mistake. They might hate the final version, and request a complete do-over, which is a waste of time and money. Think about it like this — if you're getting your hair cut, do you watch the process of your stylist, or do you close your eyes until it's all over? Unless you want to be surprised and don't really care about the end result, you naturally keep an eye on what the stylist is doing. If they start cutting your hair too short or dying it a funky color, you speak up and ask them to stop and/or rework it. You don't want to end up with terrible hair that you hate! Using Scrum Agile Framework is all about transparency; a clear vision for all involved. It also allows for all of the stakeholders to be informed, which specifically helps discover weaknesses and makes for more effective teamwork. Scrum allows everyone in the loop during a project, which means there are fewer mistakes to be made.

Quality also plays a big part in Scrum. Testing is something that happens at every Sprint, which means it happens often; usually daily! Doing this secures the quality of every product from the beginning on and allows for problems to be recognized and fixed on time and promptly.

It also helps with costs, which is something every business likes to hear. Each project usually has a fixed period, which means there's a definitive cost involved and it won't get any higher. And while the effort and little details might change thought out the process, the cost will always remain the same since the period of a project is definite.

Something the customer would really love about Scrum is that changes are always welcome! They can be shown to the Product Owner at any time, who then follows through with them in the next Sprint meeting. The Product Owner informs the Scrum Team, who then implements the changes as soon as the next day. Doing this helps the customer get the product they desire, and a happy customer is always good for the company.

Implementing scrum

Scrum can also help with efficient communication skills and creativity. It involves everyone within the project and requires strong communication, collaboration, respect, and understanding. A successful project is built off of what the customer requires and what the team develops, and Scrum can help enforce both of those.

Those in the Scrum Team especially benefit from acquiring communication skills.

They develop these skills over stages, and by the end of the process are able to communicate effectively. This can be used in both the professional and personal life.

The development of complex systems and extensively long projects can be difficult and very frustrating. Luckily, Scrum can help with the exact planning needed for these types of projects, which allows for the integration of new functionalities and a new way of thinking. Using Scrum will help things to run smoothly and won't allow for a terrible realization at the end of the project that something has gone wrong. It basically streamlines the process and makes it better for everyone involved.

There are also several instances when Scrum can help a business in very specific ways. After all, maybe your business is doing just fine, and you think it doesn't need a change. However, consider this — organizations that implement Scrum experience changes in their companies culture. They become more team oriented, more value oriented, and place more value on the customers themselves. Would you rather work for a company that cares only about profits, or work for one that cares more for its people? Businesses using Scrum teams become high performance and show results that are much higher than normal teams.

What about the other side of things? Instead of a business that's doing just fine, let's say there's an organization that could be in deep trouble, but they're willing to adopt the Scrum system. Adopting a new system shakes the company up, and allows for a new culture, process, and team environment, which then helps the business actually get out of trouble. The business completely changes around, and people actually want to start working there. The most important thing about this scenario is that the business is willing to admit they actually need the help! Sometimes organizations don't like to admit there are things wrong, which leads to bad things for the business. Using Scrum, they can get back on their feet, and back to where they would like to be.

Another way Scrum can help a business is when there is a small business that has a high-performance state but is struggling to maintain said high performance when they're also trying to grow all at the same time. They can easily implement Scrum in their organization, and it will help immensely in balancing things out. Scrum can help steam line their production so they're not so overwhelmed with everything all at once. The organization helps immensely and makes it seem like things are easier to accomplish.

Sprinting Cycle

Putting together a group of people to accomplish something as sophisticated as the Scrum process can be a difficult task. It is necessary to ensure that everyone is working towards a common goal, and requires a specific process called the Group Development Process. This process is a 5-step program that ensures the Scrum team is as successful as possible. The first 4 stages (Forming, Storming, Norming, and Performing) were developed by Bruce Tuckman in 1965. Tuckman said that these stages are necessary for the Scrum Team to grow and that using this process helps them to face challenges, tackle problems, plan work, find solutions, and deliver the best results possible. Tuckman later added in the final 5th stage (Adjourning) in the year 1977. It's interesting to note that, specifically in Agile software development, teams will exhibit a behavior called "swarming". This is a performance shown as the team comes together, collaborates, and focuses on solving a singular problem. This behavior is adapted from when a swarm of insects is focused on a common event, such as a swarm of wasps attacking a person because said person decided it would be wise to hit the wasp's nest with a baseball bat.

Using the Group Development Process method leads to maturity and a highly efficient Scrum Team. It's necessary to remember that sometimes a process like this can take time. Most companies are more concerned with immediate results and jumping into tasks right away, without thinking about how important team building is. Using a method like this will lead to positive impacts and the Scrum Team's success.

1. **Forming Stage** - It is very important to get the Scrum Team off to a successful start. This stage is used for the team members to get to know one another and find out different things they have in common. They use it to connect in a way that will allow them to work together seamlessly. If this step is skipped, the team might find it difficult to move through the later steps of the process. One way for the team to connect with each other is by doing fun ice breakers. Team members can share personal information; movies they like, their favorite music, or their favorite foods. There might be another team member who likes the same things, which will help them to connect to each other. Also, during this stage, the team members are relying on a group leader for guidance and direction. The members are looking for acceptance from the group and want to feel like it's a "safe space". They're looking to keep

things simple and wanting to avoid controversy, which means typical serious topics and feelings are avoided. Orientation also plays a big part in this stage. Team members try to become more oriented to not just each other, but the tasks as well. Usually, discussions are revolved around figuring out the scope of each task, how to approach it, and similar concerns. In order for the team members to grow from this task to the next, they must step out of their comfort box, and risk the possibility of conflict.

2. **Storming Stage** - Storming is an apt name for this stage. This one is the most likely to have arising conflicts and competition. The "fear of failure" or "fear of exposure" might come into play and increase the desire for structural clarification and commitment. Members will question who is going to be in charge, who is responsible for what, what the rules are, the reward system, and what the criteria for evaluations are. There might even be behavioral changes in attitudes based on issues of competition. Team members might ally with other team members, especially ones that they are already familiar with. It is even possible that cliques might form, which some of the team members would be against. Some members might feel more comfortable speaking up, while others would feel it

was better to remain silent. It could end up with the Scrum Team feeling splintered and not as if they are a team. It's important to figure out different working styles and other obstacles that are standing in the way of the group completing their goal. The best way to solve conflicts is through a collaborative and problem-solving based approach. It's the only way for team members to unify and work together. The only reason for skipping a step like this is if the Scrum Team is already established and has been working together for a while. It's possible they already know each other's working style and are already banded together as a team. If this step is needed, then the only way for the Scrum team to move to the next one is by adopting a problem-solving mentality. And the most important trait for each member to have is the ability to listen.

3. **Norming Stage** - This stage is all about cohesion within the group. It's important for each member to acknowledge each other's contributions, community building, and attempt to solve the group issues. Team members must be willing to change their previous ideas and opinions when presented with facts from other team members. This should go along with asking questions of each other. The team acknowledges that leadership is shared, and there is

no need for any cliques. Having all the members get to know each other and identify with each other is important in strengthening trust. which then contributes to the development of the group as a unit. It's also important to have established rules for how the team operates in each meeting. The team members need to discuss logistics, such as location of the meeting, how long the meeting will take, and what time it starts. They need to talk about how the meeting will flow, and what to do if conflicts happen. Inclusion plays an important role within the Scrum Team. Every group member needs to feel like they belong, so that they actually participate in all the activities. The main goal is to find a set of rules that everyone can agree to, and then actually follow. Doing this will help the team to operate as the best they can be. The group will feel a sense of camaraderie and almost a feeling of relief when the interpersonal conflicts are resolved. In this specific stage, creativity is high; there's a sense of openness and sharing of information, both on a personal and task level. Everyone feels good about being part of a group that gets things done. The only drawback at this stage is that the members resist change of any kind, and the ones that fear the inevitable future breakup of the group. They may decide the only way to avoid said breakup is by resist forming it in the first place.

4. **Performing Stage** - This stage is not reached by all groups. If they have reached it, the group has formed a tight knit team that trusts each other and is ready to perform tasks efficiently and effectively. Team members are able to work independently, in subgroups, or as the group as a whole with equal productiveness. Everyone's roles are able to change and adjust depending on the needs of the group and individuals. This is the stage where the group is the most productive. Each individual member has become self-assuring and feel as if it's unnecessary to seek group approval. Team members are both task-oriented and people-oriented. There is a certain feel of unity and. Group morale is high, group loyalty is strong, and everyone knows who they are as a group. Products that the Scrum Team works on can change over time, so there is a strong feel of support for experimentation in solving issues. The team is capable of working together well enough to adapt and accept that change. Everyone knows that the overall goal is productivity reached through problem-solving and hard work. Performance is also best if the team follows the rules set in the Norming Stage because it's used to solve personal conflicts. If

such a situation occurs, the team would need to review the rules and enforce what the team originally decided on.

5. **Adjourning Stage** - This stage wasn't originally a part of the process and was added in later years. But just because it was added at a later time, doesn't mean it is any less important! At this point in time, the team has most likely fulfilled the project vision. While the technical sides of things are done, the team needs to check in with things on a more personal level. They need to reflect on how they worked together as a team and see if there are any improvements that could be made. The team also recognizes participation and achievements. They can also use this as an opportunity to say personal goodbyes. The team worked closely with one another on an intense project. It's important to wrap things up on a personal level, otherwise there could be a feeling of incompleteness. And what if the team gets back together in any future projects? It's important that they discuss the process and methodologies that succeeded and the ones that failed. The team can go through and decided if there was anything that could be salvaged with a little bit of change. Information gathered during this time might even be used for

performance evaluations. So, it's important that the team takes this stage seriously.

Sometimes it can be difficult to follow the stages. There could be a person that is especially stubborn, or maybe some people just don't particularly work well with others. In order for the group to reach its best potential, they must be flexible enough to accept when they need help. There are a few different steps that a group can take to ensure they develop properly through the different stages:

1. The group needs to make sure they change up the responsibility of group facilitator. Each person should have a chance to be "in charge" and doing so creates a feeling of inclusion and equality.

2. The purpose and mission of the group needs to be clear to all members involved. And the mission should be looked over often, just in case anything has changed or any member has forgotten what it originally was supposed to be. It's entirely possible the mission changes, depending on what the customer's feedback is after a Sprint. Keeping the mission statement updated will help everyone to stay on task.

3. Rules are very important and need to be established and monitored throughout the entire process.

Having the rules helps everyone know where things stand and what to do if a rule is broken or in question.

4. The group should remember that conflict can be a positive thing and is completely normal. The conflict could even be necessary for the group's development. One member might disagree with another on how to complete a task. Because of the two members disagreeing, they might actually invent a third way to complete said task that is much more efficient.

5. The group should remember to listen to each other. Having one person to speak over everyone isn't productive and can cause the group to be upset or resent each other. If everyone remembers to listen, then everyone feels as if they are heard by the other members. People tend to respond better and are more accepting of other's if they feel as if they've had the chance to be heard.

6. Each session should end with constructive criticism instead of harsh "advice". It's important to lift each other up and be helpful towards each other, instead of putting each other down. And it's also important to remember that the constructive criticism should be about the group process and nothing personal.

7. Everyone should contribute and do the work. Having one person do all the work makes said person feel resentful toward the whole group. And if only one person is doing the work, then it's entirely possible that the product won't be finished on time and any deadlines will be behind schedule. The same thing goes for one person sitting out while the rest of the group does all the work. That one person will get credit for work they haven't done, and it's not fair to the rest of the team.

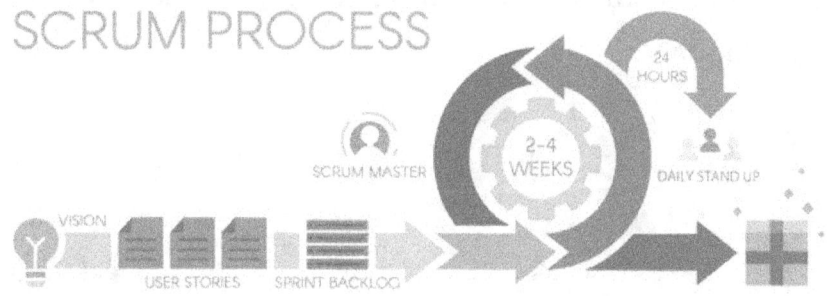

The Scrum Roles

A Scrum has three main roles or responsibilities, namely a product owner, a Scrum master, and the development team members. These roles can often get confused with actual job titles, but these are not the same thing.

Scrum Roles vs. Job Titles

The three Scrum roles involve and outline the key responsibilities within the Scrum team. They are not job titles and do not replace existing job titles. A Scrum master role, for example, can be performed by someone with any appropriate job title. The essence of the Scrum methodology is to operate with an iterative approach that involves empiricism, continuous feedback loops and improvement. What is key for the above Scrum roles is that they are able to fulfill the objectives of Scrum by performing what their role requires. Taking on these roles does not affect their job title or other responsibilities within an organization.

Tools and Methodologies

The reason why too detailed methodology approaches haven't been successful in development process is that they are not defined completely. If you act like these processes are predictable, you won't be prepared for unpredictable situations and results.

Several detailed methodologies are based on current methods of development. In the next paragraphs, we will discuss the Waterfall methodology, which is one of the first detailed and defined methodologies for system development. We will also talk about Spiral and Iterative methodologies. Finally, we will discuss more details about the functioning and phases of Scrum.

Waterfall and Spiral Methodology

The waterfall approach works on the premise that undefined processes exist and they need to be controlled. Still, this methodology has a linear nature and that is why it has some shortcomings. For example, Waterfall doesn't offer any solution for unexpected outputs. The spiral methodology created by Barry Boehm addressed this issue later. Contrarily, in each of Waterfall phases, there is an end caused by the risk of assessment or activities that suggest making prototypes.

The Spiral methodology is based on the "layers" and it predicts more aspects and variables in system development processes. For example, unlike Waterfall, Spiral methodology allows the user to try the prototype. It lets you estimate if the project is on the right path. This way you can see, firsthand, if the project needs to be returned to some of the prior phases. You can also determine if the project is successful or unsuccessful and end it. Even though Spiral principles give more insight into the development than the Waterfall method, the phases of projects still have linear construction. This means that if your requirement is designed, you have to do only design in that phase. If it is coding, you only have to do coding, and so forth. Every process is strictly defined and explained in detail without any room for flexibility.

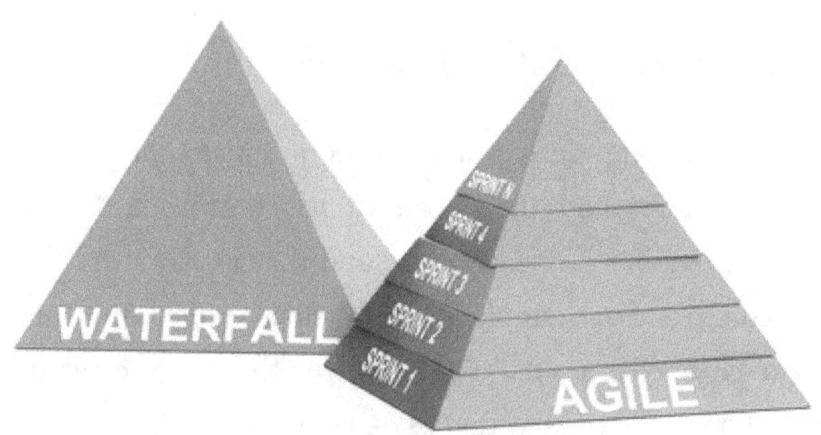

Iterative Methodology

The Iterative methodology is an improvement on the first two. Iterations have phases that are standard for Waterfall phases; still, iterations address only one set of functionalities. Deliverables of the project are divided into subsystems and ordered by priority. The interface is clear and defined for subsystems individually.

This methodology is useful to test the subsystem's technology and its feasibility. The advantage is that this can be done in some of the initial phases. As the project advances, iterations can be used to get additional resources, and it can speed up the delivery of the project. Iterative methodology means that you will have good control over your costs and improves the system of delivery and flexibility. Yet, there are some of the processes in the Iterative approach that retained its linear definition.

Scrum Methodology

The system development process is not simple. It has many unpredictable variables; therefore, its complexity requires flexible solutions.

The evolution of technology showed that to have a successful project one has to work with full flexibility.

This also means that you need to be prepared to be completely exposed to environmental changes.

In this era, it is useless to try to make your environment less complex and to try to avoid chaos. Working teams have to embrace an approach that helps them adapt to excessive changes and predict efficient solutions that are not always too precise.

It is already clear that every system development happens in circumstances that can change rapidly. This also means that even producing systems based on existent technologies under chaotic and diverse variables has to be flexible.

The team needs to be ready to work under the pressure of chaotic conditions and maintain order. Although this requires flexibility and many unknown areas, it also increases competitiveness and brings more efficient production. The complexity theory introduced by Langton was based on a modeled effect that was used in computer simulations. This simulation was later recognized as one of the fundamental discoveries that explained the principles of complexity in system developing processes. One of the most important factors in estimating the probability of success is the methodology that is used on the project. It was proven that the methodologies that promote flexible approaches have a higher degree of success and better responsiveness on changes in variables.

Waterfall, Spiral and Iterative methodology were used for software development in companies such as Easel, ADM and VMARK, and it reflected their experiences.

These companies were ready to take a risk and have built the most successful software of the moment. In this context, they increased the impact of their products and changed the meaning of deliverables by including environmental factors.

Scrum methodology defines all these processes as undefined completely. The purpose of the Scrum is to use mechanisms that will effectively improve flexibility and control. The main distinction between fully defined approaches such as Waterfall or Spiral and Scrum is that Scrum has a hypothesis that Sprint is unpredictable in terms of analysis or design. That is why Scrum has a special focus on risk control and management of unpredictable variables. The overall goal of Scrum is to enhance responsiveness and increases the results during the system development process.

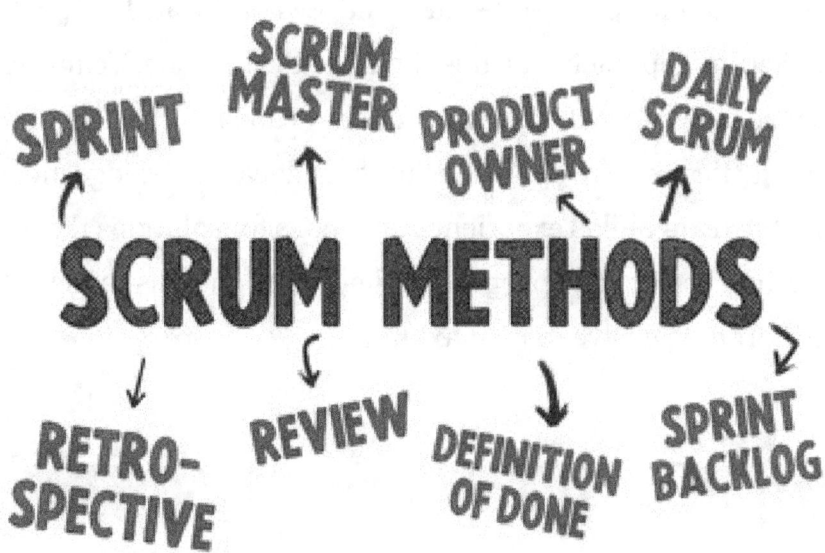

Some of the main characteristics of the Scrum methodology are:

• The only fully defined processes are the first phase called planning, and the last phase called the closure. All of the processes during these two phases need to have clear inputs and outputs. Scrum uses some of the iterations in the planning part which gives it a linear flow.

• The sprint category that we mentioned multiple times is actually an empirical phase. This is where Scrum's undefined premises are compared with the black box. These uncontrollable processes need to have external mechanisms of control. Scrum predicts this with the sections such as risk management for iterations individually during the Sprint. That is how a team can achieve maximum flexibility and reduce chaos.

• Sprint can have multiple parts and it isn't linear. It is part of the Scrum approach which is the most flexible one. Teams can use the knowledge that is explicit if they can, but if that's not the case, tactical knowledge can be used. Tactical knowledge means that the team builds experience and looks for solutions through tests and errors. The purpose of the Sprint phase is to help the final product evolve to its maximum.

- In Scrum, environmental variables can influence the project until the Closure. It also enables the change of deliverables during the whole first phase and Sprint. Variables can change during these two sections and they include time frame, resources, environmental changes and quality of the product.
- Last but not least; Scrum is different because it allows the teams to determine the deliverables following the environmental requirements.

One of the Scrum Phase divisions

Phases of the scrum can be divided into groups. The first group is the Pregame. It consists of planning that needs to provide a definition of a planned release. This definition has to be based on backlog knowledge and to have an estimated cost and schedule. If the team wants to develop a completely new system, they need to provide a concept and analysis of their product in this phase. Architecture is also in this group. It means that the team needs to provide the concept for a design for their backlog items. They also need to explain how they will implement this design.

The second group is the Game. This group includes Sprints for development. The team needs to determine the functionality of their new release.

They need to include environmental variables and to predict flexible ways to increase their responsiveness in terms of quality of their product, requirements of their product, time frame for their deliverables. They need to have a flexible plan for costs and funding during the system development phase and to include competition and its impact on the productivity of the team. There have to be multiple Sprints during this phase to evolve the system's deliverables.

The third group is called Postgame. In this phase, teams that implement Scrum approach enter the Closure. This means that the teams finished all previous stages successfully and that they are ready to prepare for the final release of their product. Once the management team sees that the variables have been successfully resolved they will declare the project as closed. Additional tasks for the Closure are preparation for integrating the product and necessary adjustments for general release. Scrum includes final tests before releasing the product. It also includes all necessary paperwork like financial reports, product licenses, patent rights, etc. This phase also covers user manuals, final system checks, documentation for training, and so forth. One of the significant aspects of Post-Game is that the team needs to prepare a marketing campaign that will launch their final product.

Avoiding chaos due to many unpredictable factors is one of the strongest features of Scrum methodology. Mature and well-structured management is necessary to empower this kind of approach. Scrum is used to provide external control for undefined inputs and outputs. The reason why Scrum is so popular is that it enables teams to have a good insight into their tasks and helps them to increase their productivity and quality of the whole system development process. In the end, successful Scrum implementation means that your product is ready to be on the market.

Planning Your Projects

The Scrum arranging process sets partners' desires. These partners incorporate the individuals who support the undertaking, the individuals who expect to utilize the usefulness made by the task, and the individuals who will be in any case influenced by the venture. The arrangement is a method for synchronizing partners' desires with the Team's desires.

On account of partners who will be clients of venture usefulness, the arrangement causes them sort out their work with the goal that they can be prepared to exploit the usefulness as it is actualized.

On account of partners who are financing the undertaking, the arrangement subtleties their desire for what subsidizing is required and when the advantages of the venture ought to be figured it out. The arrangement is additionally the premise of venture revealing. Toward the finish of the Sprint, the partners go to the Sprint survey gatherings and look at the undertaking's real advancement against its arranged advancement.

Changes in course and updates to the arrangement made in Sprint arranging gatherings are disclosed to the partners. For the individuals who can't go to the Sprint survey meeting, the venture reports contrast genuine outcomes with the arrangement—both the first arrangement and the arrangement as it has been adjusted since the task's beginning.

The Scrum arranging process includes settling three inquiries:

What can those financing the task hope to have changed when the undertaking is done? What progress will have been made before the finish of each Sprint?

For what reason should those being approached to support the venture accept that the undertaking is a significant speculation, and for what reason would it be advisable for them to accept that those proposing the task can convey those anticipated advantages?

Scrum ventures require less arranging than regular Gantt diagram-based undertakings in light of the fact that those attempting to convey the normal advantages give perceivability into their advancement toward the finish of each Sprint. Since Scrum ventures are too perplexing to possibly be depicted in incredible detail at their origin, we rather screen them and guide them with the goal that they will convey the most ideal outcomes.

The base arrangement important to begin a Scrum venture comprises of a dream and a Product Backlog. The vision depicts why the venture is being attempted and what the ideal end state is. For a framework utilized inside an association, the vision may portray how the business activity will be diverse when the framework is introduced.

For software that is being produced for outer deal, the vision may depict the software's major new highlights and capacities, how they will profit clients, and what the foreseen sway on the commercial center will be.

The Product Backlog characterizes the useful and nonfunctional necessities that the framework should meet to convey the vision, organized and evaluated.

Overseeing Cash at MegaBank:

MegaBank is one of the biggest money related establishments on the planet. We'll consider MegaBank's utilization of Scrum here and in ensuing parts. Two years after Scrum was first presented at MegaBank, 20 percent of all MegaBank software extends now use Scrum. One group had heard what a triumph Scrum had been in different pieces of MegaBank and needed to give it a shot a pilot venture that included moving one of MegaBank's applications from centralized computer frameworks to the Web. The application being referred to, known as the "money application," was utilized for recording and revealing money moves. Subsidizing had been endorsed, the group had been framed, and the arrangement had been composed. The group was given a notice that expressed that the Web-based variant of the money application would be finished and prepared for usage in five months. No more subtleties were essential in light of the fact that the new application would be a coordinated reproduction of its centralized server forerunner; subsequently, no new usefulness had been approved for this undertaking.

Runs normally start with a one-day Sprint arranging meeting. For ventures like this one, be that as it may, I add an extra day to build a Product Backlog for the task too to educate the new ScrumMaster, Product Owner, and Team how Scrum works. I see these two-day meetings as especially viable for showing Scrum—in huge part in light of the fact that the subject of the exercise is characteristically handy, concerning genuine work that must be done in the extremely close to term.

The Two-Day Sprint Planning Meeting:

The group comprised of five designers. The Product Owner, Julie, was at this gathering, as were Tom, the ScrumMaster, and Ed, the frameworks development administrator. At that point I told everybody that we were practically prepared to begin the customary Sprint arranging meeting; the main thing we were missing was the Product Backlog. Julie required a Product Backlog list so she could recognize the most noteworthy need excess.

The group expected to see the Product Backlog list so it could focus on changing it into an addition of item usefulness. I guaranteed everybody that we'd have the Product Backlog done before the day's over, yet everybody moaned in any case.

Colleagues specifically considered this to be as superfluous overhead. They inquired as to why we couldn't simply make sense of what to accomplish for the following Sprint. All things considered, that was what being agile was about, they contemplated. I advised the group that we expected to understand the undertaking inside the setting of Scrum; we would utilize the Product Backlog to set out a benchmark of desires against which the board at MegaBank could plot the venture's advancement.

We taped flip-outline paper to the divider and began posting the entirety of the capacities in the current centralized server framework, which were all to be duplicated on the Web. We likewise considered some nonfunctional necessities, for example, building up a quality affirmation (QA) and creation condition for the framework. Inside two hours, we had recorded essentially the entirety of the Product Backlog, and positively the most significant components.

Assessing the Product Backlog:

The subsequent stage was to assess how a lot of work would be associated with satisfying the necessities in the Product Backlog. The colleagues moaned once more, expecting that this errand would take for eternity.

They questioned that they could think of precise appraisals—especially assesses that were sufficiently exact to accurately set desires and guide their determination of Product Backlog at each future Sprint.

Before we continued with evaluating, we talked about the idea of intricacy and its effect on software development. To assess every necessity decisively, we would need to know the specific structure and communication of the prerequisite, the innovation used to manufacture the necessity, and the aptitudes and state of mind of the individuals accomplishing the work. We might invest more energy attempting to characterize these characteristics and their collaborations than we would spend really changing the necessity into usefulness. More regrettable yet, regardless of whether we did as such, the nature of complex issues would eventually render our endeavors useless. The idea of complex issues is with the end goal that little varieties in any part of the issue can cause amazingly huge and eccentric varieties in how the issue shows itself. So regardless of how much time we spent improving the exactness of our assessments, the evaluations would at present be fiercely incorrect.

Monitoring

The term scalability refers to the process of taking a defined process or framework and expanding upon the process so as to create a larger impact. Some processes or practices are easier to scale than others, and often the question is raised as to whether or not Scrum is scalable, and if so, how is this best done. Scaling Scrum, for example, could involve taking mechanisms from one Scrum team and implementing them in multiple teams for larger projects.

So, the question is, 'Is Scrum scalable?' Initially, Scrum was thought only to be applicable to teams who work on smaller projects, and that is was not suitable for application across multiple teams for larger projects. However, this was only based on the fact that Scrum had not yet been used on larger scale projects, and since its inception Scrum has been applied and successfully scaled.

So, when and how should a team make a move to scale a Scrum project? The answer to this question usually depends on the nature of the project and at what level a team would like to scale. Scaling usually occurs at one of three different levels as scaling can take place across projects, programs, or portfolios.

Depending on what level a team would like to scale at determines how much coordination is required. When it comes to scalability, additional resources and project managers may be necessary to ensure that development stays on track.

When it comes to Scrum teams, it is usually recommended that teams stay under ten members. In the event that an organization wishes to scale their Scrum projects, it is recommended that a bigger team is divided into smaller groups who meet regularly to discuss their progress and report any issues or concerns. Keeping cadence with these meetings and ensuring they happen at regular intervals is crucial and could be managed by a project manager.

Each Scrum team would select a team representative who join the Scrum meetings and update on the team's progress, challenges they may be facing, breakthroughs they may have had, as well as coordinate any future activities with other teams. When it comes to deciding how often a Scrum of Scrums should meet, it is the size of the project, level of interdependency, complexity, and recommendations from upper management, which should be taken into consideration.

As we know, Scrum recommends that meetings and collaboration take place face to face. Although not impossible to implement Scrum over different geographical locations, it does take a lot more coordination and effort.

When it comes to scaling a project with teams in different offices, the Scrum of Scrum meeting scan takes place using video conferencing tools.

When larger projects are deployed, a chief of Scrums will need to hire, and this person is responsible for facilitating all the sessions between the Scrum of Scrums. The chief of Scrums will determine exactly when meetings should take place and outline their agendas. These meetings, like other check-ins, will involve the sharing of updates on progress, challenges, and recognized dependencies across projects. Once teams receive an agenda from the chief Scrum master, they should prepare their updates ahead of the meeting. Should any particular members of a team be facing challenges, these should be raised in these meetings, as it is often likely that other teams may experience the same challenges. This allows teams to share in problem solving and overcome obstacles at a quicker rate.

When these meetings take place, each team representative will usually provide an update that answers four main questions. These include what the team has been working on since the last meetings, what the team plans to work on between now and the next meeting, asking other representatives if there are any other elements of development the other teams dependent on them for, and finally, what could the team be working on that would directly impact the other teams.

The outcome of these Scrum of Scrum meetings is usually better coordination of work, which is carried out across teams.
This is specifically true when there are tasks that run across different teams, and there are high levels of dependency.

This ensures that if there are any obstacles, discrepancies between expectations, or change in deliverables, they are exposed and addressed as soon as possible. These meetings also operate as an open forum when representatives can provide honest feedback and receive recommendations or input from other representatives.

In the event that a project is scaled above the capabilities of a Scrum of Scrums framework, an additional meeting framework is created where a representative from each Scrum of Scrums is sent to a larger meeting known as the 'Scrum of Scrum of Scrums.' This allows all projects that are related to each other to be coordinated in such a way that allows for maximum quality and timeous output. What is important to note is that this type of coordination, especially should the larger teams be distributed across geographical locations, will require much larger coordination and management effort.

Tips for Scrum Mastery

We will address some of the problems that might occur during the implementation of Scrum phases. For example, how can you find a solution to fund some of the problems that have to be resolved without knowing the concrete result, and how you will present the possibility of allocating the funds to the possible funders when some risks and circumstances can't be predicted, but they are still in control from ROI?

The person responsible for the project planning is the product owner as we already know. In big corporations, this role is often assigned to the head of the department. This can be the director of the manufacturing section, head of inventory control, and so forth.

When it comes to product organizations, the product owner is usually the product manager itself because he is already familiar with both software and the products. There are cases in which the product owner is an IT project manager. Usually, this person is in charge of internal infrastructure in the IT sector. For example, the role of the product owner in Scrum methodology can be assigned to the project manager in charge of consolidating servers in the internal IT sector of a concrete company. The role of the product owner is to nurture the product's vision and communicate that vision to all other team members. The product owner also needs to get the initial funding for the project and to constantly work in collecting the resources. This is achieved by making initial product backlog and initial plans for project release.

Why planning is necessary?

Having a plan is the most effective way to determine that the right vision is shared between those who fund the project and those who work on the project and deliver the desired product. The purpose of the thoughtful and carefully crafted plan is to make a bond between all the people that are involved in the project. This bond helps them to evaluate the overall progress of the project and to make decisions that will maximize production within the vision that is established and the context in which decision has to be made.

Having a plan is important in terms of assertions needed for achieving the projected value of the project while respecting the time frameset. Making a plan means that the project manager projects activities that can influence the value of the project. This includes timetables for finishing the project to deliver this value. This kind of setting becomes the benchmark against which the investors and management evaluate the overall progress of the project.

Basics in Scrum project planning

In Scrum, the planning phase is usually made of one sprint that is shorter than others and lasts for 15 days more or less. All practices used in Scrum for backlog sprints or daily Scrums apply to this planning sprint. Outputs that are defined during the planning sprint are used to prepare project documentation and project prototype. In case that prototype can't be made, the planning phase needs to deliver at least the concept proof which is usually one part of the functionality that works in a predetermined environment. So, the first thing in every project is to determine what kind of system project team will build and what the importance of that system is.

In the traditional approach, project planning is made of complete preparation of all tasks in all stages with exact instructions that every member of the team has to do and for how long. Traditional project planning means that the whole development process is predicted thus predetermined. This kind of planning requires scheduled and staffed tasks and activities and the plan itself represents a way to control the project and manage it accordingly. This way project manager has a role to assign tasks to each member of the team and give them work that is planned in advance. Scrum methodology, on the contrary, relies on agility and promotes emergence and self-organization. This way the team can build a complex system even though the business environment can be complicated.

Regardless of the initial project requests, Scrum helps developing teams to work with new and also complex, sometimes even untested technologies.

Even if the vision of the system in the planning phase has one set up, the reality of the product and its working functionality will be known after all the activities have started. That is why technology and requirements often change during the project development phase.

When there is a new business opportunity, the Product owner prioritizing of the product backlog and functionalities of the final product change.

When the Product Owner sees this new working functionality, he or she will decide how that functionality should be released or adjusted. Changes can also occur if the new technology appears in the meantime, or if the one that is already used isn't suitable for the project.

In Scrum, system functionalities are defined only on the highest level. Scrum focuses on functionalities that are first and they are the only ones detailed enough for any kind of proper estimation. Functionality that is defined represents the priority to the development team because that is the potentially shippable product they need to deliver by the end of the sprint. It is also the most valuable one for the business. These functionality details are usually given for one feature at the time. Still, sometimes there can be up to six functionalities that are prioritized in the product backlog.

We already mentioned that in Scrum, management doesn't have any influence on the definition and division of the tasks for the development phase. That is the job for development teams. They need to brainstorm and set the working schedule for themselves, which motivates them and gives them the chance to self-organize.

The team can manage itself through the whole development phase and the project manager (Scrum master) is there only to guide them if something is not right.

Nobody gives the team a project plan with working details and schedules; they just get the list of functionalities that need to be delivered. The workflow and assignments are determined by developing a team without external influences.

Scrum and new, unfunded or already funded projects

If you start with a brand-new project, you will need funding. Every investor wants to know if they will have a return on investment (or ROI for short) and how will they benefit from the project. After they are familiar with these few points, investors will make an evaluation in which they will compare the offered project to all available competing projects and their funding. For better evaluation, investors need to have enough information about the project's vision; risks that project will face and underlying assumptions about the product.

Planning a new project is a way of laying out a vision to the investors against which they can assess their vision of the investment and adjust it if they find it acceptable. It is a set of understandings that need to be common and from which collaboration and adaptation can emerge. This kind of understanding grows into the determination of expectations and measures that can be reported and reviewed.

Sometimes the project can be approved for funding but it still has to get underway. Also, some projects tried to get underway but they were too complex or its technology was stopping any kind of progress.

Some projects have already been approved and funded, but have yet to get underway. Or, perhaps a project has tried to get underway but the complexity of the technology or requirements have precluded any progress. If that is the case, your project representative should be familiar with both users and customers. In the Scrum method, this person would be your Product Owner. You'd give them the authorization to make the first requirements with high priority for the product backlog. After you have found a suitable product owner the next role you need to fill in the role of the Scrum Master. When this person is found you need to start with daily Scrums.

The first product backlog that you need make for your project needs to have basic business functionalities and requirements for technology that you will use.

Once you define the technology, the team builds a preliminary design and framework in which the system will operate. When this is over, the team needs to implement determined user functionalities into the framework.

Sometimes the team will need to connect the existing database to some functionalities or to make a preliminary database for the project. If these are the circumstances for your project, then the goal of your first sprint is defined. You need to try and deliver the key piece of user functionality using the technology that you selected.

Once when the sprint backlog is in harmony with the project goals, you can create an environment that development needs. This is the time when you set up the whole development team, define the code that will be used and discuss management and practices that will be implemented during the project. In this stage, you also need to start implementing the targeted technology and build a functionality that can be tested on the platform previously made by the team. All these activities are more or less everything that happens during the full first sprint.

There are two purposes of this initial sprint. First of all, there has to be a development environment for the team so they can build the best possible functionality. And second, working part of the system built by the development team is actually the deliverable that will be demonstrated to your customers and to the Product owner within the first development sprint.

If you deliver your first working functionality fast and successfully, you will convince both the Product owner and the customers that your project is real. You will show them your determination and real and measurable results and they will get involved. The first sprint is the most important step for every new project because it connects you and your team with the customers and product owners. It introduces them to regular sprint rhythm in which they can always expect deliverables they asked for through their requirements.

The product owner updates the product backlog while the team works on its first Sprint. Keep in mind that Scrum doesn't insist on having a complete product backlog. It only needs to have enough requirements for the duration of several following sprints. Once the customers and the Product owner get the feel from the Scrum approach, they start using longer views of the backlog. If the current vision of the project doesn't follow the reality of the project anymore, the Product owner will make a new vision along with the customers. When they forge a new vision, their product backlog requirements will change too.

In some cases, Scrum is used to get a generated code for an already existing project. In other cases, Scrum is implemented to help a project that already exists in terms of productivity and focus.

This often happens because during the development phase teams have issues with building the complex system while following the changes in technology and requirements. It can happen that the team was stuck with trying to deliver documents or models rather than the working functionality for the business. This doesn't mean that the team doesn't have a good development environment or selected technology, it only means that the priorities haven't been properly communicated.

If this is the case for your new project, you also need to appoint a Product owner that represents users and customers. Just like in the first case scenario, this person needs to come up with reprioritized requirements. The next step is also the same since you need to have a Scrum master and to start daily Scrums as soon as possible. The difference is that now you already have the development team and some deliverables. You need to use daily Scrums to find out what are the impediments. Don't be surprised if daily Scrum meetings last for hours in this phase.

The development team needs to talk about all issues and try to determine why they couldn't build the software. You can motivate the team using a simple challenge. Ask them what they can build in a month.

This can be a good way to make the team work together and to prove that they can develop the software envisioned in the project. You need to get the team to focus on building functionalities since they are important to the Product Owner. The reality is that the Product owner, in this case, will be impressed by the fact that the team built anything functional in such a short amount of time. The reason for this is the fact that the previous approach team was working for months without delivering any working functionality. This kind of unproductive team can cause the customers and Product owners to give up.

Systems of Control in Scrum

Scrum uses several methods to provide external control in the process of system development.

These controls are:

• A backlog is a form of control in which we need to address the functionality of the product and its requirements that haven't been defined right in the current description of the project release. This means that in the backlog, Scrum deals with enhancements asked for by customers and bugs or defects of the product. It also addresses upgrades in terms of technology and competitiveness of the product.

• In the phase of release or enhancement, Scrum uses backlog items. These items are improved in the release phase of the product using the info that teams gathered on variables such as quality, time and strength of competition.

• Components of every project use packet as another form of external control. If the packets are used, the product changes, following the backlog items and a new release plan.

• One of the most frequently used forms of external control in Scrum is change. It is predicted that changes must happen to every packet if they want to implement enhancements of the backlog items.

- In many cases, we meet with problems during the development processes. But if we want to have a successful implementation of the changes, we must resolve any technical problems that might occur.
- Every system in the developing process is faced with risks. Risks can seriously affect the project and its success. That is why is necessary to be prepared and to be responsive in this stage. Risk assessment can affect every other phase and it can totally change the course of the project.
- Teams are always required to provide solutions to these risks and problems. Sometimes solutions to certain risks or problem-solving lead to big changes in the product release phase.
- Teams must also be prepared to face issues that are not described in any previous method of control. There can be some overall project issues in different phases of Scrum. These issues are usually used by management to properly manage backlog items. On the other hand, teams use them to find solutions and make changes. However, management and the teams can't control risks or solutions individually. They need to work together if they want to increase their productivity. Also, these mechanisms of control are changeable. They are reviewed in every Sprint meeting when the whole team discuss, modifies and reconciles them.

Deliverables in Scrum

The product that is delivered at the end of the development process is flexible. The content of this product depends on many variables, especially the environmental ones.

As it was already mentioned, some of these variables are funding, time frame, work of the competition and functionality of the product itself. When we talk about determinants for our deliverables, we need to consider the intelligence of the market. We also need to include the contacts of our customers and the skills of our developers. In the phase of development, many changes occur. These changes or adjustments are frequent for the products. They represent the team's answer to environmental variables. Keep in mind that in Scrum, you can determine deliverables in any stage of the project.

Project Team in Scrum

The project team in Scrum is a team of developers who work full time on the product. The project team also includes external parties which will be affected by the release of that new product. External parties are customers and marketing sales. When it comes to traditional processes of product release, groups that are not developers are not included in the system development process because there is a possibility of making the project too much complicated. There is also a possibility of strong interference that is not necessary or useful for the project. On the other hand, Scrum allows external groups to be involved even though it is a controlled involvement set in short time intervals. According to the Scrum approach, this kind of feedback will increase the results of the project release. It is an object-oriented tool that helps developers address the right behaviors of the product and have a clear interface.

Scrum strategies have many resemblances with the strategies of the sport called Rugby. Scrum, the same as Rugby uses the environment (in Rugby it in the field) to set the context of their strategies. This also helps them establish their system of external controls (we compare it to the rules of Rugby). Also, Scrum uses its first cycle to move its product (ball) forward in the game (or in this case the system development process). Additionally, just like Rugby evolved because some soccer rules were broken, the Scrum used the same principle to evolve. They both succeeded to adapt to the changes in the environment. In the end, the game will not end as long as there are changes in their surroundings (in Scrum, this refers to the needs of the business, time frame, work of the competition and overall functionality of the product).

Scrum Methodology and its advantages

Unlike the traditional development methodologies, Scrum is not designed to respond to environmental changes only at the beginning of the cycle of enhancements. It isn't designed to respond to just too unpredictable external factors. These approaches that are more recent, like Boehm spiral methodology for example still have some limitations.

This is mostly because they are not flexible enough to be responsive to all variables that can change once when the project starts.

Contrarily, Scrum represents a methodology that is flexible during the whole project, in all its stages. It is a framework designed to provide mechanisms that externally control product planning and its release. Scrum manages aspects such as risk assessment, environmental variables, etc., and all other issues that can happen during the progress of the project. With this flexibility, the team can change the project at any time and create deliverables that will evolve and become more suitable for release. It enables the product to find a better place on the market.

Scrum helps developers to find solutions for many different problems or adjustments that need to be done through the whole system development process. It enables them to learn and to build experience in predicting the outcomes of environmental changes and create an appropriate response to those changes.

This has an even better result if the team is small and collaborative. Scrum also has an environmental training mode that is available to all parties involved with the project. The core principle of Scrum methodology is object-oriented technology.

According to Scrum's philosophy, objects that are actually features of the product already offer their own environment that is discrete but also manageable.

Code which has many intertwined interfaces during the procedures doesn't work well in Scrum. However, Scrum can be applied to these procedural developing systems selectively. It can be used only in sections that offer data orientation which is strong, and it can be applied only on clear interfaces.

Scrum Project

We can estimate a Scrum projects through some of the standard criteria for estimation. Still, when it comes to Scrum methodology, the recommendation is to double this estimation in terms of productivity. Rationally, all this is possible to determine only for the project to start. The real time frame and overall cost of the project are the things that can change through the course of the project, and they depend on variables and their changeability.

Scrum is considered to have both of the most important aspects of project estimation. These aspects are acceleration and velocity in all stages of the system development process. These two criteria can be predicted by their delivered functions, or the estimation can be done observing the backlog items that have completed. In these terms, we will see that the acceleration and velocity of the project are lower in the beginning since the overall infrastructure of the system is yet to be built or modified.

Also, as we put the basic function of the project into objects, the acceleration will rise. Still, acceleration will decrease when a team needs to develop new metrics for empirical processes. In this case, the velocity is high and remains sustainable until the development of the required metrics is finished.

Applications of Scrum

We are beginning to come to the stretch drive. But there is still lots more to discuss.

We will be looking at the applications of Scrum. That is, we will be discussing how and where Scrum can be applied. This will give you a broader perspective on how Scrum is not just limited to software development. Since Scrum has cross-cutting applications, it's definitely worth jumping into a deeper discussion on how Scrum can be applied to your organization.

Born out of Software Development

When Agile was developed, traditional project management methodologies had been unable to address the issues pertaining to dynamic and ever-changing environments. This led project managers to seek alternatives that would embrace change and help software developers find the right way in which they could address these dynamics while making the most out of the current project management techniques available.

Out of this need, approaches such as Extreme Programming allowed developers to find a host of principles which could better address the circumstances they face as developers in a volatility environment.

Since 2001, the Agile movement has led to the emergence of Scrum as a viable methodology which can provide developers a series of steps and procedures in order to create a project framework conducive to getting results.

Given that we have already covered the history of Scrum; it's worth mentioning at this point that the software industry is the most common place where Scrum can be found in action. But it is not the only place in which Scrum can be implemented. In fact, Scrum can be implemented in any type of industry and business.

It Starts with the Agile Mindset
In that regard, the Agile mindset is all about putting people first. In this case, the people that go first are the customer and the individual team members.
When you move away from getting results based on the cold metrics that are just numbers on a page to an approach where success is measured by the success of individuals, then you are setting yourself up for a successful run at each project.

One of the most crucial success factors in Scrum is determining if team members have the right mindset. This may imply having to "sell" individuals on the merits of Scrum especially if they have been exposed to other project management methodologies which espouse more rigid principles.

The fact of the matter is that anyone who is truly dedicated to providing the best value at all times will quickly see the merits of Scrum for what they are. As long as team members are willing to focus on delivering value at all times, and not just "getting the job done," then you can be sure that you will be successful in the long run.

A Cross-Cutting Approach
Scrum has a cross-cutting approach in the sense that it can be applied to virtually any industry and business out there. This is something which is important to take into account as project management is a diverse field.

Given that there is no, one methodology which is "perfect," new approaches are consistently being developed. As such, each approach attempts to tackle the gaps that other approaches have failed to address, either due to obsolescence or due to inadequacy on the part of their practitioners.

In any event, Scrum can be implemented in just about every walk of life. Increasingly, more and more industries are getting their staff Scrum certified so that they can tackle project management, and daily tasks, within an Agile environment.

Consequently, being "Agile" means being able to trim away the fat from your organization and focusing on getting results rather than sounding smart. In fact, you will sound even smarter when you are able to deliver on your promises as opposed to having to justify your team as to why your objectives were not met.

In this regard, you have the power to choose Scrum as a means of bringing your team into a more dynamic approach which can allow you to become faster, quicker and even get ahead of the game especially during times of uncertainty.

From pharma to manufacturing to business process outsourcing, Scrum has gained more and more traction as Scrum practitioners have been able to make headway in the application of Scrum to various facets of the business world. This is something which should not be taken lightly as most organizations are in a constant search for improving their processes in such a way that they can reduce both time and cost.

That being said, it's important to take into account that Scrum is just one of the methodologies under the Agile umbrella. Thus, you have a myriad of options which you can also check out. By learning more and more about Agile, you can see just how beneficial being Agile really is.

Other Methodologies to Consider

If you are serious about going Agile, I will encourage you to check out other methodologies which can help you get the most out of your Agile mindset.

The first is Lean Manufacturing.

This methodology is focused on trimming down the fat as much as possible during manufacturing processes. Lean Manufacturing is all about reducing errors while maximizing output. Often, this is achieved through the streamlining of processes which aren't always the most efficient.

In Lean Manufacturing, the idea of "time is money" is really taken to heart.

When you become "lean," what you are essentially doing is reducing the "waste" from your processes. So, this waste can be seen as a waste of time, a waste of money and even a waste of staff. Often, businesses will hire more people than they really need. Also, they will spend a lot more time on tasks which can be done in a reduced period of time.

Now, we are not talking about firing your staff and hiring a bunch of robots to do their job.

Hardly.

What we are advocating is for having the right amount of people, within the properly designed processes, which can yield more efficient results. Consequently, efficiency will lead to better profit margins and improved revenues for companies.

Becoming lean is all about embracing an out-of-the-box approach in which you are willing to consider different angles on processes which you might be considered to have down cold. But it's when you begin thinking outside of the box that true progress is made.

Also, becoming lean is a mindset, just like Agile, in which you are looking to maximize your uptime. As you become leaner, your uptime will yield more. Hence, you will be able to take advantage of the savings obtained in term of time and resources.

A great complement to Lean Manufacturing is Six Sigma.

Six Sigma is a methodology which tracks defects and attempts to find the best ways to reduce them. So, the first step for Six Sigma practitioners is to identify the number of defects that make up the entire manufacturing process.

Six Sigma is an ideal complement to Scrum since both Six Sigma, and Scrum seeks to find the best ways to produce given the circumstances you are dealing with. In that regard, keeping a mature attitude about the reality of a company is ideal in order to make the most of any restructuring process.

Therefore, Six Sigma seeks to encourage management teams to find ways to reduce the incidence of defects. This ties into the metrics in Scrum looking to measure defects in lines of code, for instance.

The spirit driving Scrum is continuous improvement. That is the same attitude that drives Six Sigma. As such, Six Sigma will enable you to quantify your defects in such a way that you can see where you stand, and then, make a concerted effort to improve the overall quality of your manufacturing process.

So, I would encourage you to check out these the methodology mentioned herein. They will help you find additional elements which can help you improve your overall processes in such a way that you can ensure continuous development across the lifecycle of projects, as well as, your organization's daily tasks.

As such, keeping an open mind will be just as useful to you, and your organization, as any high-priced training seminar or course you can take. Bear in mind that investing in yourself, and your team, will always be beneficial insofar as ensuring consistent results as delivered to your customers and stakeholders.

Stacking Scrum up to traditional project management methodologies

Since Scrum is relatively new on the project management scene, the more traditional project management methodologies have become increasingly scrutinized in the way they handle many of the functions associated with projecting management.

It is worth noting that the comparison that we will make in this section is not about selling Scrum as a superior means of project management. If anything, both Agile and traditional project management share many common traits.

However, it is their differences which seem to generate some controversy among advocates and practitioners of the various project management methodologies. So, I would like to point out that is it important for you to become well acquainted with the various approaches out there.

When you become familiar with the myriad of the project management approaches out there, you will be able to come up with a list of items which you can confidently apply to your own project management style, as well as, helping your team rally around what you feel to be the most effective means of carrying out projects.

Since Agile, and consequently Scrum, advocates for a flat hierarchical structure, all Scrum team members have an equal say in what is done and how it is done. This is a fundamental shift from traditional project management as a traditional approached call for a hierarchical structure in which the project manager reigns supreme.

While we have clearly established this difference earlier on, it's important to consider how traditional project management is heavy on a single point of accountability. Needless to say, this may become overwhelming to that individual who must bear the responsibility for an entire project.

That being said, it is important to consider how empowerment plays a key role in providing project teams the opportunity to do things as they see fit given the fact that it is the team members who are tasked with delivering the actual value at the end of the project.

Furthermore, traditional project management considers processes as the most important elements within a project. As such, we have stated how people are more important than processes. Of course, even the most talented individuals need to have clear processes and procedures on which they can rely on. Nevertheless, when greater emphasis is placed on processes over people, then the talents of individual team members may become stifled.

Hence, it is important to foster empowerment among team members. This can be achieved by allowing team members to use their criteria, judgment, and common sense to dictate the way in which they will approach the tasks they are to complete. This is another fundamental shift in mindset as the more individual team members are allowed to think for themselves; the lesser the burden becomes to project leaders. This is why traditional project management approaches rely so heavily on project managers. In the end, it's the project manager who bears the burden of everything that goes wrong.

Yet, if the project runs smoothly and everything comes up roses, then it's the project manager who can claim credit for everything that happened in the project.

This is another fundamental shift in mindset when dealing with Scrum. If the project is a success, then the entire team takes credit for it. In a way, it's like team sports that do not rely on one player to make the difference.

Think of Rugby.

In Rugby, one player cannot be a difference-maker. One player can come to a deciding factor, but one player is not enough to win a match singlehandedly. This is where the term "Scrum" comes from. It comes from Rugby; a true team sport in every sense of the word.

This is why the collaborative nature of Scrum is at the root of the way everything is done. If Scrum practitioners truly embrace the way of this collaborative nature, then there is a good chance that the projects you embark upon will be successful.

As for traditional project management methodologies, a more segregated, differentiated division of labor is espoused. The intent behind this division of labor is to foster specialization among team members in such a way that each individual will be in their area of expertise and thereby producing results.

While this logic makes all the sense in the world, it leads to communication breakdown and even competition among the various components of the project team. So, the project manager is often a mediator among the different sections of the project. Undoubtedly, this represents additional tasks which may not be really necessary. This is not a good example of being "lean."

How to Deal with Resistance

The last topic I would like to address is resistance.

Often, Scrum practitioners encounter resistance, especially with those folks who are unfamiliar with the principles that Agile holds true.

This resistance is mainly due to the fact that any time you ask individuals to change their ways of doing things and even approach life, you will encounter resistance. Given that this is a perfectly natural response by a human being, it is also important to consider that not everyone is open to embracing the Agile mindset.

In that sense, there are folks who would rather not be a part of Agile processes and moving away from what they know best. As such, some folks believe that advocating for the implementation of Agile methodologies is about replacing previous ideas and beliefs since Scrum is somehow much better than other methodologies.

As I have stated earlier, Scrum is not "better" than other project management methodologies. It is just "better-suited" for some types of projects and industries. This is a key difference since not all projects are created equal, and certainly not all fields have the same characteristics.

This is why Scrum's cross-cutting appeal is so useful. Nevertheless, making the most of the talent and resources available is a must for all project managers. Thus, being able to communicate the benefits of Scrum to team members is a valuable first step on the road to becoming Agile.

As you traverse through the paths of becoming Agile, your team members may bring up objections as to why Agile approaches and Scrum are not the best way to go.
One of the most common issues raised by folks is the lack of a hierarchical structure.

Since hierarchy is something that is deeply rooted in the psyche of all humans, it may be hard for some folks to wrap their mind around the fact that there isn't a boss, but rather, it is a team of "bosses" that runs the project.

In addition, some folks may resist that implementing Scrum usually requires some type of retraining or courses to be taken. As such, resistance can certainly be strong especially among older folks who may not be too keen on taking courses or go through retraining efforts.

However, it is certainly worth making the most of your time to learn more about how Scrum can have a direct impact on the way that you work and how your organization can benefit from going Agile. Moreover, teams that embrace Scrum are often closer and yield better results.

As individuals begin to see the ways in which Scrum can be implemented in a positive way, the Agile mindset will begin to take hold within your organization's culture. Eventually, Scrum and Agile will become second nature to an extent whereby everything will revolve around this newfound culture.

So, I would certainly encourage you to motivate your staff to take a closer look at how Scrum and Agile can help them become a much better team. Since Agile is all about continuous improvement, then the first important concept to embrace is exactly that: <u>continuous improvement.</u>

As such, continuous improvement begins with individuals within your organization becoming committed to continuously improve processes, outputs, and most importantly, themselves. Therefore, approaching continuous improvement and development should become the norm among all team members.

That being said, your organization will soon become a breeding ground for success as team members become more and more aware of the need to help each other improve. This is something that I cannot stress enough: the collaborative nature of Agile. Without it, the entire building comes crashing down.

Also, collaboration breeds trust among team members. The more team members can learn to trust each other, the more they will be willing to take on the roles and responsibilities that Agile asks of them. Moreover, when teammates really trust each other, they will develop keen instincts in which they will be able to sense everything that is going on around.

This is just like sports. When teammates truly know each other perfectly, they can produce those "no-look passes" simply because they know where their teammates are going to be. Thus, this connection among teammates can lead to producing results on a consistent basis.

Finally, I would like to underscore the importance that leadership has on a successful team. When the leadership of a team is able to provide an example of consistency and dedication, that is something which a team can rally around. While it is true that Agile does not advocate leadership in terms of being the boss, Agile does espouse a concept of leadership in which leaders must become set the standard by which team members must perform.

Metrics in Scrum

One of the core tenets of effective project management is producing metrics that can track the progress of a project. Without a solid, quantitative measurement of project performance, it is nearly impossible to accurately measure how effective the project actually is. In fact, offering a qualitative measure of the effectiveness of a project provides a very limited scope of just how well the project is doing.

Consequently, it is vital that project leaders develop a series of indicators which can be used to determine the progress of the project and verify how well the results of the project have been achieved. Based on that premise, Scrum, just like any other project management methodology out there, seeks to use indicators, formally known as Key Performance Indicators (or KPIs) to measure the success of the project and track its output. We will be looking at the KPIs which can be used to track project development in order to ensure that the outputs established at the outset of the project are met.

Who is in Charge of Tracking KPIs?

The first point that needs to be taken into consideration is: who is in charge of tracking KPIs?

The measurement of overall project success and progress is a collaborative effort, just like everything else in Scrum. The Product Owner is in charge of the overall reporting process, especially when reporting to the customer and other stakeholders on the progress of the project.

In addition, the Scrum Master is in charge of compiling the relevant information that is used to generate the indicators. For instance, this refers to tracking the results of individual Sprint Tasks which build up to the Product Backlog items.

The Development Team is also in charge of tracking their own progress such as the number of hours that have been worked and which are remaining in the sprint, the progress they have made in their individual tasks in addition to any bugs or problems encountered in the testing portion of the deliverables. It should be noted that even if the Product Owner is in charge of compiling the KPIs for the project, this does not mean that the Product Owner has the authority to "supervise" the project. Please keep in mind that Scrum espouses a concept of transparency and mutual accountability. What this means is that everyone is in charge of tracking the progress of the project and not just the Product Owner.

Also, the Scrum Master is just keeping track of the tasks being completed in such a way that if there are issues that arise within the project itself, the Development Team has the opportunity to bring them up at the next available time which would be the Daily Standup Meeting.

Consequently, there is no officially tracker or supervisor. Everyone is in charge of keeping tabs on everyone. If there should ever be any disciplinary issues, the team, as a whole, has the responsibility and the authority to deal with the issue among themselves. This is one of the most important features of self-organizing teams.

Scrum Metrics and KPIs

The metrics used in Scrum are part of the broader group of Agile KPIs. These metrics serve as the parameters by which the progress of the project is measured in an objective and quantitative manner. Now, there are other metrics and methodologies which could come into play such as combining a Scrum project with Six Sigma or the use of Kanban metrics which track workflow.

The fact of the matter is that there is a wide range of metrics which could be used, and all depend on the project itself. As such, Scrum practitioners quickly come to realize that no two projects are the same and they may all end up requiring different metrics to measure their output.

Nevertheless, there are three broad types of metrics which can be used to generate KPIs.

- **Measuring deliverables.** These metrics measure the output of the Scrum team and the amount of value being provided to customers. This measurement can be in terms of time saved, cost reduction, increased sales, or any other type of impact the project has had on the customer. Also, deliverables may be measured in terms of their individual functionalities. This refers to the specific characteristics of the project and how it can be tracked to ensure that the final product does what it's supposed to do.

- **Measuring effectiveness.** These metrics measure the overall effectiveness and success of the Scrum team. There is a myriad of metrics here. Some that stand out are Return on Investment (ROI), time to market, and so on. These metrics focus on the impact that the Scrum team's actions had on the business itself, or even the industry.

- **Measuring the Scrum team.** These metrics look to determine the overall health of the team in terms of member satisfaction, turnover, and even attrition. This measurement allows the Scrum

Master and Product Owner to determine if the way the project is being handled is appropriate if the tempo is moving too fast, or if there are any other considerations which must be taken into account.

The three broad categories of metrics described above are to provide a sense of what the Scrum team should be producing, where they stand in terms of the overall progress of the project and if there are any potential issues which could be caught ahead of time and dealt with in a proactive manner.

Therefore, it is up to the Product Owner to help the Scrum Master determine if the team is firing on all cylinders or if there are any issues within the team that need to be addressed at once.

In addition, it's important for the Product Owner to be aware of how metrics from other disciplines, such as Six Sigma, could potentially help the Development Team, and any other stakeholder, gain a better perspective of how well the project is doing. Ultimately, the success of the project is measured in the customer's satisfaction and the overall achievement of the project's aim. Moreover, the success of a project is measured by the amount of value that was ultimately delivered to the customer as a result of the deliverables.

Now, let's dig deeper into the specifics of each of the three broad categories we have described above.

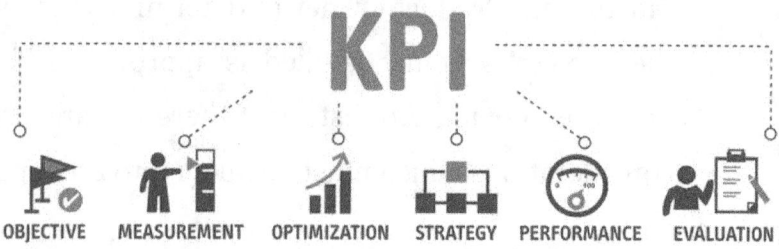

Escaped Defects

This metric tracks the number of bugs that the Development Team encountered during the development of the product. This particular metric is ideal for tracking those products which are reliant on testing in order to make sure it works well.

This metric can be used in manufacturing, software development, pharma, and even food production. If you look at it those terms, you can put Scrum to use in any field in which defects are tracked. The big difference between Scrum and other manufacturing systems such as Total Quality is that you are not waiting till the end of the production cycle to see where the defects are. With Scrum, you can gauge how many errors are popping during the manufacturing phase. Therefore, you will be able to determine if there are corrections that need to be made.

Defect Density

And, on the subject of defects, the Defect Density metric measures how many defects were found per unit of production. In the case of software, for instance, you could track the number of mistakes per lines of code. In manufacturing, you could track the number of mistakes per thousand units of production. The measurements may vary, but the concept is the same. As such, it's important to keep track of this measurement as it is vital to ensure that you have the right number of defects.

Team Velocity

This is a more Scrum-like measure. In essence, team velocity is measured by the number of user stories completed in a sprint, or the amount of Product Backlog items finalized.

Now, this metric is not an exact metric in the sense that some sprints may yield the completion of a significant number of products while other sprints may produce a very limited number. This all depends on the actual work breakdown that has been determined at the outset of the sprint.

Nevertheless, it is a useful measurement in tracking the actual work that the Development Team is achieving per sprint.

However, it might be unfair to compare one sprint with another since conditions may be changing and the dynamics of the project may require one set of tasks over another.

Thus, this may lead the team to produce a high number of outputs in one sprint while the remaining number of sprints may yield a lower amount of outputs.

At the end of the day, the team serves as a means of tracking the amount of work being done. As the completed work piles up, the Scrum team can see the success of their actions.

A word of caution though: in the case where there are multiple Scrum teams, it's important to avoid the sure of team velocity as a means of comparing team performance.

Unless you have multiple teams completing the exact same tasks (which would be pointless) you would not have an "apples to apples" comparison.

This means that while one team is apparently getting more work done than other teams, this measurement is not fair since each team is working on completely different tasks. As such, this is a flawed metric in terms of using it as a comparison among teams.

Sprint Burndown

The Sprint Burndown is a measure in which the sprint's total working hours are divided by the number of work days available.

Let's assume that a Scrum team has four weeks to complete a sprint. Then, let's assume they are working 8 hours a day over a 5-day week, that's 20 work days at a clip of 160 total hours of work.

This means that each day, 8 hours will tick off the Burndown Chart. If the team is humming along, there may be no need to work overtime. However, it could be that the Development Team has encountered issues and needs to put in a few extra hours. This would be reflected in the number of hours the team is working on a daily basis.

Consequently, you can chart the team's work by generating a bar graph representing the number of hours worked per day. The trend line for the chart would gradually wind down to zero as the number of hours run out.

The Sprint Burndown Chart serves as a graphic organizer in which the team can see where they are heading in terms of the remaining hours in the sprint versus the amount of work remaining. It should be said that if everything is humming along perfectly and the work assigned to that sprint takes less time than anticipated, the leftover time is automatically assigned to testing. That way, no time is wasted.

Time to Market

This metric tracks the amount of time the Scrum project actually takes before the product begins to generate income for the customer. So, this would be the number of sprints it would take the Scrum team before the final product is officially released and begins to generate income for the customer.

Let's consider a software release such as a video game. The Scrum team has determined that it would take four, four-week sprints before the Scrum team would have a demo version available for testing. At this point, the game would not be up for sale yet, but the advance speculation would provide the customer with some traction. As such, value is being created without actually being up for sale.

When the video game is fully operational and ready to generate income, then the Scrum team will have the final release of the product to the customer. At this point, the customer can begin to generate income off the product's final release.

This measure is also depending on the Scrum team's alpha and beta testing procedures. It could be that beta testing may take up an entire sprint since the product itself is so extensive. And once beta testing is complete, the product may enter the market under alpha testing guidelines. As such, this may represent another full sprint while the final bugs are worked out for the product.

As you can see, time to market becomes more and more critical as the project grows in size and scope. Therefore, it's crucial for the Scrum team to set realistic timelines so that the customer can be aware of the amount of the time the project will need before the final product is released.

Return on Investment (ROI)

This metric can be used on both sides of the ball.
For the Scrum team, their work generates an income to the company which has employed them to deliver the service to the customer.

As such, the ROI for the company employing the Scrum team may be measured in terms of the costs associated with each sprint versus what the customer has actually paid for the services rendered.

This is fairly straightforward, and the Scrum team would most likely generate costs in terms of wages, equipment, and other materials used to produce the final product for the customer. Since the Scrum team may be employed by a company external to the customer, this external company, perhaps a consulting firm would have to make an upfront investment in equipment and training in order to get the Scrum team fully operational.

On the customer's side, the customer will measure the expense that arose from the actual payment of the services rendered by the Scrum team. This payment could be calculated and agreed upon in a number of ways. At the end of the day, the customer hopes to generate much more income as compared to the expense it incurred in during the production of the project's outputs.

The easiest way to breakdown costing for a Scrum project is per sprint. Since each sprint may have very different activities attached to them, the Scrum team may reduce or increase costs depending on the actions that are done.

How to build a Scrum Team

Scrum is an overall framework that different project managers can use to application processes. It provides the structure needed to run successful projects, which are complex in nature. While Scrum is incredibly useful in its adaptability to the different subject matter, it is not a one size fits all approach. As a project and its stakeholders vary, so the team members and the appropriate roles they should fill will differ. When building a Scrum team, this is something to be carefully considered. For example, a Scrum team working on an application for an online store will vary significantly from a Scrum team working on developing the integration of an Xbox Game. One will require technical knowledge of backend systems and ecommerce while the other will require graphics designers and sound engineers.

Depending on the complexity of a problem, building and selecting a team may be more challenging. Some projects may include many unknown variables that could leave a team without relevant and more specialist skills. In order to cater to a variety of challenges and subject matter, the Scrum framework outlines three main responsibilities to ensure most bases and responsibilities are covered.

1. The Product Owner

The product owner plays a vital role in framing a project and ensuring that it's key objectives are achieved by the team. They are responsible for the business side of the project in terms of accountability of the project as a whole, and to ensure that the vision for the project remains clear to all team members. One of the main tools a product owner uses to achieve this is through a product backlog. With a well-organized list of priorities which is consistently reviewed and amended as needs change, the product owner is able to control and steer the team's focus more effectively. Communication within the Scrum team is also the responsibility of the product owner. They need to ensure that all team members clearly understand the overall project's objectives, as well as any required changes that are made to the scope of the project.

The role of the product owner is best taken up by someone who fully understands what the final end product such looks like the functionality it is expected to offer. It is ideally best suited to someone who has a product testing or marketing background, although this is not a strict requirement. The ability to clearly communicate is the most important attribute for a person to have. They need to not only ensure they fully understand what is expected from the client but also need to clearly convey this message to the team and maintain communication throughout the development process. The ability of a product manager to forecast and measure what future market conditions may be or what competitors are developing may aid in their success in guiding a Scrum team.

The approach that a product owner takes in managing a team can also be a determining factor in the team's success. They should not take a micro-managing or dictatorship approach and allow the team to own their space and tasks with autonomy. This role should ensure they work with all team members to provide clarity when needed and continuous communication.

Another important responsibility of the product owner is to assess the completion of user story criteria within a sprint and whether or not it is "Done."

They are the quality assurance measure within Scrum teams and need to constantly assess whether the quality provided is up to the standard, which is expected.

Having skills related to making business decisions regarding functionality and profitability will also be pertinent to the success of a product owner.

One of the final key responsibilities of the product owner is to assess and maintain return on investment. They are required to view the project from the end user's point of view and ensure that the product being developed provides a credible solution to the problem they are trying to solve. The product owner will also need to prioritize the development of single features and steer the team with a clear vision to ensure the final desired product is achieved. They will be required to respond quickly and efficiently to any setbacks or obstacles, which the team may face, again highlighting the importance of this team member to maintain communication.

Even if all the other team members are efficiently fulfilling their roles, an ineffective or incompetent product owner can derail a successful project. They are, therefore, the cornerstone of the project's success. The product owner is involved in every step of the project and maintains this involvement throughout the project. They are required to wear many hats by representing the interest of all parties involved in the development process.

2. *The Scrum Master*

The Scrum master is responsible for making sure that every team member understands their specific role and the overall objectives of the project.

Throughout a Scrum project, they will mentor, coach, and provide support to all team members while ensuring that they stick to the specific practices and theory of Scrum methodology. They should always lead by example and exercise patience while balancing the consideration of all aspects of the project and their task owners. The Scrum master works in collaboration with the product owner to manage the product backlog and find ways to ensure it is continuously streamlined.

The Scrum master is also responsible for ensuring that all team members have a clear understanding of exactly what is to be achieved and by when. This is a crucial task when it comes to changes within a project and the iterative approach of Scrum. They are expected to take any action necessary to assist the team in successfully completing a project. Along with the product owner, they should ensure that any impediments or obstacles to the team's success are removed.

A Scrum master should always be conscious of what a team can create within a specified time so that they can prevent a team from over committing what they can realistically achieve within a specific sprint.

Over-committing on delivery can cause stress and anxiety within a team, something which the Scrum master should ensure to avoid wherever possible. This unnecessary stress will hinder a team's progress and lead to reduced productivity.

The Scrum master should challenge the other team members to think out of the box in terms of innovation and what is possible. They should ask questions in a coaching way, which encourages team members to answer their own questions so as to facilitate the learning and development of teams.

Although the Scrum master is not responsible for the successful execution of a team, their role is vital in supporting and mentoring the team. They are pivotal in the backstage operation of a project. The most significant difference between a team leader and a Scrum master lies in the fact that a team leader physically leads the team while a Scrum master observes the team, ensures they adhere to Scrum processes, and that the Scrum methodology is successfully realized. The Scrum master should not interfere with the decisions made by the team around development specifics. Instead, they operate in an advisory capacity. They will only actively intervene when it is clear that the processes required by Scrum methodologies are not followed.

The Scrum master shares a responsibility with the product owner to remove obstacles from a team.

These generally fall within three different categories with the first being problems which the team cannot solve.

These problems could be delayed infrastructure, last-minute additions to functionality from external stakeholders or insufficient hardware needed to test developed products.

The second type of problem, which could arise, relates to the unintended consequences of strategic decisions. Conflicts of interest may arise, or team members may be adversely affected by decisions that are made. This leads to the third type of problem, which a Scrum master will be responsible for managing, and that is handling the more personal element of leadership relating to the team members themselves.

3. *The Scrum Development Team*

The actual development of a product is carried out by the Scrum development team, who is a group of individuals who work together to develop and deliver a final product. This team could include team members such as business analysts, software developers, or product testers.

In order to ensure that these team members work cohesively, it is important that all members understand the common goal. This team is responsible for the actual product delivery and so also needs to answer for ant delivery failures but will also share in the recognition and celebration of project successes. The development team is required to report on their daily progress in the daily Scrums as well as share any successes or challenges they are facing.

It is usually expected that it will take a few weeks for a new Scrum team to get into its stride and deliver product increment, which is 100% on brief.

Team members need time to adjust to working together and building interpersonal relationships that allow for great teamwork. This team has a significant amount of autonomy that they can decide independently how much work they can deliver in an upcoming sprint and commit to that accordingly. How a Scrum team operates in this may, by essentially deciding on projects and self-managing, is the perfect example of the essence of Scrum in action. The Scrum manager does not delegate the work needed to be accomplished. This is done by the development team themselves.

Scrum Master vs. Project Manager

Through all of these different roles and teams, you might be wondering what the main differences are between a Scrum master and a project manager. When overviewing the various roles of a Scrum, it may appear that the project management role would be redundant. However, the entire premise of Scrum is to handle the process of project management in an entirely different way. Traditionally, project managers were responsible for the ultimate decision making and the one who needed to take responsibility for failures. In this sense, a traditional project management role shares responsibility with a project manager. A project manager, by role definition, will make decisions on problem solutions whereas a Scrum master will provide coaching and guidance to a development team in problem-solving.

Project managers usually follow a more traditional approach to problem-solving. Essentially, Scrum works to distribute the tasks usually undertaken by a project manager, to various Scrum team members. This can leave project managers feeling out of place, but it does not necessarily make them redundant. Project managers still have a big role to play in the implementation and transition of a team in implementing the Scrum methodology. One key way in which a project manager would do that is through the training of employees in the transition and understanding of Scrum. They could either handle the training themselves or hire an external trainer.

Once Scrum has been implemented and is in full swing, it is the project manager's responsibility to assist in reporting and compliance issues relating to all projects. They need to ensure that the teams adhere to industry standards through compliance audits and the identification of risks. These are crucial tasks that are not fulfilled by members of a Scrum team, and so the project manger's role remains pertinent to the team's overall success.

The Project Managers Role within Scrum

As you have read through this guide and the roles specific to a scrum team, you may have started to question what role a traditional project manager takes on during Scrum.

At first glance, it may appear as though this role becomes redundant when Scrum is implemented. The need for a project manager in Scrum is often debated, especially since the ultimate goal of Scrum adoption is for teams to be self-organizing and be able to navigate much of their development without too much guidance.

The role of the product owner and Scrum master, by definition, include responsibilities, which are typically carried out by a project manager, which is why the function of a project manager within Scrum continues to be debated. We know that a product owner is responsible for understanding a client's needs, benchmarking competition, and ensuring the development team has a clear picture of the client's expectations. The Scrum master is an internal servant leader and works closely with the product owner and development to support the development process while the development team gives input on what can be achieved within given time frames, and once approved, they work to achieve the agreed outputs. This appears to leave very little room for a project manager as the duties traditionally carried out by the project manager are done by the Scrum team. Many of the roles and responsibilities of a project manager are covered by the three main roles within a Scrum team:

• Determining and setting the project focus (Scrum Master)

• Allocating Tasks (Development Team)

- Addressing any obstacles or issues (Scrum Master/Product Owner)

- Prioritizing the requirements of a project (Product Owner)

- Managing the project's risk (all Scrum team members)

Redefining the Project Manager's Role in Scrum

While it is true that Scrum teams can operate without the role of a project manager, a skilled project manager is still an asset to the Scrum management process. Project managers, through a diverse and valuable skill set, can fulfill a role within the Scrum team, whether that be as a product owner, Scrum master, or the development team.

Project Manager – Scrum Master

Project managers are skilled in communicating and negotiating with stakeholders, implementing change management, and managing timelines and expected deadlines. The Scrum master role is a popular one for a project manager to take on as the roles are relatively similar.

If there are existing reporting lines between the project manager and the rest of the Scrum team, the Scrum master would not be a great fit for a project manager.

This is due to the communication and feedback (and possibly pushback) that may be necessary amongst team members and the fact they may feel comfortable pushing back against their manager.

Project Manager – Scrum of Scrums Master

Large organizations may have many teams working on large development projects across multiple teams where coordination related to planning and testing must take place. Dependencies between the teams and possible roadblocks should be carefully managed. A Scrum of Scrums master has the responsibility of reviewing dependencies that may exist between teams and coordinate activities to prevent these from delaying the progress of the Scrum teams. This is a role that requires negotiation skills and advanced communication and could be great for an advanced project manager.

Project Manager – Programs Manager

Although the Scrum roles cover a large number of areas and duties required for development, there are a number of decisions or tasks, which are often overlooked.
These include budgeting, hiring and firing, and performance reviews. Should disputes arise between the team, a person outside of the three main roles may be instrumental in reaching resolutions.

This is a role that a project manager could undertake in support of the Scrum team.

As Scrum teams are built to be self-organizing and relatively self-sufficient, the transition to Scrum may leave a project manager feeling out of place. However, project managers often have valuable skills that complement a Scrum team and make the process more seamless. There are a number of elements of a project, which should be considered in determining how a project manager could fit into either of the three main roles or an additional support role. These elements include the scale and complexity of the project, the size of the project, the risk profile, the geographical location of the team, governance, and commercial consideration.

1. Scale and Complexity

Should a project involve a small team operating from the same location on a relatively simple project, a project manager is not usually deemed necessary. As we have mentioned, all of the elements of the project will be covered by the Scrum roles. However, projects, which are more complex and have multiple components place different demands on the team, and a project manager could be vital to addressing and undertaking support tasks that are crucial to the team's success.

2. Project Size

As a project gets bigger in size and scope, it inherently becomes more complex. Some projects may involve multiple teams and require an additional layer of coordination and support. For these larger projects, the support of a project manager is very useful.

3. Risk Profile

One of the benefits of implementing the Scrum framework is the manner in which risk is decreased through the iterative approach and opportunities for course correction. That being said, there are still additional risks that may present themselves throughout a project which require identifying, reporting, and being actively managed. The risks identified at the beginning of a project need to be monitored throughout, as well as focusing on any the identification of risks that appear as the project progresses. This bigger picture thinking when it comes to risk is ideal for a project manager to take on.

Non-Core Roles in Scrum

Just as there are essential core roles in Scrum, there are also non-core roles. While these roles are not mandatory for a Scrum project and might not even be as involved as the other roles, they are still very important because they can play a significant part in the projects. These roles include the Stakeholder(s), the Vendors, and the Scrum Guidance Body.

Stakeholder

Stakeholder is a term that collectively includes customers, sponsors, and users who frequently collaborate with the Product Owner, Scrum Master, and Scrum Team. It's their job to come up with ideas and help start the creation of the project's service or product and provide influence throughout the project's development. The customer is the specific person who buys the project's product or service. It's entirely possible for an organization's project to have customers within that same organization (internal customers), or customers outside of that organization (external customers). A user is an individual or organization that uses the project's service or product. Just like customers, there can be both internal and external users. It's even possible for customers and users to be the same person. The sponsor is the person or organization that provides support and resources for the project. They are also the person that everyone is accountable to in the end.

Vendor

Vendors are outside persons or organizations. They provide services and products that are not usually found within the project organization. They help bring things in that might not have been there otherwise.

Scrum Guidance Body

The Scrum Guidance Body is optional and is made up of either a group of documents or a group of expert individuals. It's their job to define government regulations, security, objectives related to quality, and other parameters seen in the organization. It's these guidelines that help the Product Owner, Scrum Master, and Scrum Team to carry out their work in a consistent manner. The Scrum Guidance Body is also a good way for the organization to know what the best practices are, and which ones should be used in all Scrum projects. It's important to note that the Scrum Guidance Body doesn't actually make any decisions related to the project. It's instead used as guidelines and a structural way for everyone in the project organization to consult the portfolio, project, and program. It's especially useful for the Scrum Teams, who can look at or ask the Scrum Guidance Body for advice whenever they might need it.

Scrum Management Errors to Avoid

Although the Scrum principles are simple and relatively easy to grasp, there are a number of common errors that occur. These are relatively easy to avoid once they have been identified.

1. *Underestimating the effort involved in switching to Scrum/Agile*

After getting an initial understanding of Scrum and its key principles and tools, a project manager may be of the impression that making the transition to Scrum may be a seamless process. Although Scrum is a simple framework to grasp, a successful transition involves more conscious effort and determination that anticipated. In more complex situations, the problems to be overcome may require greater levels of Scrum management expertise and commitment to follow through until the initial speed bumps are overcome.

The fast pace of Scrum with an expected high level of outputs can take a team some time to adjust to. There may also be higher levels of stress associated with the move to agile, which a project manager may not anticipate.

The recommended approach is to expect the transition to be messy and allow for extended lead times due to delays and frustrations with the change.

Changes to the way a team collaborates can often undercover underlying organizational issues that need resolving. These commonly include poor communication, lack of trust, and lack of accountability.

Encountering these issues and overcoming them may seem daunting at first, but by approaching them head-on, a team will be more successful in the long run. The key to overcoming these challenges is to expect that they may arise and initially delay the effects and implementation of Scrum. Do not be deterred as the nature of Scrum and its focus on teamwork, transparency, and accountability will continue to address and eradicate common problems within teams that may have already been present.

2. Implementation without adhering to the Rules

Many teams will implement Scrum under the direction of a project manager, and initially be educated and well-versed in all the key elements and practices of Scrum, including making use of Scrum artifacts, having daily Scrums, and ensuring consistent communication between team members. As projects progress and teams become fatigued, it is tempting for teams to slowly loosen the practices and use of the tools, which they initially abided by. Many organizations fall short of the requirement to consistently implement all the elements of Scrum.

Not only is it important that the practices that are integral to Scrum are followed, but it is important that the principles explained at the beginning of this guide, which underpins these practices, are consistently discussed and understood.

3. Creating Unnecessary Complications

As you implement Scrum and get used to using as an overarching framework, it may be tempting to allow other practices and smaller frameworks to creep into your everyday operations. While facilitating the parallel use of other frameworks with Scrum is one of its many positive attributes, it is important to keep the implementation of Scrum as simple as possible.

Collaboration and enhancement tools are constantly being released to make Scrum easier to implement. Although it may be tempting to delve straight into buying or to use these tools, make sure you do not spend precious time implementing tools when refining the simple elements of Scrum would be a better use of your time and energy.

4. Using the Scrum Master as a Messenger

As the Scrum master communicates with the team as a whole, and individually on a one on one basis, it may occur that team members start to use the Scrum master as a messenger, as opposed to exercising their duty to communicate openly and honestly with other teammates.

Developers could also, through their naturally more regular interaction with the Scrum master, direct any questions they have relating to, for example, a user story, to the Scrum master as opposed to directly to the product owner.

This kind of communication should be prevented at all costs as it undermines one of the key principles of Scrum relating to always having open channels of communication. This indirect communication can also relate to timewasting as, in this example, the Scrum master would have to contact the product owner first and then relay the answer to the developer. A must more efficient option would be for the developer to contact the product owner directly. If indirect communication is left to continue, it could cause miscommunication between the team as a whole.

Useful Resources

So, at this point, I hope that I have managed to paint a clear picture of what Agile is, and how Scrum can become an effective methodology for you and your organization. Thus, this implies embracing the Agile mindset and making changes in your overall mentality to embrace the finer points of Scrum.

However, you might be asking yourself where you can begin. This is especially true if you are not familiar with Scrum or Agile. If this is the first time you have seriously dug into the Agile mindset, then you might be eager to learn more about how you can set down the path toward embracing Agile in order to harness its full potential.

You might be looking for additional resources which can help you get your journey in Agile off to a rocking start.

Please feel free to share the knowledge you have learned here with your colleagues and teammates. You can become an agent of change by implementing this knowledge in such a way that those around you can learn more about the Agile mindset and the finer points of Scrum.

You might also be interested in holding some training sessions or meetings in which you can discuss how Agile may benefit your organization and if Agile is truly right for you and your organization. While it is true that Agile has a cross-cutting application across various fields, there may be valid reasons why Agile might not be a good fit for your organization.

Nevertheless, I am sure that the more you learn about Agile, the more you will see how many of the underlying principles in Agile, and by extension Scrum, can be applied to your organization. Of course, this is not the type of process that can happen overnight, but it is worth taking a deeper look.

By giving Scrum some serious consideration, you will be opening the door to making some interesting changes in the way business is conducted in your organization. Of course, I have no doubt that your team is currently engaged in making the most of their opportunity to deliver value, they may not be fully aware of the potential that lies in embracing a framework, such as Scrum, which can bring a certain, "logic to the madness."

However, you might not feel entirely confident about leading a Scrum-oriented process. At least not yet. Hence, you might be looking for other sources in which you can gain further insights and perspectives on implementing Scrum in your organization.

Find a Great Agile Coach

One of the best sources of knowledge and experience in the Agile world is an experienced and reputable Agile Coach. A good Agile Coach will take you and your teammates through the rigors of Agile, more specifically Scrum, and help you see how implementing Scrum can help you improve your overall processes.

Also, an Agile Coach will work with you and your team in helping you improve your overall knowledge and understanding of Agile. In doing this, the Agile Coach will help all of the members involved in this transition process become keenly aware of how Agile can be put into practice in virtually all facets of your organization's operation. Therefore, you can rest assured that you will be able to make a strong case for the implementation of Agile within your organization.

In addition, a good Agile Coach is a type of person who can hold your hand through an entire Scrum project. They can sit on the sidelines while your team takes the field. When mistakes happen, the Agile Coach will be quick to help you find the proper solution to the shortcomings your team has made. This will enable your teammates to find their rightful place within the Agile mindset in such a way that you can take full advantage of their strengths while allowing them to grow out of any limitations they may have.

Of course, an Agile Coach may not come cheap, but the overall investment would certainly be worth the time and money. Nevertheless, your organization may not be in a position to take on a full-time consultant in this capacity.

So, what other options are out there for your team to become versed in Agile and Scrum?

The Multiplier Effect

One workaround that companies and organizations use when they don't have the means to bring in full-time consultants or expensive training companies is to have a handful of staff members get trained by the experts and then multiply their knowledge and expertise.

In doing this, the organization can ensure that growth as a result of the implementation of Agile and Scrum methodologies can be born from within the company. Considering that experts and consultants have the know-how to help your organization get off the ground, it's worth mentioning that there are equally qualified individuals within your organization who can also learn from the pros and then become excellent coaches in their own right.

So, your organization might choose to send some staff off to a training course, take a class at a local college, or take an online training course. These options open the discussion to some interesting possibilities.

First, does your staff really need to take time off work in order to attend a training seminar or a class?

If you believe that it is worth giving some staff members time off to attend in-person training, then you can certainly go down that path. However, you might find that taking time off from work may not be the wisest course of action. After all, the time that staff is not working means that it is time in which tasks are not getting done.

Now, you could ask the staff to go in their free time. This may, or may not, be appealing to some. But you can be sure that if someone takes a class in their free time, it is because they are committed to learning. But this brings us to another interesting possibility: online courses.

There are several companies which offer online training courses in Agile and Scrum. They offer a number of courses and certifications which you can pursue. While not all folks are interested in becoming officially certified, holding one such certification is a great way in which you can earn some valuable credentials. Consequently, some folks are keen on becoming certified in the fields of Agile and Scrum.

Here are some of the most renowned companies in the online Agile training business:

- **Scrumstudy.com.** They offer all sorts of courses and training programs ranging from free introductory courses to full-fledged certifications. I would encourage you to check out their free courses and then look into their paid options. I believe you will find some interesting options for yourself and your teammates.

- **Scrum.org**. This company is very similar to Scrumstudy. They offer a learning path which leads to certification in addition to providing some free content to learners. This company also provides classes and training seminars which you can book in-person depending on your location.

- **Scrum Alliance.** This is one of the largest players in the Agile training world. They have a series of courses and training seminars which you can attend both online and in person. So, I would encourage you to take a closer look at how the Scrum Alliance may be able to offer you the right training solution.

- **Project management Institute (PMI).** PMI is the company behind the traditional Project Management Professional (PMP) certification. This is the most widely-respected project management certification out there. Holders of the PMP certification are heralded as pros in their field. However, PMI was a bit slow in embracing the Agile movement. Nevertheless, PMI has its own Agile training program now which is certainly worth checking out.

- **Agile Alliance.** Just like the Scrum Alliance, the Agile Alliance is focused on the broader Agile movement. So, their focus is not just on Scrum, but on all things Agile. This is a great source of information which you can check out. They have a very extensive repository of information which can check out for free. So, I would highly recommend their website for your Agile research needs.

So, there you have it. I hope you are eager to get started on the road that leads to an Agile mindset.

As I have mentioned earlier, Agile isn't for everyone, and it certainly isn't for every organization. Nevertheless, I hope that you will give Agile and Scrum a chance. After all, you have nothing to lose but everything to gain in a new, dynamic Agile world.

Conclusions about SCRUM

I hope this book was able to help you to gain an understanding of Scrum principles, practices, and underlying values. By taking the opportunity to learn more about Scrum, you are starting the journey of bigger opportunities as you execute on project delivery of the highest standard, relying on the values which underpin Scrum. You should have the knowledge to not only teach members of your team about Scrum and its events and processes, but also have the foundation to continue to build upon for your Scrum and project management career.

If you are an individual looking to become skilled in the realm of project management, then you have taken a big step towards being a seasoned professional on the execution of agile, and more specifically, Scrum. The next step is to continue to learn about Scrum through the process of implementation and continuous learning and education. Pursuing a formal certification is one way to take the next step in your project management career. Alternatively, you could simply use what you have learned through reading this guide to implement the valuable processes and practices of Scrum in any of the projects you may work on going forward.

The agile framework is an advocate for continuous learning and improvement of teams and what they can produce.

Whether you strictly follow the rules and guidelines you have read here to implement Scrum, or simply extract only those that are applicable to you specifically, you will be taking a positive step towards you and your team's growth and improvement. What is important is that, in line with agile learning precept, you should pass as much knowledge to your team members throughout the Scrum process.

Once you have created your Scrum team and initiated the development process, you can fine-tune and tweak the process to correct for any inconsistencies or challenges you or your team may face. Keep in mind that you may have a number of different challenges, which you may face in the initial stages of Scrum implementation. This is par for the course and over time will lead your team to be more established and effective in product development. Remember to be patient, get help from an agile coach if needed, and enjoy the process and newly acquired skills.

The next step, following the mastering of this guide, could be to enlist in a Scrum project management certification of which there are many. These are most commonly divided into the three main roles within the Scrum framework, depending on which role you choose to pursue, as well as qualifications.

For example, implementing Scrum and integrating it with Kanban. Although the implementation of Scrum is relatively easy, the mastering of Scrum takes more patience and effort. Pursuing a qualification may provide you with further confidence to confidently lead a Scrum team, and complex development process as well as successfully scale the process for larger projects across multiple teams.

If you are a project manager in the traditional sense, you will still be able to use your broad set of skills to complement any Scrum team. Although debates still continue as to how your role may fit into Scrum, depending on your key skills, you will be a valuable asset to any Scrum team.